DI020067

THE VOLGA RISES IN EUROPE

Birlinn Limited
8 Canongate Venture
5 New Street
Edinburgh
EH8 8BH

© The Estate of Curzio Malaparte 1951

All rights reserved. No part of this publication may be
reproduced, stored, or transmitted in any form, or by
any means, electronic, mechanical or photocopying,
recording or otherwise, without the express written
permission of the publisher.

ISBN 0-7394-1930-7

Printed and bound in U.S.A.

The Volga Rises in Europe

CURZIO MALAPARTE

Translated by David Moore

Birlinn

CONTENTS

CONTENTS

FOREWORD

WHEN, in June, 1941, at the outset of the German war against Soviet Russia, my despatches from the Ukrainian Front began to appear in the *Corriere della Sera,* the Italian public was filled with utter amazement—almost, one might say, with shocked indignation.

Quoted at length in the press of Britain, America, Switzerland and Scandinavia, my messages were welcomed by international public opinion as constituting the only objective document, the only impartial testimony, to have come out of Soviet Russia since the beginning of the campaign. Nevertheless, it seemed to a great many people in Italy that my observations and reflections were inspired not by an honest and courageous desire to tell the truth but by a personal sympathy with Communist Russia, and that, in consequence, the view of events which they presented was both biased and arbitrary.

Since my writings were completely at variance with the line that was being taken at the time by the Italian press—to wit, that the war against Russia was likely to be short and "easy"—and since they even contradicted the opinions expressed by all the other special correspondents of my own newspaper, many of my readers came to the conclusion that I was animated by a spirit of partisanship; and there were not a few who denounced me as a defeatist, and loudly demanded that I be at once recalled from the Russian Front and placed under arrest. Today, all are in a position to appreciate that I saw things clearly, and that the "sympathy" for Communist Russia with which I was reproached was nothing more or less than objective reporting, as Togliatti himself was forced to admit to me personally when, on Easter Day, 1944, he came to

1*

my house to congratulate me on the despatches in question.

But objective reporting was a crime even in those days. In September, 1941, by order of Goebbels, the German military authorities expelled me from the Soviet war-zone, notwithstanding the protests of General Messe, Commander of the Italian Expeditionary Force in Russia. Although the Fascist censors, both military and political, had, albeit with the greatest reluctance, permitted the publication of my despatches, Mussolini first threatened to send me back to Lipari, then kept me under house-arrest for a period of four months. But in January, 1942, by which time military events had confirmed the soundness of my judgment and the accuracy of my forecasts, he ordered me to be sent back to the Russian Front. This time, however, fearing German reprisals, I asked to be sent to Finland, where Hitler had no authority. My request was granted, and I remained in Finland for two years, until Mussolini's arrest. Then, on July 27th, 1943, I returned to Italy in order to assume my post of responsibility in the struggle against the Germans, which I considered both inevitable and imminent.

During the summer of 1941 I was the only front-line war-correspondent in the whole of the U.S.S.R. (I should add that I was accompanied throughout by Lino Pellegrini, whom I had selected as a companion so that I might have a reliable witness to the truth of all that I wrote.) At the time there were no other Italian war-correspondents either in the Ukraine or on any other part of the Russian Front, from Murmansk to the Black Sea. Even the British and American correspondents, who were forbidden by the Soviet authorities to go to the front, had remained in Moscow, with the result that their writings were characterized by the forced tone, the episodic manner, the vague language and the rhetoric of men who write from hearsay and not from personal experience. To confirm this one need only read the despatches which the American writer Erskine Caldwell, author of *God's Little Acre* and *Tobacco Road,* subsequently assembled in a volume entitled *Moscow*

Under Fire (Hutchinson, London—New York—Melbourne, 1942). I record these facts not out of vanity but in order to emphasize what the Anglo-American press itself freely admitted at the time—namely, that the only objective writing on the German war against Russia came from an Italian and that, unlike the British and American correspondents, citizens of free, democratic countries, I did not undertake to describe events of which I had no first-hand knowledge, nor did I stoop to make propaganda in favour of one side or the other.

Apart from the fact that I was the only front-line war-correspondent in the whole of the U.S.S.R., and hence the only one in a position to see how matters really stood, I should mention that my long-standing acquaintance with Soviet Russia and her problems helped me greatly to assess the significance of events and to foresee the inevitable course of their development. What I observed on the battlefield merely confirmed in the most damning fashion what I had been saying and writing about Communist Russia for the last twenty years and more.[1]

In the course of my long personal experience of things Russian I have always refused to judge the Soviet Union from what might be termed a " bourgeois " viewpoint—in other words, from a viewpoint that is necessarily not objective. " Objectivity is not the prime characteristic of the bourgeois outlook," I wrote in my preface to Fülop-Miller's *Il volto del bolscevismo* (Bompiani, 1930). And I added that " the surest defence of the bourgeois way of life against the dangers of Bolshevism ought to consist in an understanding of the revolutionary phenomena of the modern age. Failure to understand these phenomena is the surest sign of bourgeois decadence " : and this not only in Italy (where the *bourgeoisie* has remained faithful, so far as Russia is concerned, to those naïve prejudices

---

[1] See *La rivolta dei santi maledetti,* 1921 ; *Intelligenza di Lenin,* 1930 ; *Sodoma e Gomorra,* 1931 ; *Technique du coup d'Etat,* 1931 ; *Le bon-homme Lénine,* 1932 ; various essays in *La Ronda,* 1921, and in *Rivoluzione liberale,* 1922 ; and my preface to Fülop-Miller's *Il volto del bolscevismo,* 1930.

so egregiously exemplified in the short essay of Francesco de Sanctis, *Il testamento di Pietro il Grande,* written in 1864 and published in the journal of the Constitutional Unitarian Association of Naples, *L'Italia*), but in all the countries of Europe, England especially. As to the English *bourgeoisie,* the judgment formulated by the liberal English economist Keynes in his famous little book, *A Short View of Russia* (Hogarth Press, London, 1929) is still of unique interest, and in a sense represents the last word on the subject. I declare that it is impossible to understand Soviet Russia without first ridding oneself of bourgeois preconceptions; and it is obvious that those who do not understand Soviet Russia are not capable of fighting her, still less of prevailing over her.

Among the many bourgeois preconceptions that exist about Communist Russia the most persistent is that of the man who regards Bolshevism as a typically Asiatic phenomenon. This explanation of the Bolshevik revolution and its problems is too simple and convenient to be accepted with safety. The title of this book, *The Volga Rises in Europe* (the original title, which the Fascist censors vetoed, was different, as I shall explain in due course), is in fact intended to draw attention to this childish preconception. As long ago as 1930, in the preface to Fülop-Miller's essay mentioned above, I wrote that " the face of Bolshevism is not, as so many believe, an Asiatic face. It is a European face." The truth is that Bolshevism is a typically European phenomenon.

Behind the Doric columns of the *Pyatlyetki,* the Five Year Plans, behind the rows of figures of the *Gosplan,* there stretches not Asia, but another Europe : *the* other Europe (in the sense in which America too is another Europe). The steel cupola of Marxism + Leninism + Stalinism (the gigantic dynamo of the U.S.S.R. according to Lenin's formula : Soviet + electrification=Bolshevism) is not the mausoleum of Genghis Khan but —in the very sense that bourgeois folk find so distasteful—the *other* Parthenon of Europe. " The Volga," says Pilnyak, " flows into the Caspian Sea." Yes, but it does not rise in Asia :

it rises in Europe. It is a European river. The Thames, the Seine, the Potomac are its tributaries.

This truth should have been remembered in 1941 (as, indeed, it should be remembered today), when many people abandoned themselves to the facile assumption that the German war against Soviet Russia was simply a war between Europe and Asia. In 1941 German Europe was fighting against European peoples, against European ideologies—whether in fact it was fighting against Britain and America or against Soviet Russia.

" One day," I wrote then, " when the din of battle has subsided, and it is possible to review the situation calmly, it will be seen that this war against Soviet Russia should be regarded not as a struggle against the Mongolian hordes of a new Genghis Khan, *but as one of those social wars which always precede, and clear the ground for, a new political and social world-order.*"

If these words, which I wrote in 1941, were true then, they are even truer today; for the slogan *Europe against Asia,* the slogan of the German war (and it was essentially a bourgeois war) against Soviet Russia, has today become the slogan of the Atlantic Pact. Today, as in 1941, the two forces in conflict are not Europe and Asia, but the bourgeois ethic and the proletarian ethic.

This is the first, and so far the only, book that has revealed the underlying significance of the colossal European tragedy implicit in the German war against Soviet Russia. It therefore remains highly topical, not merely because it stresses the " social " character of that war, and of any possible future war against Soviet Russia, but because it poses the fundamental problem of contemporary Europe : the incompatibility of the bourgeois ethic and the proletarian ethic, which is the ethic of the modern world.

The reader of these pages should never forget the expression " proletarian ethic." Apropos of which, this seems to me a fitting moment to mention that I originally intended to entitle my book *War and the Strike Weapon*. I chose this title not because it carried a faint echo of *War and Peace,* not because I presumed to see in these pages, and in their avowed purpose, some kind of a reflection of Tolstoy's novel, least of all because I thought that the German war against Soviet Russia was even remotely comparable to the equally unfortunate and senseless campaign of Napoleon. I chose it because I felt that the title *War and the Strike Weapon* brought out in full relief the social character of this war and the fundamental importance of the " proletarian ethic " as a factor in the Soviet military power, to which all those social elements of the class struggle and of the technique of the proletarian revolution embraced by the word " strike " made, and would continue to make, as significant a contribution as the weapons of war and the various aspects of the military art, such as discipline, technical training, tactical organization, etc.

The Fascist censors vetoed the title *War and the Strike Weapon,* no doubt because of a legitimate fear that readers of the book might see in it a deliberate and dangerous juxtaposition of the words " strike " and " war " and that they might in consequence be led to think that the most effective means of opposing this or any other war was the strike weapon. In choosing such a title this was in fact what I had in mind— *but not only this.* And I am bound to admit that, from their own point of view, the Fascist censors were right.

My book was to have been published by Bompiani, and it was all ready to be despatched to the booksellers when, on February 18th, 1943, the printing-works was destroyed in a British air-raid and the entire edition of *The Volga Rises in Europe* went up in smoke. Newly set up and printed by another firm, the volume finally appeared at the end of August, 1943. But a few days later, on September 15th, the German authorities, who in the meantime had made themselves masters of Italy, ordered the book's seizure. It was condemned to the flames; and so it may be said that *The Volga Rises in Europe* is now seeing the light for the first time in this new edition.

In order not to mislead the reader by giving him the

impression that this is a new work I have resisted the temptation to restore the original title, vetoed by the censors, of *War and the Strike Weapon*. I have done so with reluctance; for by reverting to the title in question I should have been able to confront the honest and intelligent reader in the most immediate way with the necessity of reflecting seriously on the hidden meaning of this war, of considering with an objective eye its significance as a social conflict, and of recognising in Germany's ferocious struggle with Soviet Russia all those social elements which make of it an episode—the most terrible yet—in the European class-struggle.

CURZIO MALAPARTE.

Forte dei Marmi,
   1951.

BOOK ONE

IN THE STEPS OF NAPOLEON

I

THE CROWS OF GALATZ

Galatz, June 18th, 1941.

SITUATED between the Prut and the Danube, in the middle of a group of lagoons, Galatz diffuses an odour of mud, fish and rotting canes. (On these damp June evenings the languid odour of silt clings to the leaves of the trees, to the hair of the women, to the manes of the horses, to the long velvet robes of the *scopzi,* the eunuch cab-drivers belonging to the famous Russian sect of which Galatz is the last refuge, the last temple.) From Braila to Galatz, from Sulina to the mountains of Dobrudja, the huge delta of the Danube is a single vast expanse of shining water. The spring floods have transformed the region into an enormous fen. Here the flat Wallachian plain undulates like a gigantic curtain stirred by the wind. At intervals it rises from the boundless marshes in languid waves of yellow earth, then finally subsides in a series of gentle folds, forming a sort of shallow basin, within which lie the placid waters of Lake Bratesc, eternally veiled in a transparent, pale-blue mist.

Galatz stands on the edge of this basin, at the apex of the triangle formed by the Danube and the Prut, which converge a few miles below the town. The mountains of Dobrudja, far away on the horizon, form a backcloth to this fluid landscape, with its low houses, its marshes, its light mists. From a distance they resemble Mount Tifata, which dominates Capua; they reveal the same languid shades of blue and green, the same romantic and delicate innocence. Every so often they disappear, merging into the horizon, leaving behind them in the shimmering air a sad, blurred memory, a memory that has about it an almost feminine quality.

(Between my hotel room and Soviet Russia there is only the stream of the Prut : a sluggish, yellow river which at this point, near its mouth, broadens to form the vast, turbid pool of Lake Bratesc, whose smooth surface is broken here and there by the reeds and rushes that rise in thick green clusters from the mudbanks. The Prut seems strangely deserted these days. Not a tug, not a lighter, not even a rowing-boat cleaves its surface. Only a few Rumanian fishing-smacks are to be seen, bobbing up and down amid the lazy muddy whirlpools that form near the water's edge. But woe betide the man who ventures out into the middle of the stream : the Russians will fire at him for a certainty. After dark the Soviet sentries open fire at the first rustle of a leaf, at the first crack of a twig. The faint plopping sound which the water makes from time to time as it laps the shore is enough to put them in a state of alarm.)

From the window of my room it is possible to see with the naked eye the houses on the Russian bank, the timber-yards, the smoke from the handful of tugs anchored in the river harbour. On the road that runs beside the river one can distinguish with binoculars groups of people—soldiers perhaps— columns of vehicles, patrols of cavalry. During the night the Soviet shore appears black and blind. One has the impression that night begins over there on the other bank, that it rises, hard and smooth as a black wall, over there, opposite the Rumanian shore with its twinkling lights. At dawn the Soviet shore resembles a closed eye that gradually opens, to survey the river with a pale, wan, extraordinarily sad and disquieting expression.

Gangs of children chase one another along the avenues of the public gardens. Groups of people lean on the parapet of the Belvedere, which rises sheer above a bare, reddish expanse of marshland traversed by the railway-embankment, and, shielding their eyes with their hands, scan the Russian shore.

Over there, on the far side of the Prut, a cloud of silky blue smoke ascends from the houses of Reni and lazily dissolves in the dusty air. (Two more days, perhaps one more day, perhaps only a few hours.) I catch myself looking at the Town Hall clock as I drive in a cab down to the bridge that links Galatz to the Soviet town of Reni.

A strong smell, a pungent, greasy smell, rises to greet me from Lake Bratesc. It is the stench from the carcases of some animals that lie buried in the mud. Great blue and green flies, their wings shot with gold, buzz around insistently. A party of Rumanian sappers are laying a mine preparatory to blowing up the bridge. The soldiers talk and laugh loudly among themselves. The muddy waters of Lake Bratesc diffuse a yellowish light which illuminates a countryside in agony, a torpid, impermanent, decaying countryside. The imminent war is perceived as a storm that is about to break, as something independent of man's will, almost as a fact of nature. (Here Europe is no longer amenable to reason, it no longer knows any moral code. It is but a sham—a continent of putrid flesh.) At the far end of the bridge, on the threshold of the U.S.S.R., rises the Soviet triumphal arch, a rustic structure surmounted by the ritual trophy of the hammer and sickle. I need only cross the bridge, I need only walk a few hundred yards, to leave this Europe, to pass the frontier of that other Europe. From one Europe to the other it is but a step—though much too long a step, I would say, for mortal legs.

Truly, this landscape conveys an impression of insecurity, of impermanence. The earthquake of last November has left the town littered with ruins and rubble, with the result that the very sight of the place suggests to the eye images of a fleeting world, of a tottering civilization. Many of the houses have collapsed, nearly all reveal deep scars. Some are without a roof, some have a wall missing. Some have lost their balconies, some their entire façades. And some are disfigured by wide cracks through which one glimpses bourgeois interiors—floors covered with Turkish carpets, Viennese beds,

the hideous oleographs which adorn the walls of all oriental
houses. There is a street near the Brascioveni where the fronts
of all the houses have collapsed; one sees people moving
behind cloth or paper screens, as on the boards of a stage,
before a noisy and indifferent audience. It is like a scene
painted by Piscator. The beams that prop up the façades or
the sides of the houses form a sort of continuous, oblique
pergola stretching from end to end of the pavements, a
pergola beneath which people of every race and tongue shout
and yell, jostle and pursue one another, collect into momentary
groups, into sudden struggling masses. At many points,
especially in the area surrounding Colonel Boyle Street, the
alleys which lead down to the harbour are still cluttered up
with fallen masonry. And amid those ruins, beneath those
oblique pergolas of beams, among those deeply-scarred, tottering walls, before the stage of those gaping houses, a crowd of
Greeks, Armenians, gypsies, Turks and Jews swarm in a cloud
of yellow dust, in a tumult of raucous voices, of yells, of
laughter, of shrieks, of songs blaring from gramophones. And
pervading everything is that smell of horses' urine and attar of
roses which is the smell of the Levant, the smell of the Black
Sea.

The pavements of every street are flanked by hundreds and
hundreds of cafés, haberdashers' shops, perfumeries, barbers'
saloons, *croitoris'* window-displays, confectioners' shops,
dentists' surgeries. The Greek barbers with their olive complexions, their enormous black eyebrows and their huge black
moustaches glistening with brilliantine; the women's *coiffeurs*,
their thick jet-black hair curled with hot irons and arranged
in baroque styles; the Turkish pastrycooks, their hands dripping with honey and butter, their arms plastered up to the
elbows with grated almonds and pistachio-dust; the perfumers,
shoemakers, photographers, tailors, tobacconists and dentists—
all greet you in sing-song voices, with solemn gestures and
deep bows. All invite you to come in, to sit down, to try a
comb, a razor, a suit of clothes, a pair of shoes, a hat, a truss,
a pair of spectacles, a set of false teeth, a bottle of perfume,

or else to have your hair curled, cut or dyed. And all the while
the Turkish coffee foams in the little pots of gleaming copper,
and the newsvendors shout the headlines of the *Actiunea* or
recite in loud voices the latest *communiqués* on the "*situatia
pe fronturile de lupta,*" and interminable processions of hairy,
painted, curly-headed women pass to and fro along the pavements in front of the café tables, which are crowded with fat
Levantines sitting with legs wide apart, as in the drawings of
Pashin, who came from Braila.

It is not yet time to go to lunch at Suré's. Accordingly, I
leave Manzavinato's Greek *cofetaria* and walk down to the
harbour by way of the Domneasca, the fashionable street of
Galatz, which is over a mile long. In Brascioveni Street the
shrill squealing of the tramcar wheels makes the window-panes
vibrate; the cabs of the *scopzi*, drawn by pairs of glossy,
panting horses, rush past in clouds of dust (the *scopez* sitting
on his box, swathed in his long robe, his eunuch's face soft
and very thin, with what I would term a flabby, sagging thin-
ness). Swarms of dogs and boys pursue one another from
pavement to pavement. I look up, and observe that the
inscriptions above the shops are written alternately in Hebrew,
Armenian, Turkish, Greek and Rumanian. Eventually I
emerge into the street that leads down to the harbour.

The Danube is swollen with rain, the massive lighters tied
up alongside the moles move gently up and down in the water.
The street flanking the harbour is a sort of endless terrace of
low houses, half ruined by the earthquake and now shored up
with beams. The most sumptuous of these hovels are built of
brick; others, of earth mixed with lime; the most wretched, of
straw-pulp overlaid with plaster. At street level the stranger
is confronted with a succession of gloomy warehouses, the doors
of which stand wide open to reveal great piles of casks containing pitch, tar, pepper, copper-sulphate, dried fish, raisins and
all kinds of spices. This vast trade in imported goods is mono-
polized by Greeks. Some lean and dark, others fat and very
pale, they stand in the doorways of their shops, arms folded
across their chests, cigarettes dangling from their lower lips,

enormous black eyebrows protruding above lack-lustre eyes and long, aquiline noses with quivering red nostrils, which give to those sepia-coloured faces an air of vitality and refinement that is otherwise lacking.

The usual bustle prevails throughout Badalan, as the district surrounding the harbour is called. The river bank swarms with soldiers. A company of territorials is unloading cattle, bales of hay, sacks of cereals and bundles of firewood from some of the lighters. The soldiers are old, they have white hair. They hurry to and fro between the lighters and the mole, passing up and down the gangways like yellow insects. Some women with green, yellow and red silk sunshades are sitting in a group on the deck of a lighter, eating sweets. They are the wives of the captains, the pilots and the owners of the vessels.

On the shore, near the cattle-pen, a group of soldiers are preparing a meal. They are young men, and they laugh and joke as they work. Some scrape the soil from onions and garlic, some throw kidney beans into pots, some peel potatoes, some smear the interior of large frying pans with lard, some cut meat into slices ready for cooking. The bean-soup bubbles in the pots. The whole operation is supervised by a captain, who from time to time turns his head and apathetically surveys the harbour, the women sitting on the decks of the lighters, the cattle, and the Russian shore of Lake Bratesc, beyond which rise the Titan-Nadrag-Calan Foundries, guarded by sentries with fixed bayonets.

A huge cloud of black smoke belches from the squat chimneys of the foundries, enveloping the harbour, the houses, the soldiers, the cattle and the lighters. At times one has the impression that the docks are burning, that the whole district of Badalan is in flames. Soldiers can be seen running after fleeing cattle, driving horses before them with the aid of whips. A goods train whistles incessantly as it carries out shunting operations near the station, which has also been destroyed by the earthquake. In the district of Badalan everything is painted blue—windows, Persian blinds, doors, balconies, railings, shop signs, even the fronts of the houses. Here, on the bank of this pale, almost white river, one is obtrusively reminded of the sea.

Near the silos, beyond the foundries, a group of soldiers and workers stand motionless, gazing up at a manifesto which a bill-poster has just finished sticking to the wall. It is a proclamation by the Government announcing that Horia Sima and the other legionary leaders have been condemned to forced labour. The men stand motionless in front of the poster, as if they were looking at a picture. The thought occurs to me that perhaps they cannot read. Their eyes are expressionless, their faces blank : no, they cannot read. Then, suddenly, one of the soldiers laughs, and the others begin to talk among themselves. They talk of the prices paid by the Government for requisitioned cattle, they talk of the impending war. While I am walking back to my hotel a dark cloud rises from Lake Bratesc—a huge black pall that obscures the sky above the river, above the harbour, above the city : a cloud of crows. The funereal birds caw sadly from the rooftops. I walk up Brascioveni Street. All of a sudden something falls from the sky on to the pavement, right into the midst of the crowd of pedestrians. No one stops, no one looks round. I walk over to the object and inspect it. It is a piece of rotting flesh, which a crow has dropped from its beak.

II

THE RED WAR

THE war against Soviet Russia began at dawn today. It was the first time for two months that I had heard the guns speak. (The last time was in April, beneath the walls of Belgrade.) Amid these vast expanses of corn, in these boundless " forests " of sunflowers, I see the war once again in all its metallic precision, in the glitter of its steel machines, in the continuous, uniform roar of its thousand engines (Honegger, Hindemith). Once again the smell of men and horses gives way to the overpowering reek of petrol. (Yesterday, as I drove north-west along the Soviet border from Galatz to Iaşi, following the line of the Prut, I came upon groups of stern, impassive *Feldgendarmen* standing at the various crossroads, armed with their red-and-white indicators, their brass discs dangling from their necks.

Once I was held up for two hours at a crossroad while a German column went by. It was a mechanized division, preceded by a fleet of heavy tanks. It came from Greece. It had crossed Attica, Boeotia, Thessaly, Macedonia, Bulgaria, Rumania. From the Doric colonnade of the Parthenon to the steel colonnade of the *Pyatlyetka*. The soldiers rode in open lorries, sitting on benches with their backs to the driver. Their faces were white with dust. Each lorry had a likeness of the Parthenon painted in white lead on its bonnet—a childish representation of Doric columns portrayed in white varnish on the dark-grey metal. Instinctively one knew that beneath the

26

mask of dust the soldiers' faces were scorched by the sun, pinched by the Greek wind. The men sat in strangely stiff attitudes; they had the appearance of statues. They were so white with dust that they looked as if they were made of marble.

One of them had an owl, a live owl, perched on his fist. Moreover, the bird undoubtedly came from the Acropolis, it was one of those owls that hoot at night among the marble columns of the Parthenon. (And I remembered that the owl was sacred to Pallas Athene, to "owl-eyed" Athene, γλαυκῶπις Ἀθήνη.) Every so often it fluttered its wings to shake off the dust; and against that vague white background its eyes shone forth clear and lustrous. The German soldier had the same clear, lustrous eyes. And there was in them a mysterious, timeless look—a look pregnant with a timeless, mysterious sense of the inexorable.

Vehicles of grey steel roar past the hedges of willows that grow along the banks of the Prut. The exhausts of the panzers belch out blue tongues of smoke. The air is filled with a pungent, bluish vapour that mingles with the damp green of the grass and with the golden reflection of the corn. Beneath the screaming arch of Stukas the mobile columns of tanks resemble thin lines drawn with a pencil on the vast green slate of the Moldavian plain.

Right Bank of the Prut, June 23rd.

I spent the night in a village on the right bank of the Prut. From time to time, above the frenzied lashing of the rain and the din of the unleashed elements, I heard the thunder of the guns on the horizon. Then a dense, opaque silence fell upon the plain. Through the darkness broken by periodic flashes of lightning, along the road that crosses the village, passed columns of vehicles, battalions of infantry, pieces of artillery drawn by powerful lorries. The roar of engines, the tramp of the horses, the raucous voices of the soldiers filled the night with that sense of restless anxiety which characterizes any period of waiting near the front line.

Then, as the first pale streak of dawn appeared in the eastern sky, the mutter of the guns was heard once again in the distance. Through the grey, soundless mist, which hung from the branches of the trees like cotton-wool, I saw the sun slowly rising, yellow and flabby as the yolk of an egg.

"*Inainte, inainte, baètzi! Sa mergem, sa mergem!*" Standing up in their waggons, the soldiers crack their whips, lash the steaming flanks of their horses. "*Inainte, inainte, baètzi!* Gee up, lads—gee up!*" The wheels creak, sink in the mud up to their axles. Along all the roads adjoining the Prut stretch unending columns of Rumanian military waggons drawn by pairs of shaggy, stunted horses. (They are *caruzze* of the type used by peasants, with a single long shaft and rack-shaped sides.) "*Sa mergem! Sa mergem!*" German mechanized columns roar past these streams of waggons, the drivers lean out of the lorries shouting : "*Weg! Weg!* Make way! Make way!*" The waggons slither into the ditches, the horses flounder in the deep mud, the Rumanian soldiers yell, swear, laugh, crack their whips, lash the steaming flanks of the skinny, shaggy animals. The heavens are scored by the metal wings of the German planes, which pass overhead in a continuous, swift stream, cleaving the glassy sky as incisively as cutting-diamonds. The hum of their engines descends upon the steppe with the soft hissing sound of rain.

Near Huşi, June 25th.

Although the war has now been in progress for three days the Red Army has not yet joined battle. Its masses of tanks, its mechanized units, its assault-divisions, its squads of specialists (who in the Army, as in the field of industrial production, go by the name of *stakanovitsi* or *udarniki*) have not yet gone into action. The troops facing us are covering troops. There are not many of them; but they make up for their lack of numbers by their mobility and stubbornness. For the Russian soldiers are fighters. Their retreat from Bessarabia is very far from being in the nature of a headlong flight. It is a gradual withdrawal of light rearguards, consisting of machine-gunners, squadrons of cavalry, specialists of the corps of engineers. It is a methodical retirement, long prepared. Signs of a hasty abandonment of positions, signs that the enemy has been caught unawares, are apparent only at a few points, where unmistakable traces of the battle remain in the shape of burned-out villages, dead horses left to rot in ditches, and gutted vehicles, with here and there a few corpses (though these are encountered so rarely that one might almost suppose the Soviet troops had been ordered to take their dead with them). It is, in short, clear that the war has come as no surprise to the Russians, at any rate from the military standpoint.

The character of the struggle during these early days has, however, been such that for the moment it would be rash to attempt to draw any conclusions. So far the German and Rumanian divisions have only come up against the Soviet rearguards. It is unlikely that the main body of the Russian Army on the Ukrainian Front will join battle west of the Dnieper, which constitutes a natural line of defence. The enemy will try to slow up the German advance by clinging to the left bank of the Dniester; but the real clash, the real battle, will take place along the line of the Dnieper.

Near Stefanesti, June 27th.

I have today met a group of Soviet prisoners. They climbed out of a lorry which had stopped outside a German Tactical Command post. They were tall young men, with shaven heads, and they wore long leather cloaks. They looked more like mechanics than soldiers. I went up to the youngest and asked him some questions in Russian. He looked at me without replying. When I persisted, he gazed at me for a moment with cold, lack-lustre eyes. Then, with a note of irritation in his voice he said: "*Nye mogu*—I can't." I offered him a cigarette: he accepted it with an air of indifference. After two or three puffs he flung it to the ground, then, as if to excuse his insolent gesture, as if to justify himself, he gave me such a strange, shamefaced smile that I would rather he had looked at me with an expression of undisguised hatred.

III

WORKERS IN UNIFORM

Left Bank of the Prut, June 29th.

AMID this vast expanse of green that stretches for miles in every direction one is hardly conscious any longer of the smell of humanity. (Only of the stench of an occasional corpse, near the villages, near the holes and ditches where the Soviet soldiers have resisted to the last man : and it is almost a living smell, the smell of something endowed with life.)

All night long the dark, heavy, rugged sky, a sky of cast iron, has borne down upon the plain like the press of a foundry. The German camp, situated on the banks of the pool, within the wood, awoke at dawn with a roar reminiscent of a factory-workshop. Strictly speaking, it is not a camp but a bivouac, inasmuch as it consists merely of a fleet of vehicles—some twenty lorries and four heavy *Panzerwagen*—drawn up in the form of a square in a clearing, near the road. As soon as they were awake the German soldiers got to work on the engines with pliers, pincers, screwdrivers, spanners and hammers. The coughing of the carburettors drowns the neighing of the horses of a squadron of Rumanian lancers, who have spent the night near the German bivouac. From the pool comes a merry sound of voices—the voices of the German soldiers, who are bathing, splashing themselves with water, chasing one another along the bank. Farther off, the Rumanian horses, assembled at their drinking-place, paw the ground impatiently, kicking up lumps of mud. In the Rumanian camp the soldiers have lit a fire and are making coffee. A German corporal, covered with a camouflage-net which comes down to his knees, walks through the grass towards the road, head down, possibly looking for something. The *Panzerwagen* and the lorries are also enveloped in large camouflage-nets. Tree-branches have been thrown across the piles of boxes and petrol-tins dumped near the bivouac.

Dressed in black, their big berets tilted over their ears (each beret has a steel badge in the form of a death's head), the German crews move around their tanks, bend down to examine the tracks, tap the wheels with heavy hammers like railwaymen checking the brakes of carriages. From time to time a man climbs on to a tank, raises the hatch, pops in and out of the giant's belly. A temporary smithy has been erected under a large tree. A soldier turns the handle of the bellows. Another beats with a hammer on an anvil. A third dismantles an engine, others check the pressure of the lorries' tyres. A smell of burning oil, carbonic acid, petrol, and white-hot metal re-creates in the wood the characteristic atmosphere of a smithy. (This is the smell of modern war, this is the authentic smell of mechanized war.) One has to retreat a hundred yards in order to detect the strong smell of horses' urine and human sweat. Seated on the grass outside their tents, the Rumanian soldiers clean their rifles, talk loudly and laugh among themselves. They are all young, and they are all peasants. One has only to hear them speak, one has only to observe their gestures, their movements, the way they walk, one has only to see how they grasp their rifles, how they remove the bolts, how they peer down the barrels, to realize that they are peasants.

Their officers—a captain and two subalterns—walk up and down along the edge of the pool, flicking their riding-boots with their canes. (Near the top of each boot, just below the knee, is a gold rosette, the badge of the cavalry.) A group of peasant girls has appeared in the vicinity of the camp. I watch them distribute cherries, strawberries, and bowls filled with that species of *jogurt* which in these parts is called *lapte batut*. From the sky there comes a sound like a prolonged, intense buzzing of insects. The soldiers look up. The sound emanates from three Soviet planes. They are very high. They are flying in the direction of Huşi. During the night the Soviet aircraft sleep. They take off at dawn, circle around overhead all the morning, then, towards mid-day, disappear, returning at sunset. They are going to drop bombs on Iaşi, Galatz, Braila, Tulcea, and Bucharest. The Germans also look up. They gaze at the enemy planes in silence. Then they resume their work.

I watch them working; I note the way they use their hands, the way they hold things, the way they bend their heads over their implements. They are the same soldiers as I have seen " working " in the streets of the Banato, outside Belgrade. They have the same impersonal, alert expressions, the same calm, deliberate, precise gestures, the same air of unsmiling equanimity. They reveal the same indifference to everything that is unconnected with their work. It occurs to me that perhaps the pecularly technical character of this war is leaving its mark on the combatants. Rather than soldiers intent on fighting they look like artisans at work, like mechanics busying themselves about a complex, delicate machine. They bend over a machine-gun and press the trigger, they manipulate the gleaming breech-plug of a field-gun, they grasp the double handle of an anti-aircraft weapon with the same delicate *gaucherie,* or rather with the same rude dexterity, as they reveal when they tighten a nut, or when, with the palm of the hand, or merely with two fingers, they control the vibrations of a cylinder, the play of a large screw, the pressure of a valve. They climb on to the turrets of their tanks as if they were clambering up the iron ladder of a turbine, a dynamo, or a boiler. Yes, indeed—they look more like artisans at work than soldiers at war.

Their very gait, their very manner of speech, their very gestures are those of workmen, not of soldiers. The wounded have that tight-lipped, slightly angry air of workmen injured in an industrial accident. Their discipline has about it the same flexibility and informality as the discipline maintained by a gang of workmen. Their *esprit de corps* is an *esprit d'équipe,* a team spirit, and at the same time it is an *esprit de métier.* They are bound to their unit by the same bonds of loyalty and affection as unite a team of factory-hands to their machine, a team of electricians to their dynamo, a team of artisans to their lathe, to their boiler, to their rolling-mill. In the mechanized armies of today the officers are the technicians, the N.C.O.s are the foremen, the gangers. This small formation of *Panzerwagen* is commanded by a sergeant, not by an officer. A corporal is in charge of the twenty lorries. All the men are specialists—that is to say, they are experts at their various trades. They all know what they are expected to do, where they are expected to go, how they are expected to conduct themselves in any given circumstances.

Now the column is ready to start. The mechanics have filled the petrol-tanks, three *Panzerwagen* have taken up positions in front, the fourth at the rear. The engines tick over, emitting a gentle hum. At this point, however, the sergeant notices that the despatch-rider has not yet returned. He orders his men to switch off the engines. Then they all sit down on the grass and begin their breakfast.

The sun has barely risen, the wood echoes marvellously to the singing of the birds, the leaves of the trees are tinged with pink, the water in the pool is gradually turning green. The tree-trunks glisten, they look as if they had been newly varnished. The soldiers invite me to join them in their meal. I sit down on the grass, the corporal squeezes a little cheese from a tin tube, resembling a tube of tooth-paste, on to a slice of black bread and spreads it with a knife. I start to eat. In my car is a bottle of *zuica*—a kind of Rumanian brandy made from plums. " Would you like a drop of *zuica*?" I ask. The soldiers talk and laugh as they eat and drink, and suddenly I become aware that there is a stranger seated among them, a fair-haired youth with a shaven head, wearing a khaki uniform. A prisoner.

Undoubtedly, he is a workman. He has a strong jaw. thick lips and bushy eyebrows. His expression is obstinate, and at the same time abstracted. From a few small indications I gather that the German soldiers feel in duty bound to treat him with a modicum of respect. The reason : he is an officer.

I ask him, in Russian, if he would like something to eat. " No, thank you," he says, " I'm not hungry." He will only accept a little *zuica*. " Ah, you speak Russian?" says the sergeant to me. " This fellow doesn't speak a word of German. We can't make ourselves understood." I ask the sergeant where they captured him. " We picked him up last night on the road," comes the answer. He gave no trouble. As soon as he saw the tanks he made a gesture, as much as to say: " What's the use?" He was armed with a pistol, but he had run out of ammunition. While I am talking to the sergeant the prisoner gazes at me intently, as if he were trying to guess what we are saying. Then, suddenly, he stretches out his hand and plucks at my arm. " We did all we could," he says. " My men fought hard." " There were only two of us left at the end," he adds, throwing away his cigarette. " The other chap died on the road." I ask him if the other chap was a soldier. " Yes, he was a soldier," he answers, looking at me in surprise. " He was a soldier," he repeats, as if the significance of my question had only just dawned on him.

We begin to talk. I speak slowly, seeking the Russian words. The prisoner answers me slowly, as if he too were seeking the words, but for a different reason. His eyes express distrust: I would say that he distrusts not only me but himself. I ask him again if he would like something to eat. He smiles. " Yes," he says, " I would indeed. I haven't had a bite since yesterday morning." The corporal offers him a piece of sausage-meat sandwiched between two thick slices of bread. " *Ochen spasibo* —thank you," says the prisoner. He starts to eat greedily, fixing his eyes on the track of a tank. The sergeant follows the direction of his gaze, then smiles and exclaims: " *Ach* !" He gets up, takes an adjustable spanner from a pouch, bends over the track and tightens a bolt. All the soldiers laugh. The prisoner laughs too. He is a trifle embarrassed, he feels that he has put his foot in it, that he has been guilty of an indiscretion; he wishes he hadn't noticed the loose bolt. " Thanks !" shouts the sergeant. The prisoner blushes and joins in the laughter. I ask him if he is a regular officer. He replies that he is. Then he adds that he has been in the Army only two years. " And before that?" I ask. Before that, he was working in a machine-shop in Kharkov, in the Ukraine.

He was a stakanovite—an *udarnik*—in other words, an " industrial commando ". To reward him for his services they sent him to a school for officers. The mechanized units of the Red Army are full of ex-stakanovites from the engineering industry. " It's a shame," says the prisoner, shaking his head sadly, " to deprive industry of its best elements." He speaks slowly, with an almost imperceptible note of vexation. His tone is that of a man who has lost interest in everything. I have no idea what he is thinking and feeling at this moment.

While we are talking the despatch-rider returns. " Off we go!" says the sergeant. The prisoner gets to his feet, passes his hand over his shaven head, gazes with intense interest at the *Panzerwagen* and the lorries. Yes, now I understand. Nothing else matters to him now, all that interests him is the machine. He looks intently at the tracks, at the open turrets, at the anti-aircraft machine-guns mounted on the backs of the lorries, at the light anti-tank guns strung out behind them. He is no longer an officer; he is a worker. The only things that interest him now are machines.

" Off we go!" says the corporal. I ask him what they intend to do with the prisoner. " We shall hand him over to the first *Feldgendarme* we meet," he replies. " Goodbye," I say to the prisoner. " *Do svidanya*," he answers. He shakes me by the hand, then he climbs on to a lorry. The column moves off, reaches the road, rumbles away into the distance and finally disappears.

The horses of the cavalry squadron neigh loudly and impatiently paw the ground, tearing at the resplendent, emerald-green grass with their hooves. At a word of command from their officers the soldiers climb into the saddle. The squadron moves off at a walking-pace. " *La revedere*!" I cry. " *La revedere*!" reply the soldiers. And as the mounted figures slowly recede into the distance I hear the guns calling, calling softly, from somewhere far away on the horizon.

IV

BEYOND THE PRUT

Shante-Bani (Bessarabia), July 2nd.

YESTERDAY the weather was unsettled, and a cold, biting wind whistled across the vast wilderness of rushes, in the midst of which multitudes of cattle and horses could be seen grazing. For a distance of some fifty miles the road from Iaşi to Stefanesti follows the right bank of the Prut, passing along the top of the broad marshy valley which until a few days ago marked the boundary between Rumania and Russia. By about ten o'clock, after we had been travelling for five and a half hours, we found ourselves within a few miles of Stefanesti. The corrugated-iron roofs of this large village—indeed, it might almost be described as a small town—had already begun to appear through the morning haze, now penetrated by innumerable shafts of sunlight, when a roar of engines and the characteristic sound of anti-aircraft shells bursting overhead warned us to stop and hide our vehicles beneath a clump of trees. A few moments later we heard the first Soviet bombs exploding ahead of us among the houses of Stefanesti. It was a violent, intensive raid, which ended only when the outlines of a patrol of Messerschmitts appeared against the background of the grey sky. The unseen battle that now developed among the dense clouds gradually moved across the border into the sky above Bessarabia. We were able then to resume our journey, and soon we entered Stefanesti.

As a result of the continuous Soviet air-raids nothing now remains of this pretty little town on the Prut but a heap of smoking ruins. When we arrived many of the houses were in flames. From time to time groups of German soldiers passed along the deserted streets carrying stretchers which they had reverently draped with groundsheets. In a little square behind the church two large German lorries which had sustained direct hits were now no more than twisted masses of metal. A heavy bomb had fallen just in front of the entrance to the kind of garden which surrounds the church, a few yards from the little cemetery where the German soldiers killed in the air-raids of the past few days have been laid to rest. In the middle of the crossroad stood the *Feldgendarme*, rigid and motionless, his face streaming with blood : he had not moved from his post.

" How do we get to the bridge?" we asked him. He raised his red-and-white indicator and pointed in the desired direction. As he turned he noticed five or six boys—the eldest could not have been more than ten years old—huddled in a terrified group in the doorway of the café which stands at the corner of the street. (Mechanically I read the words on the smashed sign-board which hung above the door : *Café Central de Iancu Liebermann*.) The interior seemed to have been completely destroyed, and even as I looked a few wisps of smoke drifted slowly out into the street. *" Weg, weg, Kinder !"* shouted the *Feldgendarme* in a voice that was at once severe and amiable, and he smiled as he wiped his blood-stained face with the back of his hand. At the sound of that voice the boys silently fled and concealed themselves among the ruins of a nearby house. The *Feldgendarme* laughingly explained to us that they used to stand there all day and watch him raising his arms, waving his indicator, turning abruptly to let through a waiting stream of traffic. " They don't go away even when the bombs are falling," he added. " They're more afraid of me than of Russian bombs. But as soon as I turn my back . . ." And even as he spoke we could see them, cautiously emerging from behind a ruined wall. *" Nichts zu machen,"* said the *Feldgendarme* with a laugh.

Until recently there were two bridges over the Prut at

Stefanesti, both built of stout wooden beams. On the outbreak of hostilities, however, the Russians succeeded in blowing them up, and for a while it seemed that they had made it impossible for the Germans to cross the river. Indeed, during the first few days of the war the German troops on this sector were completely inactive. Not a single shell, not a single bullet was fired from the Rumanian bank in the direction of the Soviet bank. Life was truly idyllic. Military operations were restricted to aerial battles between the Soviet planes that periodically bombed Stefanesti and formations of German fighters supported by flak. But two days ago the German engineers, undeterred by Russian artillery-fire, suddenly began to build a bridge of boats, and three hours after the commencement of the battle the tanks of a *Panzerdivision* were deploying along the Soviet bank.

This morning we crossed the bridge of boats, near which the Todt Organization is already building a second bridge. Although constantly interrupted by air-raids the work is proceeding rapidly and methodically, as if there were no Soviet troops within sixty miles. And yet the Russians are no more than a dozen miles away, on the far side of the hills.

We pass beneath one of those rustic triumphal arches, surmounted by the emblem of the hammer and sickle, which the Bolsheviks have erected at all their frontier-posts. Not a single house in the Soviet village facing Stefanesti seems to have been destroyed. The Germans have deliberately spared the homes of the poor Rumanian peasants of Bessarabia. With a coolness amounting almost to insolence they have crossed the river without firing a single shell. A dozen white crosses of acacia-wood are ranged along the side of the road near the intact village. I stop to read the names of the fallen. They were all mere boys, from twenty to twenty-five years of age. The German soldiers get out of their vehicles, pick wild flowers and lay them on their comrades' graves.

I look about me. The houses of the village look very neat and tidy with their whitewashed walls and thatched roofs. The wooden window-sills are adorned with beautiful inlaid designs worked by hand. Groups of women and boys stand behind the palings of the little gardens that surround all the houses and watch the motorized column go by. The old men sit motionless in the doorways, their heads sunk upon their chests. There are no youths to be seen, nor any men between the ages of thirty and forty. There are, on the other hand, a great many children, as well as a lot of girls, all very young and not unprepossessing with their brightly-coloured dresses and their red-and-white kerchiefs. All are merry-eyed, but their faces are pale and sad, with a sadness that is almost bitter. Their pallor is indicative not of under-nourishment but of an emotion which I cannot define. It is the physical expression of a whole mental complex, of which, perhaps, I shall speak in due course, when I have succeeded in probing the mystery of those merry eyes set in those pale, sad faces.

It is astonishing to see the cattle grazing in the meadows, the fields of golden corn nodding in the breeze, the hens scratching among the tracks of the tanks parked on the dusty road. The Rumanian bank, which we left only a few minutes ago, was thick with mud, but here we find dust. That, I think, is due to the fact that the Rumanian bank is low-lying and marshy, in contrast to the Soviet bank, which gradually rises in a series of ample folds through the vast, ever-widening circles of an amphitheatre of hills covered with woods and fields of ripening grain.

Just outside the village we join the German motorized column which we are to accompany throughout the rest of our journey to the front.

Shortly before noon the column gets under way. As it rolls through the Bessarabian countryside it leaves in its wake a huge cloud of dust which darkens the green of the hills like the smoke of a great fire. The advanced elements passed this way only a few hours ago, and there are traces of the fighting all around us—the scent, so to say, is still warm. All the indications are of brief, violent clashes rather than of full-scale battles. The German forces in this sector have advanced slowly but inexorably, overcoming by an uninterrupted series of encircling movements and fierce assaults the mobility of the Russian defence which, supported by tanks, launches frequent counter-attacks against the head and flanks of their columns.

But these counter-attacks are conceived on a very modest scale: they are clearly designed to delay rather than to arrest the German advance. It seems, nevertheless, that since this morning the Soviet troops have been reacting more violently on the hills to the east and north of Zaicani, which is situated about six miles from here. The deep boom of the artillery, to which the sharp crackle of anti-aircraft fire provides an accompaniment, becomes more muffled every hour.

We advance slowly, both on account of the weight of the traffic and because we have to surmount the obstacles with which the retreating Russians have strewn the ground. At intervals the road is pitted with mine-craters. The grass for miles around is littered with steel helmets, twisted motor-cycles, and the remains of vehicles gutted by shells and bombs. As we climb towards the top of the hill that dominates Stefanesti the terrain begins to reveal more frequent and more pronounced traces of the struggle. Every yard of ground is pitted with shell-holes. Presently, as we round a bend, we come upon a Soviet tank lying on its side right at the edge of the road, the long barrels of its twin cannon pointing towards the valley. Here the battle has been prolonged, fierce and bitter. The Russian tank was supported only by a few small detachments of fusiliers from Turkestan, entrenched here and there in the corn-fields and the woods. The air seems to be filled even yet with the din of the explosions, with those lingering reverberations which always follow the muffled roar of artillery. Clouds of small grey birds fly low over the corn with a whirring sound as of machine-gun bullets.

During the brief halt, enforced upon us by one of the numerous craters in the road, we get out and view the scene of the struggle. The Soviet tank has a gash in its side from which protrude its entrails of twisted steel. However much we look around us we can find no trace of any Russian dead. When possible the Bolshevik troops take their dead with them.

2*

Always they remove their papers and their regimental badges. A group of German soldiers carefully examines the tank. They look like experts conducting an on-the-spot inquiry into the causes of an accident. What interests them most of all is the quality of the enemy's material and the manner in which that material is employed in the field : in other words, Soviet technique in its twofold aspect—industrial and tactical. They examine the small trenches dug by the Russians, the ammunition-boxes, the abandoned rifles, the shell-holes, the steel of the tank, the structure of the twin cannon. Then they shake their heads and murmur : " *Ja, ja, aber* . . ." The whole secret of the German successes is implicit in that " *aber* . . .", in that " but . . ."

Our column gets under way again, overtaking battalions of infantry, trains of artillery, squadrons of cavalry. The roar of engines cleaves the red cloud of dust which covers the hills. Cold shafts of sunlight cut through that dense fog, glinting on the steel of the tanks and on the foaming cruppers of the horses. Icy gusts of wind form sharp ridges in the thick dust. Our mouths are filled with sand, our eyes smart, our eyelids bleed. It is July, and the cold is intense. How many hours have we been on the road? How many miles have we travelled? The sun is already setting, the moisture of early evening permeates the cloud of dust and dulls the steel of the tanks. From the horizon comes the rhythmic boom of the guns, like the pulsations of a giant piston. The sound grows louder and softer by turns, in an alternation of sonorous and muffled echoes.

Presently a despatch-rider conveys to the column the order to stop and to deploy in a meadow flanking the road, under cover of a wood. Within the space of a few minutes the column has assumed the formation prescribed for overnight halts. The drone of engines is heard in the sky above the hills and valleys, which are already deep in shadow and moist with the dews of evening. " They're fighting over there," says Lieutenant Lauser, a young man from Leipzig with an athlete's shoulders and boyish eyes behind his thick spectacles (he is a *Dozent* in some university, if I am not mistaken), and he indicates a point on the near horizon where the cloud of dust is higher, denser, like the smoke from a fire.

A green twilight settles lightly on the trees and the corn. A line of ambulances laden with wounded passes along the road. How different are the wounded of this war from those of the war of twenty-five years ago! I have said it before: they look more like workers who have been injured in an industrial accident than soldiers wounded in battle. They smoke in silence, their faces a little pale, a little strained. A corporation bus from Bucharest, requisitioned by the Army Medical Corps, stops for a few moments near our column. It is full of walking wounded, many of them with their heads swathed in bandages. A German tank-driver has both arms bandaged up to the shoulders. A comrade puts a lighted cigarette between his lips. His large black beret tipped over one eye, the tank-driver smokes in silence, glancing idly about him. One would not say that they were suffering. Perhaps pain has no power over the minds of men so preoccupied with the physical fact of their wounds, men so abstracted, so turned in upon themselves. The bus moves off, and those pale faces are swallowed up in the green twilight.

The soldiers of our column sit on the grass, eat slices of bread and marmalade, drink the tea which they have brought with them in thermos-flasks, shout, joke among themselves, talk in low voices. They do not speak of the war. I have noticed that they never speak of the war. They sing—but to themselves, as it were, not in chorus. Having finished their brief meal they busy themselves about their vehicles, tightening nuts and bolts, lubricating the mechanism, lying down beneath the bellies of their tanks to check, to adjust. Then, when night has fallen, they wrap themselves in their blankets and go to sleep on the seats of their vehicles. I too wrap myself in my blanket and try to sleep.

Gradually a pale glimmer appears in the sky: the moon is rising. I think of the retreat of the Soviet troops, of their tragic, lonely, desperate struggle. It is not the classical Russian retreat of *War and Peace*—a retreat amid the glare of fires, along roads jammed with refugees, with wounded, with abandoned weapons. The atmosphere of this battlefield is that of a factory-yard after an abortive strike : cold, empty, desolate. A few weapons lying about the ground, a few military capes and greatcoats, a few gutted vehicles. A colossal strike has failed. On this battlefield there is, perhaps, no Andrew Bolkonski lying amid the corn, as on the night of Austerlitz; only a few stakanovite tank-crews, a few riflemen from Turkestan. Suddenly there is a sound of men passing along the road. Then I hear a hoarse, sad voice. It is a Russian voice, it says : " *Nyet, nyet* "—insistently, like a cry. It says : " *Nyet* —no," in a tone of protest. I cannot see the prisoners' faces. The tramp of feet recedes into the distance, and gradually I fall asleep, lulled into oblivion by the voice of the guns.

V

TECHNOLOGY AND "INDUSTRIAL ETHICS"

Zaicani (Bessarabia), July 6th.

YESTERDAY, as our column advanced from that nameless village on the Russian bank of the Prut in the direction of Shante-Bani, through a green countryside fringed with red clouds (the clouds really were red: they looked like Communist propaganda-posters glued to the sky), there unfolded around me, on the screen of the corn-fields, amid that marvellous abundance of crops ripe for harvesting, the squalid film of the battlefield, strewn with Soviet tanks gutted by bombs and shells; with smashed rifles, boxes of ammunition, and overturned vehicles. And at a certain point I found myself thinking that this was no ordinary kind of war, and that the task of a diligent observer, a dispassionate, objective witness of this Russian campaign, " 1941 model," would perhaps be very different from that of a dispassionate and objective witness of any other war.

I told myself that the important thing was not to describe the shells of the tanks, the carcases of the horses—in short, the outward and visible signs of the battle now developing—but to try to grasp the underlying significance, the hidden meaning of this singular war, to explain its peculiar, indeed its unique character, to note objectively, with a mind free from futile, stupid prejudices, all the characteristic elements of this war, elements not present in any of the campaigns so far fought in Poland, France, Greece, Africa, and Jugoslavia. Overturned tanks and dead horses, I thought to myself, are encountered

45

on all battlefields. They are essential elements of any war. But if the reader is to be furnished with the material on which to base an objective judgment—moral, historical, social and human, as well as strategic—there is much else, of a wholly different character, to be said about this campaign against Soviet Russia.

In the first place, it must be emphasized that the Germans are not here engaged in an " easy " war against a weak enemy. A possibly negative moral judgment on the Soviet State is not incompatible with a recognition of the enormous difficulties with which the German Army has to contend in this war. The Soviet troops fight hard and bitterly, they defend themselves gallantly and tenaciously. (It must, however, be added that, even if the Russian divisions were retreating without offering any resistance, the tempo of the German advance on this front would be no different. As things are, it is a miracle that we are able to progress a few miles a day over this frightful terrain.)

There was a moment yesterday when I feared that we should have to stop, that we should have to give up the idea of advancing any further. Imagine thousands and thousands of heavy vehicles—tanks, loaded gun-carriages, mobile smithies, convoys of lorries laden with munitions, anti-aircraft weapons and petrol, ambulances, field-kitchens, etc., etc.—stretching in an endless procession along narrow beaten tracks, where one sinks knee-deep into a black, sticky, extremely tenacious clay which the German soldiers call *Buna,* the name of the synthetic rubber. Add to the difficulties of the terrain an extremely mobile, stubborn and technically efficient Soviet defence, and then judge whether that is not enough to explain the apparent slowness of the German advance.

On the other hand, in order to appreciate the true reasons for the Red Army's inferiority to the *Wehrmacht* it is totally unnecessary to resort to polemical arguments—to the convenient device (which I myself shall never adopt on any account) of denigrating one's enemy, of branding him as cowardly or inept. It is enough to see this terrible war-machine that is the German Army at close quarters. This morning I was standing on the brow of the hill that slopes down to the village of Zaicani. Before me the cloud of red dust which covered the battlefield swirled and eddied in the wind. The cannon thundered ceaselessly. Far above my head formations of German and Soviet aircraft weaved in and out of enormous banks of fleecy white clouds. And below me, on both sides of the hill, down in the valley and again on the opposite slope, I could see, slowly advancing, not an army, but an immense travelling workshop, an enormous mobile foundry that stretched as far as the eye could reach in either direction. It was as if the thousands of chimneys, cranes, iron bridges and steel towers, the millions of cog-wheels, the hundreds and hundreds of blast-furnaces and rolling-mills of the whole of Westphalia, of the entire Ruhr, were advancing in a body over the vast expanse of corn-fields that is Bessarabia. It was as if an enormous Krupps Steelworks, a gigantic Essen, were preparing to launch an attack on the hills of Zaicani, of Shofroncani, of Bratosheni. Yes, that was it: I was looking not at an army but at a colossal steel-works, in which a multitude of workmen were setting about their various tasks with a streamlined efficiency which at first sight concealed the immensity of their effort. And what amazed me most of all was to see this gigantic mobile steelworks leaving behind it no trail of smoking ruins, no heaps of rubble, no blackened fields, but only peaceful villages and unscathed expanses of corn.

I was standing next to Karl, an anti-tank gunner. "The Reds are retreating," Karl said to me, indicating the red cloud that was rising three or four miles ahead of us from the hill behind Zaicani, a little to the east of Bratosheni. I thought at first that it was a cloud of smoke, that the retreating Russians were setting fire to the fields and villages. "*Nein, nein!*" exclaimed Karl, shaking his head. No, no, the Reds are not destroying the fields and villages. It is in no way to the credit of the Soviet troops that they spare the crops and the villages. It is part of the strategy of modern armies to spare the countryside. Only the towns are exposed to their assaults. The towns are centres for the storage of grain and for the production of technical equipment, munitions, machines, etc. They are a war-machine in themselves. Modern armies aim to destroy the enemy's industrial capacity, not his fields and villages. It is a case of the machine—in the literal sense of the word—destroying the machine. After the din of battle has died down, after the gigantic mobile steel-works has passed, we hear once again, as after the storm in Leopardi's poem, the cries of the animals, the murmur of the wind in the corn-fields.

Yesterday morning, as soon as we had crossed the Prut, and again in the evening at Shante-Bani, the cows brushed against the steel sides of the heavy lorries with their horns, the hens scratched about among the tracks of the panzers. Pigs grunted in the farmyards. The peasants offered the soldiers large slices of white bread. A few hours ago, in a village near Zaicani, a pig finished up beneath the wheels of a lorry. A group of soldiers gathered round the dead animal; it was obvious that they were desperately keen to take it away so that they could enjoy a meal of roast pork. And take it away they did, but not before they had recompensed the owner, an old peasant, to the tune of several hundred *lei*. That amiable transaction, that quiet deal on the edge of the battlefield seemed natural enough to everyone, and to none more than to the peasant.

Having collected the pig, the Germans returned to their vehicles, laughing and joking with that simple gaiety which is the most striking characteristic of these soldier-workers. I was astonished both at the way in which they instinctively respected the peasant's rights and by the fact that he for his part clearly regarded their scrupulous honesty as something quite normal and natural. Perhaps in all this there was at work not only a moral principle but also that subtle influence which the precision of modern technology, modern machines, and modern industrial processes exerts on the ethics of the people. For it is undoubtedly true that in the last analysis the machine profoundly influences the moral outlook of these soldier-workers—in other words, it becomes itself a moral factor.

It is only a few hours since we left the village of Shante-Bani, yet already specialists of the corps of engineers are busy installing a telephone line which will extend along the route of our advance almost to the front. Squads of soldiers are sawing up the trunks of acacias with portable saws powered by small petrol-engines. Others remove the bark with small bill-hooks, others plane away the rough edges, others perforate the wood with augers before screwing on the porcelain insulators. Meanwhile, holes are being dug in the ground at regular intervals, and soon a very long, straight line of white poles stretches down the hill into the valley, then up the other side and through the wood, finally disappearing from view in the direction of Stefanesti. Already engineers are scrambling up the poles with the aid of climbing-irons and are putting up the gleaming copper wires. It is hard to decide which aspect of the operation is most admirable—its speed, its precision, or its orderliness.

Close to the point where the engineers are erecting the last pole, the one nearest us, a squad of soldiers is hard at work constructing a little cemetery—digging graves, fashioning crosses of white acacia-wood, carving the names of the fallen on the crosses with red-hot irons. And the movements of these soldiers, their postures, have the same harmony, the same simplicity—in a word, the same precision—as the movements and postures of the engineers who are installing the telephone line, or of those mechanics whom I can see over there repairing an engine, or of the machine-gunners who are oiling the parts of an anti-aircraft weapon mounted on this lorry here beside me. There is in the movements, in the postures of all these soldiers an alertness, a sobriety, which seem to me the expression of a humanity no longer founded on sentiment alone, but on a moral principle rooted in technology. It is something profound and at the same time intangible, something profoundly intimate and pure.

We reach Zaicani in the early hours of the afternoon. The Soviet troops left the village only a few hours ago. I start to

wander among the houses and the allotments. In the pond
behind the beautiful white church with its gleaming zinc-plated
cupolas hundreds of ducks drift idly among the tall weeds.
Flocks of horses graze in the meadows. The hens flap about
their runs, throwing up clouds of dust. The cows are splashes
of white on the green canvas of the hillside. Troops of boys
rush forward to admire the German vehicles, the women lean
over the palings and laugh, the old men sit in the doorways of
the houses, their faces half-hidden by large woollen caps. It is
the usual scene, the usual absurd scene that one finds in these
villages—still quiet and contented, albeit a little nervous, after
the tide of battle has passed them by.

I stop outside a chapel, one of those rustic chapels which
are to be seen at any mountain crossroad, even in our own
province of Alto Adige. But there is no cross above it, no
painted wooden figure of Christ. The devout villagers seem to
have given the chapel a fresh coat of varnish: but the figure
of Christ has disappeared, the cross is no longer there. An
old peasant walks up to me, removes his woollen cap—his
caciula—and crosses himself. He says to me : " The Bolsheviks
wouldn't allow any icons or images of Christ in our church.
Eh, they wouldn't allow them." And he starts to laugh, as if
one could only laugh at Communist impiety. Later, a German
officer tells me that the young men in the villages seem to differ
from the old in their attitude to religion. They appear to
despise it.

I enter the church. Everything is in order, everything is
spick and span, the walls look as if they had been newly
whitewashed. But there are no icons to be seen, no crosses;
there is nothing here to remind one of the religion of Christ.
Even the crosses on the cupolas of the churches have disappeared. Some women I meet tell me : " It was the Bolsheviks
who pulled down the crosses. Eh, they wouldn't be doing
with them !" And they laugh, as if they too found Communist impiety ridiculous. But at the same time they each hold
up three fingers and cross themselves, then they kiss the tips of
their fingers.

Our commanding officer has set up his headquarters in the village school. We shall remain at Zaicani for a few hours only; but already the telephone exchange is functioning, the clerks are hammering away on their typewriters. The school hall looks very smart, the walls have only recently been white-washed. The desks are new, but already they are splashed with ink and defaced by the children's pen-knives. Hanging on the wall is a time-table, printed in Russian. It is rather a complicated time-table for an elementary school situated in the country. An astonishing number of hours a week are devoted to "proletarian ethics." While I am on the way back to my place in the column the *flak* batteries begin firing furiously. A formation of twenty-three Soviet bombers passes directly above our heads at an altitude of about five thousand feet. The outlines of the "Martin Bombers" are clearly distinguishable against the blue-and-white sky. The anti-aircraft shells burst very close to the planes, the rear patrol breaks up, then re-forms. They are heading east, they are returning from some bombing operation directed against our lines of communication.

A few seconds later two German fighters dart across the sky in hot pursuit of the Soviet formation, which disappears into a cloud-bank away on the horizon.

"The Russian Air Force is very active these days," says Captain Zeller, a staff-officer attached to our unit. "They bomb the bridges over the Prut, they attack our lines of communication. They cause us a certain amount of inconvenience, but they do little damage."

He comments on the resistance of the Soviet troops, and he speaks as a soldier—objectively, without exaggeration, without expressing any political opinions, without using any argument not of a strictly technical order. "We take few prisoners," he says, "because they always fight to the last man. They never surrender. Their material can't be compared with ours; but they know how to use it."

He confirms that on this front the Soviet divisions are composed mainly of Asiatic elements. Only the specialist units are

Russian. We go to see two officer prisoners—two lieutenants, a pilot and a tank-commander.

" They are very primitive," remarks Captain Zeller. It is the only opinion of a non-technical character he has so far vouchsafed. And it is, in my judgment, erroneous: it is a " bourgeois " opinion.

The pilot officer puffs slowly at a cigarette, eyeing us intently the while. He gazes with unconcealed curiosity at my uniform, which is that of an officer in the Alpini. But he does not say anything. They tell me that of the two he is the more reluctant to talk. He has refused to make any statement. He looks like a man of the people : possibly he comes of peasant stock. He is clean-shaven, with angular features and rather a large nose. He baled out of his aircraft after it had caught fire. Russian airmen forced down behind the German lines usually defend themselves with their revolvers. This one was unarmed : during his parachute descent his revolver had slipped' out of its holster. He gave himself up with an air of indifference. The tank-officer is a man of solid, massive build. He has a hard, coarse face; possibly he is of working-class origin. He has fair hair, bright eyes, rather large ears. He smokes placidly, his features set in a smile. He looks at me. I address him in Russian. He tells me that he is sorry he has been captured.

" Do you wish you were still fighting?" I ask him.

He does not answer. Then he tells me that it isn't his fault : he has done all that was expected of him, he has no cause to reproach himself.

" Are you a Communist?" I ask. He does not answer. After a while he tells me that for some years he worked in a ball-bearing factory at Gorki—formerly Nijni-Novgorod. He watches some soldiers tinkering with an engine. It is obvious that he would like to get to work on that engine himself. He throws away his cigarette, takes off his cap, scratches his head. He has the air of an unemployed workman.

Towards evening the column moves off again. Goodbye, Zaicani. The vehicles sink in the mud up to their axles.

Everyone has to get out and push. We pass a long train of artillery; every piece, every crate of ammunition, is drawn by six, sometimes by eight pairs of horses. A squadron of cavalry appears on the brow of the hill. The mounted figures stand out in sharp relief against a sky covered with white clouds lit by the oblique crimson rays of the setting sun. After a few miles we sight the village of Shofroncani, nestling in a green hollow. The hills around are still bathed in sunlight, but already the hollow in which the village lies is deep in shadow and moist with the dews of evening. All of a sudden the drone of aircraft is heard amid the tangled mass of clouds. A bomb falls on the houses of Shofroncani. More follow, and still more. The red flashes cleave the darkness below us. Suddenly a scarlet column of flame rises from the edge of the village, a terrible explosion reverberates from hill to hill. I would say that there were two or three aircraft engaged in the operation—not more. But now two German fighters dart across the purple sunset sky and hurl themselves at the Soviet bombers. A " Martin " dives in flames behind a wood over towards Bratosceni. Shortly after, a despatch-rider comes up to tell us that the bridge at Shofroncani has been destroyed and that a bomb has fallen on two ammunition lorries. There are many dead. Our column will have to wait on the hill until the bridge has been rebuilt. We shall undoubtedly be held up for many hours. A number of houses in the village are burning. A little way to our right some howitzer-batteries are firing continuously, the noise of the explosions can be heard in the distance. At intervals, through the clear night, there comes the sound of rifle-shots fired by Russian stragglers. A pale, solemn moon rises slowly from the corn.

VI

LOOK CLOSELY AT THESE DEAD

IT is midnight before the column moves off again. A chill wind cuts diagonally across our path. The air is smooth and transparent as glass, it sparkles like water in the moonlight. We coast down the hill in the direction of Shofroncani. A house at the edge of the village is still burning. In fact, Shofroncani is more than a village, it is a small country town, with white houses visible here and there amid groves of flowering walnut trees, acacias and limes. We have orders to deploy on the hill opposite, so that we may protect the left flank of the heavy column at present engaged in a stern battle near the village of Bratosheni. It is necessary for us to act quickly. We have already lost too much time waiting for the engineers to rebuild the bridge. The vehicles sink in the mud. The road, if this species of cattle-track may be so described, is covered with a thick layer of fine dust, which with every breath of wind rises in dense red clouds. But in places, where the clayey soil has failed to absorb the rain-water, or where a stream crosses the track, the sticky, tenacious mud grips the wheels of the lorries and the tracks of the tanks, which sink slowly into the *Buna* as into a quicksand.

The soldiers have to get out and push their vehicles. Amid the frantic roar of the engines their stertorous breathing has about it an almost brutish quality.

By now the moon is setting, and already the night is as black as pitch. In the darkness the Russian soldiers scattered about the woods and the corn-fields are sniping at us. Their bullets whistle high over our heads. No one seems to notice them. It would take something more than this to distract these soldier-workers from their immediate task. While Lieutenant Weil's despatch-rider was carrying an order to Zaicani he several times became a target for machine-gun bullets. The snipers are not *francs-tireurs* in the strict sense of the term; they are Red Army stragglers. They fire at isolated individuals, at the flanks and rear of the column.

Thus we reach Shofroncani. We cross the narrow wooden bridge which the engineers have erected in the space of a few hours. The tree-trunks, supported on trestles of rough beams, sway, groan and bend beneath the weight of the vehicles. The villagers have fled into the woods to escape the Soviet bombardment. Only the dogs are left; they rush about the gardens of the empty houses, barking furiously. It takes us more than an hour to pass through the village. We have to push and drag our vehicles with our bare hands. The mud trickles down my legs, fills my boots. I am hungry. I still have a few slices of bread left, also a little cheese.

Ahead of us, the night is lit up by the brilliant red flashes of exploding bombs. The crash of heavy shells drowns the roar of our engines. An officer is shouting, his voice harsh, metallic, penetrating. At one point our car plunges into a hole full of mud. A score of soldiers rush up and help us in our efforts to put it back on an even keel. All to no purpose. We have to wait until a lorry equipped with tracks takes it in tow, wrenching it by main force from the tenacious grip of the *Buna*. My camera is left at the bottom of the hole. I am vexed because it contains a roll of undeveloped film. I try to console myself with the thought that things might be worse. We pass the last houses of Shofroncani and start to climb the hill. The road becomes impossible. The vehicles struggle up the slope, skidding and sliding backwards. We find it easier to cut diagonally across a field of soya-beans. The wheels secure a purchase on the ample leaves, on the long fibrous stalks.

One of our machine-guns starts to sweep the vast undulating expanse of fields to our left with concentrated bursts of fire, seeking to disperse a few isolated groups of Russians who are lurking amid the corn. Dawn is already breaking when the column reaches the brow of the hill. Ahead of us, at the top of a pleasant treeless slope covered with golden grain, the outline of a Soviet tank is plainly visible against the clear sky. It moves slowly, lumbers down towards us, its guns blazing. It stops, fires at us with its front cannon. Then it continues on its way, and I hear distinctly the clatter of its tracks. It seems to be sniffing the air, trying to locate an invisible trail leading through the corn.

Suddenly it starts firing with its machine-guns, but half-heartedly, as if it merely wanted to test them. It advances swiftly down the slope towards us, then, without warning, it describes a wide half-circle and doubles back on its tracks, blazing away with its cannon. One could almost believe that it was looking for someone, that it was calling someone. Presently some men emerge from the corn and proceed to wander about the hillside, making no attempt to conceal themselves. Others emerge at various points : all told they must number about a hundred. Evidently this is some rearguard detachment, or perhaps a detachment that has been cut off from the main body. The men seem to hesitate. They are seeking a way of escape. "*Arme Leute*—poor b—s," says Lieutenant Weil in my ear.

And now the Russian soldiers advance down the hill towards us, firing their machine-guns. Then, suddenly, they vanish. There must be a dip in the ground at that point, a depression in the hillside. Around the tank can be seen the tiny chunks of turf thrown up by the shells from our mortars. The stutter of machine-gun fire spreads along the flank of the column like a message tapped out in morse. Then some German soldiers appear over to our right, walking with their heads down, firing at the Russians. They advance in a line, blazing away with their tommy-guns. An anti-tank gun fires a few rounds at the Soviet tank. And now the outlines of two panzers appear on the brow of the hill, immediately behind the Russian tank.

The column receives the order to advance in support of the leading elements. The Reds retire slowly, firing all the while.

We reach the hilltop, go down into the valley and up the other side. A German soldier is sitting on the ground; he has been wounded in the leg. He laughs, wiping the mud from his face with the back of his hand. A medical orderly goes up to him, also laughing, kneels beside him, starts to clean his wound. The Russians retreat slowly; they walk upright through the corn, firing as they go. The gutted Soviet tank lies on its side.

Suddenly a stentorian voice bellows from a loudspeaker: "*Achtung! Achtung!*" And immediately the strains of a tango, accompanied by a series of metallic whistles, issue from the mouth of a large horn attached to the roof of the loud-speaker-van of the P.K.—The *Propaganda Kompanie*. The soldiers yell with delight. That ear-splitting music provides an accompaniment to the roar of the engines, the stutter of the machine-guns, the clatter of the tank-tracks.

"*Ich habe dich lieb, braune Madonna* . . . ," sings the brutal voice over the loudspeaker. The column stops; a hail of machine-gun bullets passes high above our heads with a furious whistling sound. I walk over to the lieutenant commanding the P.K. squad attached to our unit. When I offer him a cigarette I notice that he stretches out his hand and gropes for it like a blind man. He has lost his spectacles. He laughs, caresses his eyelid with two fingers and says: "It's the second time since the war started that I've lost my spectacles. I had to grope my way into Paris."

The column moves off again. After a minute or two we pass close beside the gutted Russian tank. A number of Soviet dead are lying near it in the corn. Two are stretched out on their backs, their legs wide apart. The others are lying on their sides in grotesque postures. There must be about a score of them scattered around the tank. Nearly all are Mongolians. Only two appear to me to be Russians. An orderly falls out of the column, walks over to the corpses, touches them, examines them one by one. The column comes to a halt. The soldiers lean out of their vehicles, gazing at the dead.

" *Nichts zu machen*—there's nothing we can do," says the orderly.

Some of them are clad in uniforms of dark grey material tinged with blue and red, others in khaki. All wear jackboots. On their heads are caps, not steel helmets. Two of them—one a Mongolian—are wearing a leather headgear of the type used by airmen. There can be no doubt that they too were members of the tank-crew. They are strange, the dead of this war. They lie amid the corn like ghostly intruders. They have nothing in common even with this boundless sky that rests so lightly on the hilltops. The corn diffuses an ethereal radiance of green and yellow. The wind passes over the fields like a wave, a wave that breaks on the horizon. During the brief interludes of silence one hears the long mysterious rustle of the ripening corn. These dead men are like shipwrecked mariners washed ashore by the tempest, washed ashore by the gentle undulations of this sea of grain.

The sun rises, bright and crystal-clear in the chill of early morning. From the village of Bratosheni, a mile or so to our rear, comes a strident crowing of cocks, a bellowing of oxen. Groups of frightened peasants line the palings in front of their houses, others crawl out of enormous stacks of straw. The women and children have been hiding in the straw all night. This is a strange war. The grey steel of the armoured columns skirts the villages, skirts the delicately-waving corn, skirts the fragile houses built of straw and mortar—skirts them without touching them. It seems a miracle, yet it is only the fruit of a technique that has been brought to perfection, the fruit of a scientific method of waging war.

An armoured column is a precision instrument *par excellence*. In this extraordinary war it seems that only machines are vulnerable, that human life must at all costs be respected. That is why, on these battlefields, death assumes the character of an accident, of something outside the logic of events. There is something absurd about the dead of this war.

Even among the soldiers they occasion a momentary feeling of surprise, almost of bewilderment. They are a reality that knows no rule, no law. Their appearance comes as a shock : it is like the unexpected revelation of the failure of an experiment, of a defect in the war-machine itself. That which restores to the dead a semblance of reality, that which reintroduces them into the logical scheme of things, is the illogicality, the absurdity of their death.

At one point during that brief skirmish with the Soviet rear-guard I had a vivid impression that the machines were behaving like living creatures, almost like human beings, that they had a will, an intelligence. And those men who walked amid the corn, firing at the hard steel shells of the panzers, seemed to me extraneous to that violent episode, to that terrible clash of machines. I walk over to the Soviet dead, I examine them one by one. They are Mongolians, nearly all of them. They no longer fight as once they did, mounted on the scraggy horses of the steppe, armed only with rifles or long lances. They fight with machines, oiling the parts, listening intently to the throb of the engines. They no longer crouch over a horse's mane, they bend over a dashboard covered with instruments. The Stakanovites of Stalin's Army, the *udarniki*, the authentic creatures of the *Pyatlyetki*, the product of Lenin's famous formula, " Soviet + electrification = Bolshevism," prove their ability to sustain the terrible, bloody struggle against the soldier-workers of the German Army. (The mechanization of armies involves not only the " specialization " of labour but the technical training of the masses through the industrialization of agriculture. Here is the essential meaning of this war, the essential significance of this conflict between Germany and Russia—a conflict not of men alone but of machines, of techniques, of systems of industrialization; a conflict not only between the engineers of Göring and of Stakanov but between National Socialism, with its stupendous feats of reconstruction and organization, and Soviet Communism, with its *Pyatlyetki*, its Five Year Plans; a conflict, in short, between two peoples who, through industrialization, or rather through the " mechanization of agriculture," have acquired not only technical proficiency but that industrial "morale" which is indispensable to those called upon to fight in this war. The protagonists in this Russian campaign are two armies consisting primarily and essentially of specialized workers and "industrialized" peasants.) From the manner in which the Soviet soldier fights it is clear that the modern *muzhik* too is a skilled craftsman, a typical product of the machine age. This is a conflict—the first in history—between two armies in which the military spirit is allied to the industrial spirit, to "industrial morale," and in which military discipline is blended with technical discipline, with the discipline of organized labour, with the discipline of the team of specialists.

From the sociological standpoint too this fact is undoubtedly of singular interest. And I am thinking of the mistake made by those who hoped, at the beginning of the war against Russia, that at the first impact revolution would break out in Moscow—in other words, that the collapse of the system would precede the collapse of the army. These people showed clearly that they had failed to understand the spirit of Soviet society. Rather than the *kolkhozi*—the great collective farms—rather than her giant factories, rather than her heavy industry, the supreme industrial creation of Soviet Russia is her Army.

Everything in it, from its weapons to its spirit, is the result of twenty years of industrial organization, twenty years devoted to the training of skilled craftsmen. The true essence of Soviet society is the Army—and I say this not because I wish to imply that the régime is fundamentally militaristic in character but because the Army is the sole yardstick by which one can measure the degree of social development and industrial progress achieved by the citizens of this Communist State. (Just as, on the other hand, the German Army is the measure and the sum of the technical progress achieved by modern German industry.) The Russians themselves have always insisted on this concept. It is right that this unexpected confirmation of its truth should come from a serene and objective witness of the reactions and the resistance of the Soviet Army in its clash with the German Army, of the manner in which the industrialized peasants, the specialized workers, the great Stakanovite masses of the Soviet Revolution comport themselves on the battle-field.

I have already mentioned that among these Soviet dead are two Russians. They are tall and powerfully-built, with long arms. Their eyes are wide open, and very bright. They are two specialists, two Stakanovites. A group of German soldiers gaze at them in silence. One of the Germans looks around for some flowers; there are only red flowers in the corn, a species of poppies. The soldier hesitates before those flowers; then he gathers an armful of corn, with which he covers the faces of the two dead Russians. The other soldiers look on in silence, nibbling hunks of bread. (Look closely at these dead, these Tartar dead, these Russian dead. They are new corpses, absolutely brand-new. Just delivered from the great factory of the *Pyatlyetka*. See how bright their eyes are. Observe their low foreheads, their thick lips. Peasants, are they? Workers? Yes, they are workers—specialists, *udarniki,* from any one of the thousands of *kolkhozi,* from any one of the thousands of factories of the U.S.S.R. Look closely at their faces, their narrow, hard, obstinate faces. They are all the same. Mass-produced. They typify a new race, a tough race, these corpses of workers killed in an industrial accident.)

The loudspeaker-van starts up again: "*Ich liebe dich so tief* . . ." The soldiers laugh. They are sitting on the mudguards of their lorries, they are sitting on top of their tanks, their legs dangling through the hatches. And they are eating. In this fluid type of warfare there is no fixed time for meals. One eats when one can. Every soldier carries with him his ration of black bread and marmalade, his thermos of tea. Periodically, even during the heat of battle, he will take a slice of bread from his haversack, spread it with marmalade, raise it to his mouth with one hand, while with the other he grips the steering-wheel of his lorry or the butt of his machine-gun. The officers eat with the men, they eat the same as the men. "*Ich liebe dich so tief* . . ." sings the voice over the loudspeaker.

The air is warm. The corn nods in the wind. The fields of soya-beans rustle like silk. The forests of sunflowers turn slowly on their long stalks to greet the sun, slowly open their great yellow eyes. Huge white clouds drift across the sky. The Russian soldiers lie sleeping in the furrows, their faces covered with wisps of corn.

On the hill facing us fountains of earth are thrown up by the Soviet shells. From time to time a Russian straggler concealed amid the corn fires a shot from his rifle. The bullets pass above our heads with a faint whistling sound. The soldiers laugh, they eat and laugh. The engines drone. The soldiers' faces, their hands, seem pinker, more alive, more delicate by contrast with the steel armour of the vehicles.

VII

RED FARM

WE shall remain on this farm all day. A few hours' rest at last! We are about six miles north-east of Bratosheni, between the villages of Ketrushika Nova and Ketrushika Stara. The locality in which the farm is situated is called Skuratovoi; possibly it is the farm itself that has given the place its name. From a distance Skuratovoi resembles a wood, or rather, I would say, the park of a Venetian villa. This wood, however, is surrounded not by a wall, as in the Veneto, but by a palisade. The cottages, stables and other farm-buildings are such low, squat structures that they cannot be seen from a distance, they are obscured by the vast green mass of leaves and branches. But as one approaches—it was about half-past three this morning that our column, leaving Ketrushika Nova away to its left, arrived in the vicinity of Skuratovoi—the roofs and white walls of the cottages, stables and barns gradually appear among the trees. The countryside stretches for miles all around, green and spacious, undulating like a sea of corn. It is a most beautiful landscape, extraordinarily feminine in its symmetry, in its fertility, and in that suggestion of motherhood, I mean of expectant motherhood, which cornfields seem to convey when the harvest is near.

We entered the farmyard. There was not a soul in sight. The place seemed to be deserted. A motley collection of ducks, hens and cats scattered at our approach. A bitch lay on a heap of straw close to the wall of the stable, suckling three

63

puppies. She looked at us without stirring. As the sun climbed higher its light gradually spread over the wall like a warm patch of oil. But the air was cold: the wind, which had dropped during the night, was now slowly rising in a series of long, icy gusts. As we crossed the yard an old man appeared in the doorway of the stable. A party of some ten women and children emerged from behind a barn, followed by a man of about fifty, leading by the bridle a horse harnessed to a small cart. They were obviously dead tired, they looked as if they had just returned after a long day's hard manual labour. They were heavy-eyed, their faces were spattered with mud, their clothes and hair were covered with pieces of straw and blades of grass. I thought that they must have fled into the fields, that they must have remained hidden for two or three days in the corn, fearful lest they should be submerged by the tide of battle, which from Shofroncani had rolled north-east to Bratosheni, whence it was advancing inexorably on Skuratovoi. Now they had returned, to find the farm intact, the cottages, stables and barns undamaged.

And I was astonished, almost offended, by their indifference. They seemed not even surprised, not even relieved to see us. They did not even bid us good day. The old man removed his large woollen cap, the others gave us a stony stare. Then they all moved off in a body. The children fled across the yard, the girls disappeared behind a cottage, the man untied the horse and set off in the direction of the stable. When they had gone the old peasant came up to me, crossed himself, and wished me good day in Russian, immediately adding in Rumanian: " *Sanotate*—how do you do?"

This, I thought to myself, is a Soviet farm. A few hours ago the Bolsheviks left the district, for a few hours it has been no longer subject to Soviet laws: for a few hours only. These villages, this farm, are no longer part of the economic, political and social system of the U.S.S.R. Here, the structure and organization of the Communist régime is still intact: there has been no time yet to efface the Soviet imprint, to blur the lines of the Communist edifice. This farm appears to me in this moment, I thought to myself, as the sons of Atreus appeared for a brief moment, before they crumbled into dust, to Heinrich Schliemann, when he crossed the threshold of the tombs of Mycenae. I wanted to examine it closely, as closely as possible. For this farm was a cell in the economic and social organism of the U.S.S.R. It was a microcosm, intact and perfect, of Communist society, of the Soviet agricultural economy. I had been granted the unexpected privilege of witnessing the passage, so to say, of that cell from one body—the social, political and economic body of the U.S.S.R.—to another. It had been my good fortune to arrive just as this metamorphosis reached its most critical stage. It was a unique moment, that through which I was now living : an experience historically unique. Of Communist society I could discern, in that " cell," nothing but a mass of details. But it is by minutely examining the details (which I will describe objectively and without polemical intent, since a polemical attitude to this question would be wholly inappropriate), rather than by standing back and looking at the picture as a whole, that one can best appreciate the significance of such a metamorphosis.

While the column deploys in " camping order " (even " camping order " is a battle-formation) and the soldiers cover the grey steel vehicles with handfuls of wheat and rye, with bunches of sunflowers and the stalks of soya-beans, and distribute their small anti-tank cannon and their anti-aircraft machine-guns about the fields (the vehicles are assembled in a vast enclosed space immediately behind the farm, screened from view by a line of trees), I start to wander about the farm, observing all that goes on around me.

On the left, as I enter the forecourt, is a building, a cowshed. I look inside. Standing in front of a trough filled with hay is a cow. It gazes at me, placidly chewing the cud. The shed is in disorder : the floor is littered with hay, forks, overturned buckets. I go outside, and find myself face to face with the old man whom I had first encountered. At the end of the yard a man and a girl are harnessing two thin, shaggy horses to a small cart. The man is about forty years of age, his

3

movements are slow. The girl's face is hard, strong, intelligent; her movements are violent, almost angry. She does not even turn to look at me. A woman appears in the doorway of the cottage. Her hair is dishevelled, her face is smeared with mud, her eyes are red and swollen. She gazes at me for several seconds, then she turns and closes the door behind her.

I ask the old man where the hay is stored.

" In here," he tells me. " But there's none left."

" You have no hay left? None at all?"

" No, sir."

In fact, he does not say : " No, sir "; he says : " *Nyet, tovarish.*" But he at once adds in Rumanian : "*Nu, domnule.*" Then he mutters a few words in German which I fail to catch.

" The Russian soldiers took the hay," he tells me.

" Were there some Bolshevik cavalry here?"

" Not here. They were stationed at Ketrushika Nova. They have a lot of horses to feed. They called at every farm for miles around and took all the hay they could lay hands on, mine included."

" Did they pay you for it?"

" Of course."

" Did they give you a requisition-warrant or pay cash?"

" They gave me a warrant."

" How will you cash it?"

" I shall take it to the Agricultural Centre at Shofroncani."

" The Germans are at Shofroncani now. The Communists have gone. Didn't you know?"

" Yes, I knew. But do you think the Centre has closed down?"

" The old one, yes. But we'll soon open another in its place."

" The same Centre?"

" Not the same one. Another one."

The old man looks at me, he says in Russian : " *Da da, ponimayu*—yes, yes, I understand." Then he adds in Rumanian : " *Es, inteleg*—I understand." It is obvious that he is thinking, that he is trying hard to understand. But he does not seem to be concerned about that warrant which he will be unable to cash. I have the impression that he is thinking of something else, something less definite and yet more important, more urgent. Next to the stable is a large barn, a kind of granary. Nearly the whole of the barn is occupied by a mountain of little round seeds, dark grey in colour. I ask the old man what those seeds are called, and what purpose they serve. "They are oil-seeds," he replies. They must be soya-seeds. Resting against one wall is an enormous pile of empty sacks. Along the opposite wall stretches a line of sacks filled with seeds. "We were putting the seeds into the sacks," says the old man, "but we had to interrupt the work. We had to run for our lives."

We pass through a little door into another barn of which by far the greater part is occupied by an enormous heap of sunflower-seeds.

"Did you have to hand over all these seeds to the State each year?" I ask the old man.

"To the State? No. We had to take them to the Centre."

"It's the same thing."

"No, not to the State. We used to take them to the Centre," repeats the old man.

"Did they pay you for them?"

"Of course."

The old man adds that there has been an excellent crop of oil-seeds this year. The wheat-harvest also promises to be plentiful. "But now that everything is topsy-turvy," he says, "now that this *war* has started—and here he says first, in Russian, "*voinà*," then he adds, in Rumanian, "*rasboiu*"— "we just don't know what will happen. It will be disastrous for us if we can't sell the crops. The Communists used to buy up everything," he concludes.

"You'll find you can still sell your stuff," I assure him.

"You think so? Who to?"

"You'll have to take the seeds and the wheat to the Centre, and the people there will pay you for them."

"To the Soviet Centre?"

"No, to the German one."

" Ah, *you* have agricultural clearing-centres too?"

" Of course."

The old man looks at me hard, turning his cap over and over in his hands. I can see that he would like to ask me something, but he can't summon up the courage.

" How many horses have you?" I ask him.

He replies that until recently there were fifteen horses all told on the farm. " The Bolsheviks have taken the best of them," he says. " We have nine left." The old man and I cross the yard and enter a large stable, where we find seven horses feeding from the hay-racks. In a corner of the stable is a heap of fresh fodder—a mountain of grass, green oats and clover. The horses are thin, undersized, shaggy, with hollow flanks. I am astonished that, with such an abundance of fodder available, all the horses one encounters in these parts should be so emaciated. " It's the stock," says the old man : " it isn't good." We recross the yard and enter the shed in which the agricultural machines are kept. There are two threshing-machines, four or five mowers and a self-propelled tractor. Ranged along one wall are numerous tins containing petrol, oil and paraffin. The threshing-machines seem to me to be in a particularly bad state. " Ay," the old man tells me, " to get them repaired, or even to get a spare part for an engine, was the devil's own job. We had to wait until a mechanic turned up from one of the *kolkhozi*. The *kolkhoz* at Shofroncani never let us have a mechanic. We used to have to send to Khishinau for one, sometimes even to Balta. When I went to Shofroncani they used to say to me : ' Tomorrow—come back tomorrow.' And so the machines went to rack and ruin."

He shakes his head and scratches the white stubble that covers his chin.

" Are these machines yours?" I ask.

" The threshing-machines belong to the *kolkhoz*. We have them on loan. We have to lend them to the other farms at harvest-time. The rest of the machines belong to the farm."

We inspect more stables, more barns, more stocks of oil-seeds, two huge granaries. The farm is quite large, and also, it seems to me, quite well-equipped. But I have counted in all only three cows. This seems to me rather a small number for such a prosperous farm.

The farm-buildings also include a " villa "—in former days the residence of the proprietor. It is a low house, with walls of straw and mortar covered both inside and out with a thick layer of plaster. At the front is a veranda with a balustrade of small wooden pillars. The house is surrounded by a kind of garden, littered with refuse, stinking rags and mouldy straw. A few hens are scratching about amid the garbage.

The old man tells me that the former squire was a Rumanian Jew. I pause in the doorway and burst out laughing. The word " squire ", uttered at that moment, in that place, under those circumstances, seems to me absurd, ridiculous : a grotesque, incongruous word, an utterly obsolete word, a word culled from a dead language. I burst out laughing. To both of us, I fancy (albeit for different reasons, undoubtedly for very different reasons), that word has a strange sound—indeed, I almost feel that for us it no longer has any meaning. But the old man does not appear to be worried about the possible return of the former owner. (It seems to me, however, that he utters the word " Jew " in a somewhat bitter tone.) " The officials at the Agricultural Centre were all Jews too," he goes on. He turns his cap over and over in his hands and looks at me. I understand perfectly what he is thinking; but I pretend not to understand. What he is anxious to find out from me is whether the estates absorbed by the *kolkhozi* will be restored to their former owners. This farm is one of several which have had to surrender part of their lands to the *kolkhoz* at Shofroncani. I don't know the answer to the question. It all depends on how the war ends.

I sit on a chair in a room which I think must have been the " squire's " study. The room also contains a divan. There is a large bookcase, the shelves of which are lined with about a hundred miscellaneous volumes. Not surprisingly, many of these are French editions. There are a lot of books by Paul de Kock and several by Max Nordau. For some time past two

Soviet officials have been living in the " villa "—two inspectors from the Agricultural Centre, I gather.

" Are you tired?" the old man asks me. He advises me to lie down on the divan. I thank him, but prefer not to risk it. " You know," I tell him, " if you were to collect all the bugs you've got around here they'd make a tidy pile." The old man laughs and scratches his beard.

" Have you a bit of bread and cheese?" I ask him.

" Yes, I think so," says the old man.

We leave the " villa ". At the end of the yard a girl with a red kerchief on her head is supervising the work of three elderly peasants who are putting oil-seeds into sacks. She is the girl I saw earlier helping the man harness the horses to the cart. Every so often she raises her voice. The three peasants continue to work without answering her. The old man goes over to the girl.

" Bread, but no cheese," the girl says curtly. The old man looks mortified.

" Could I have a little milk?"

" Milk? You'll find the cow in that stable over there."

At this I put my hand on her arm and say to her: " *Domnisciaara bolscevika,* I don't know how to milk a cow." The girl laughs. " Forgive me, *domnule,*" she says, " but you know . . ."

" I'll pay you for the milk."

" I don't mean that. . . . You needn't pay me for it."

She sets off in the direction of the stable, goes inside, seizes a bucket that hangs from the wall, has a quick look to see if it is clean, goes outside to wash it at the well, comes back, kneels beside the cow. After a moment she gets up and offers me the bucket with a couple of inches of milk in it. The old man brings me a generous chunk of white bread. A little dry, but good.

I dip the bread in those two inches of milk at the bottom of the bucket. The girl watches me eat. Then she goes out without giving me so much as a nod. I think to myself: " They've brought her up badly." Then I smile. She must be a fine girl. She is the one who does the work, she is the one who keeps the wheels turning. Really and truly, I am rather taken with her. I tell myself that I could quite well have milked the cow myself.

" She's a lovely animal," I remark.

" We paid three hundred roubles for her," says the old man.

" Where did you buy her?"

" We got her from the *kolkhoz*."

" Three hundred roubles, you say? Only three hundred roubles?" (Three hundred roubles are equivalent to about a thousand lire.)

" It's a lot, I know. But she's a lovely animal."

A German soldier appears in the doorway of the stable. He asks the old man if he can sell him a goose. The old man says: " Yes, I think so." The two go outside. I watch them cross the yard and disappear behind the cottage at the end.

Then I go into the barn where the seeds are stored and fling myself down on the heap of sacks. I wake up after a couple of hours to find the old man standing in front of me, together with the girl. He removes his cap and hands me a piece of paper.

" How much did you charge that soldier for the goose?" I ask him.

" Fifty *lei*," says the old man. " Fifty *lei* is a lot, I know, but everything is dear today."

Fifty *lei*? That's five lire. I glance at the piece of paper. It's a requisition-warrant for two horses. It is written in German, it bears the signature of a German officer.

" They've just requisitioned them. Do you think they'll pay us for them?" the girl asks me.

" Of course," I reply. " This warrant is quite in order. It's issued by the German Military Command."

" And do you think they'll give us a good price for them?"

" A little more than they gave you for the goose, at any rate," I say with a laugh.

The girl looks at me with an air of embarrassment. She is blushing slightly. " You see," she says, " maybe the old man asked too much for that goose. Fifty *lei* is too much, I realize. But you must forgive us. What can you expect us to know about prices? The Bolsheviks used to tell us: 'This costs so much, that costs so much.' You ought to do the same yourselves. You ought to begin by telling us how much the *lei* is worth in relation to the rouble."

She talks in an earnest tone, knitting her brows. " She's an intelligent girl," I think to myself, " a fine girl." " My advice to you is this," I say to her with a laugh. " Go at once to Command Headquarters and ask the Colonel to fix the price of geese—otherwise the whole unit will be here inside five minutes offering to buy your geese at fifty *lei* a time." The girl laughs, slapping her thigh. Then her brow darkens and the colour gradually mounts to her cheeks: I have the impression that she has something on her mind, something she is afraid to put into words. At last she plucks up her courage and asks: " Do you think the old landlord will come back?"

" The old one, no—because he was a Jew. Someone else will come in his place."

" Won't they let us keep our land?"

I don't know what answer to give her. I would like to be able to tell her " yes ". Broadly speaking, the agrarian reforms effected by Bratianu in Rumania (the boldest agrarian reforms that have ever been carried out in a European country in the interests of the small farmer) may be said to have achieved their purpose. I tell myself that in the case of Bessarabia, which was annexed by the U.S.S.R. only a year ago, the difficulties involved in a return to the bourgeois economic system are not so great as they would be in Soviet Russia. For in the Ukraine, and indeed in the whole of Russia, the problem would undoubtedly present itself in an infinitely more complex form and would have to be tackled with the utmost circumspection.

" Everything will turn out all right—you'll see," I tell the girl. " Naturally, there will be some uncertainty at first. It isn't possible to change everything overnight."

Meanwhile, a small crowd has gathered outside the door,

in the yard. It is composed of elderly men (all the young men have been called up), women, girls, children, and a few youths, too young, perhaps, to serve in the Army, or else rejected as unfit. They all gaze at me intently. The older men stand bareheaded; the youths look more self-assured, their expressions and general demeanour betray no hint of anxiety.

" What do they want?" I ask the girl.

" They are waiting for someone to tell them what they must do."

" They must go on doing what they were doing before, what they have been doing until today," I reply in a somewhat embarrassed tone. " It seems to me that that is the best thing, at any rate for the present."

The girl knits her brow and looks at me without replying. " She is an intelligent girl," I think to myself, " a fine girl. It is she who has kept the farm going until today. It is she who has stood up to the inspectors from the Agricultural Centre, to the requisition-officers, to the officials from the *kolkhoz*. She's a fine girl," I think to myself. It was she who gave the orders, it was she who told the peasants what they must do, it was she who defended the farm. Now she no longer counts for anything, now she can no longer give the orders.

" Carry on exactly as before," I advise her, " until they tell you what new arrangements have been made, what changes have been ordered."

The girl smiles. " We have defended our fields," she says, flushing slightly. " We haven't done anything wrong."

It is just as if the farm at Skuratovoi, as if the villages of Ketrushika Stara and Ketrushika Nova, as if Bratosheni and Shofroncani and Zaicani, as if all these peasants, all these villages, all these fields, all these vast expanses of corn, were delicately poised between two diametrically-opposed social, political and economic systems, as if this were the anxious, perilous moment of their metamorphosis, the critical moment of their transition from one system to the other.

" No, you certainly haven't done anything wrong," I reply.

3*

(The following lines were suppressed by the censor.)

A few hours later I emerged from the barn and crossed the farmyard. I had fallen asleep in the barn, and when I awoke my mouth felt full of dust, I had a raging thirst. A strange silence brooded over the farm. The old man was sitting in the doorway of the stable. I asked him to give me a glass of water. He looked at me with a vacant expression and did not answer. I set off in the direction of the well. Suddenly, on the ground beside the wall of the stable, I saw a red handkerchief and two bare legs. It was the girl. Her face was steeped in blood. I covered her face with my handkerchief. "No, you haven't done anything wrong," I said to myself.

VIII

THE STEEL HORSES

Cornolenca, July 14th.

IT is not yet dawn when we leave Skuratovoi Farm. The engines cough and splutter. I am reminded of the famous sneeze of the Greek hoplite in Xenophon: " Χαῖρε! χαῖρε !" The sky to the east has a silvery pallor. The corn makes a faint murmuring sound, as of water flowing between soft banks. Little by little the hills become less steep; they have now the form of breasts, each of those ample undulations is separated from the next by a slight fold in the ground—not a valley, but just a shady hollow, peaceful and somnolent. The slopes are dotted with patrols of infantrymen. They are engaged in mopping-up operations. Slowly they make their way along the furrows, their figures sharply outlined against the pale sky.

Ahead of us the battle rages. The Russians are counter-attacking. The counter-offensive of the Soviet troops is developing not only on this front but farther to the south-east, over towards Beltsy, in the sector held by the Rumanian divisions. Patrols of Rumanian light cavalry appear fleetingly away to our right. They form a link between our column and a mixed German-Rumanian column that is advancing obliquely to our line of march.

Above the steady roar of the artillery one hears the sharp bursts of anti-tank shells and the duller sound of the panzers' cannon. Our column advances slowly across the cold, glistening grass. The sky to the east looks like crinkled parchment. Flights of larks burst from the corn. Each of the vehicles has

75

a faint blue aura formed by the smoke from the exhausts. Suddenly, as we make our way down a gentle slope, we are enveloped by a cloud of red dust and the air is filled with the rumble of wheels, the clatter of tank-tracks, and the roar of engines.

An armoured column is like an armoured train. I have climbed on to Oberleutnant Schultz's lorry; I have taken my place beside him, squatting as comfortably as I can on a box of ammunition. I ask him if he has read *Armoured Train No.* 1469, the famous book by the Communist writer Leonov.

" Yes," he says, " you are right—an armoured column is exactly like an armoured train." Woe to the man who gets off the train, who leaves the column. The fields around us are full of hidden perils. Our armoured train runs on invisible rails. The bullets of the Soviet stragglers lying in ambush amid the corn (I was about to say " along the railway-embankment ") flatten themselves against the steel sides of our vehicles. " Do you remember the attack on Train No. 1469?" I ask. But it would be impossible to halt the advance of our column, it would be impossible to blow up the invisible track on which our armoured train runs.

We discuss Communist literature.

Oberleutnant Schultz is a *Dozent* in a university. Before the war he concerned himself with social problems, and he has published a number of essays on Soviet Russia. Now he is in command of the anti-aircraft section of our mechanized column. He tells me that in all probability Russia, after her defeat, will live through another period very similar, in a sense, to that described in Pilnyak's *The Naked Year.* " With this difference," he adds : " that the drama described by Pilnyak unfolded, as it were, in an experimental laboratory. Russia will relive the same drama, but this time it will be enacted in the yard of a factory or of a steel-works, against the sordid background of a workers' rising that has been nipped in the bud." Then he looks at me, smiles shyly, and says : " From the social viewpoint, machines are very interesting and very dangerous characters." He confesses to me that he finds this problem extraordinarily fascinating.

The soldiers, standing up in the backs of their lorries, shout, gesticulate, and throw all manner of objects at one another, including combs, brushes, tins of cigarettes, pieces of soap, towels. The order to move has come unexpectedly, and many have not even had time to wash and shave. Now they are smartening themselves up as best they can. Some stand with legs wide apart on the platforms of their anti-aircraft lorries and, stripped to the waist, wash themselves in canvas buckets. Some kneel before mirrors inserted in their rifle-racks or suspended from the tripods of their machine-guns and somehow contrive to shave. Others wash their jackboots with soap and water.

The sun breaks the shell of the horizon, climbs into a sky all streaked with green, timidly illuminates the armour of the vehicles. A light pink down appears on the surface of the grey steel plates. The heavy tanks at the head of the column are enveloped in a pink aura, they emit a delicate yet vivid radiance. And suddenly, far ahead of us, on the distant horizon, amid that vast expanse of waving corn that seems to flow like a golden river—suddenly, in the distance, on the slope of a hill, there is a glint of steel, a glitter of armour.

A cry passes down the column: "The Mongols! The Mongols!" By this time the German soldiers can distinguish the Mongolian units from the other Soviet units by the way they fight, even by their tactical dispositions. As a general rule tanks manned by Asiatic crews fight not in formation but singly, or in groups of two or three at the most. (It is a tactic that recalls, in a sense, that of the cavalry-patrols.) The German soldiers call them *Panzerpferde*—roughly, " armoured horses ". Something of the old spirit survives in these Tartar horsemen, whom Soviet industrialization and military Stakanovism have made into specialized workers, mechanics, drivers of tanks.

Some Tartar prisoners, captured last evening and brought to the farm at Skuratovoi, have confirmed that the Soviet troops entrusted with the defence of the Ukraine (and therefore of the industrial and mineral basins of the Dnieper and the Don and of the roads that lead to the Caucasus and to the oil of Baku) are for the most part Asiatics. They comprise Tartars from the Crimea, the remnants of the Golden Horde; Kurds from Turkestan; and Mongols from the banks of the Don and the Volga, from the shores of the Caspian, from the Kirgizian steppes, from the plains of Tashkent and Samarkand. They represent the best that the Five Year Plan of the Mongolian Republic has produced, they are the choicest products of the industrialization of Asiatic Russia, the young recruits of military Stakanovism.

The prisoners, who numbered about fifteen, were assembled in the farmyard. They were a little above medium height, lean, but with sturdy, loose and well-proportioned limbs. At first sight they appeared very young, but their faces gave a false impression. Their ages ranged, I would say, from twenty-five to thirty. They wore a very simple khaki uniform, without any distinguishing mark, not even a number on the collar of the jacket. The forage-caps which partly concealed their glossy black hair were of the same khaki colour. They wore very soft grey leather boots of Tartar design, equally suitable for riding or for crouching inside a tank. They had narrow, slanting eyes and small mouths. About their eyes and extending all along their temples was a fine network of wrinkles, alive and sensitive, which palpitated like the nervures in the wings of a dragon-fly.

They were sitting on the ground with their backs resting against that part of the stable-wall which was illuminated by the rays of the setting sun. They were eating sunflower-seeds. They appeared apathetic, and at the same time extremely watchful. Suspicion lurked beneath that air of cold, blank indifference. The patch of sunlight on the wall grew ever smaller, until at last it was no more than a bright spot on the face of one of them.

That yellow mask, brilliantly illuminated by the last fires of sunset, was fixed, immobile : the narrow mouth, the smooth brow, the bright eyes might have been hewn from marble.

Only those two fine, delicate networks of wrinkles quivered incessantly. The prisoner's face reminded me, I know not why, of a dying bird. When the sun finally disappeared the bird folded its wings and lay inert.

They had been captured while trying to make their way back to the headquarters of their unit in two armoured vehicles. The tank that was escorting them had been gutted by a bomb in a field a few miles east of Skuratovoi. They had defended themselves fiercely against a heavy panzer which had cut off their retreat. But their resistance had been in vain : against panzers machine-gun fire is ineffectual. Some of them had been killed, and the survivors were now sitting in the farm-yard, resting their backs against the wall of the stable. Pensively they chewed their sunflower-seeds, screwing up their small, slanting eyes the while.

They seemed to rouse themselves from their lethargy only when one of those miniature tractors equipped with caterpillars and drawn by a kind of motor-cycle, likewise equipped with caterpillars, suddenly appeared in the yard. This type of vehicle is something new in the German Army—indeed, it has only made its appearance since this Russian campaign began. It is not, strictly speaking, a motor-cycle with a tractor attached; it is, rather, a tractor guided and at the same time drawn by a sort of powered monocycle which projects from the front of the vehicle. The driver sits astride the monocycle with his back resting against the bodywork. Superficially it looks a makeshift sort of vehicle, very light and of no great power. But the Germans speak highly of its exceptional pulling and climbing capacity. It will climb anything. Its inventor intended it for use in mountain-warfare. Employed for the first time on these Russian plains, it has surprised the experts by its remarkable qualities, both mechanical and practical. It serves in the main for the transport of munitions and supplies of petrol. During the actual fighting these strange vehicles follow close behind the tank-formations, moving swiftly from one panzer to another. Some of them are used for the purpose of towing light anti-tank artillery. They are very fast, and as they make their way through the corn they are almost invisible.

The Tartar prisoners looked at this strange machine with intense interest. I observed their hands. They were small and stubby, horny-thumbed and grimy with oil. The skin between thumb and forefinger seemed to be scored with deep black furrows, as is always the case with men who are in the habit of wielding metal implements. They were mechanics' hands. Mongolians, it appears, make excellent mechanics—and by that I mean genuinely skilled craftsmen. Many young Mongolians are employed nowadays in the Russian metallurgical industry, especially in the Kharkov district. They have an extraordinary passion for machines. Among the youth of Soviet Mongolia the traditional passion for horses has given way to an interest in the precise working of engines, gears, mano-meters, and so forth. They seem naturally suited to this extremely mobile type of warfare, to this technique of offensive thrusts by tanks, which are very similar to the cavalry-thrusts of earlier wars. I would say, indeed, that they use tanks as they once used horses. They employ the same tactics, based on free-dom and independence of action. Herein lies the novelty of this war of tanks which the Mongols are waging on the plains of the Ukraine. They come forward not in a body but singly. They advance through the cornfields in a series of broad sweeping movements, like horsemen performing evolutions in some gigantic circus. And their audacity is reminiscent of that for which the old-time cavalry were famous.

"The Mongols! The Mongols!" cry the German soldiers. They have sighted three small tanks swiftly climbing the gentle slope of a hill barely two miles ahead of us. Two large panzers detach themselves from the head of our column. We watch them advance diagonally through the corn, one to the right, the other to the left, gradually widening the distance between them as if they were seeking to check the enemy's advance by means of a pincer movement. The three small Mongolian tanks abruptly disperse. They begin a series of strange evolutions, each describing a broad spiral upon the surface of the plain, whose undulations periodically hide them from view. One has the impression that they are trying to gain time, to engage the German tanks in a kind of gymkhana, so as to give the main body of their formation an opportunity to come to their assistance, or to retreat. Suddenly the two heavy panzers open fire with their cannon.

The bursting shells throw up high fountains of earth around the small Soviet tanks. The battle only lasts ten minutes. The three Russian tanks are far more mobile than the panzers, they evade their fire and disappear behind the hill. " It is a technique of enticement," says Oberleutnant Schultz. " In this war of mobile columns the Mongolian *Panzerpferde* are doing an imaginative and extremely hazardous job of work. One has to be very careful not to swallow the bait—not to allow oneself to be lured on to ground that has been mined or ambushed by large armoured formations concealed in a wood or behind a hill."

After a few hours we reach the village of Cornolenca. It is intact, but deserted. A few hundred yards beyond the village we come upon a group of burning houses. Our column has received orders to take up a position behind a hill, about half a mile outside Cornolenca. We spent a nerve-racking afternoon awaiting developments. One of our medium guns, sited among the houses of a village, fires a shot at intervals of three minutes. Numerous batteries concealed in the woods to our right keep up a continuous bombardment.

Towards evening we see a column of approximately ten German vehicles coming in our direction, escorted by a panzer. Six prisoners dismount from a lorry—four Mongols and two Russians.

After the interrogation, while the prisoners are being locked up in a room of a house situated in the village, Oberleutnant Schultz comes over to me and says : " I have a suspicion that one of those prisoners is a political commissar. Did you notice his uniform ?"

It is already dark when I discern a strange coming and going outside the house in which the prisoners are confined. While I am walking towards the house I run into Schultz. He tells

me that the "political commissar" has been found dead—
strangled. And he shows me a pencilled note, written in
Russian. It reads as follows: "I personally gave my men the
order to kill me." The signature is clearly legible: "Basil
Volinski, political commissar attached to the 15th Armoured
Division."

IX

BEHOLD THE DNIESTER!

Soroki (on the Dniester), August 4th.

BEHOLD the Dniester! Behold the mighty river, flowing through a deep, narrow valley whose slopes of hard clay are traversed by white ridges and red gullies! And behold, on the Ukrainian bank, amid the green of the maize and the gold of the wheat, stretching through the woods of acacias and the fields thick with sunflowers and soya-beans, the labyrinth of iron and cement that is the Stalin Line!

The Stalin Line is a complex system of concrete redoubts, winding trenches and steel-domed bunkers. From here, from the top of the cliff that overhangs Soroki, it resembles a series of white letters of the alphabet inscribed upon the clayey blackboard of the river-bank. That T which can just be seen in the middle of a field of soya-beans is an anti-tank gun-emplacement. That A, that C, that inverted D, that Z, that I are miniature forts, bunkers, communication-trenches, machine-gun nests. The Stalin Line is, so to say, a code, a conventional language, a mysterious script, which the German artillerymen are patiently deciphering with the help of their range-tables, in readiness for the final assault. Already the siege-trains are arriving on the scene of the battle. The dust-filled air vibrates with the strident roar of tank-tracks. On this enchanted summer day great teeth of steel seem to be grinding the ordered countryside to pulp. The cannon beat like hammers on the burnished steel of the August sky. Huge castles of white cloud tower above the horizon at the edge of the green Ukrainian steppe.

Behold the Dniester! Two days ago we left the mechanized division to which we were attached and moved farther south to join a column of assault-troops. This war is profoundly different from that of which I have been a witness in recent weeks. It is no longer a war of machines, a clash of great formations of heavy armoured tanks. It is, instead, an old-fashioned war of infantry battalions, of gun-batteries drawn by horses. The odour of horses' dung is welcome to me after the constant smell of oil and petrol. The voices of the soldiers sound in my ears like the voices of a humanity that has finally rediscovered itself.

From the Mogilev Front to Soroki, where we are at present, the journey was long and rather hard. We had to make our way along roads jammed with baggage-waggons, with artillery-trains, with columns of infantry, with interminable convoys of vehicles, through dense, blinding clouds of red dust. From time to time we saw at the edge of the road twisted cars, charred lorries, Soviet tanks lying on their sides. As we approached Beltsy the signs of the struggle became more frequent. Already groups of prisoners were busy repairing the road. They watched me pass with undisguised curiosity, gazing intently at my Alpini officer's uniform. They would pause for a moment and lean on the handles of their picks and shovels, only to be recalled to their tasks immediately by the shouts of their German guards. Every so often I would notice a Mongolian with narrow, slanting eyes, small mouth and shaven skull standing in the midst of a group of prisoners, his face a circular patch of yellow against a white background.

A few miles from Flahesty, near some gutted Russian tanks, we come upon the first Soviet graves. They consist of simple mounds of earth, without a cross, without a name, without any distinguishing feature save only a Soviet helmet, a cap with a leather peak, or a tattered khaki jacket resting on the newly-turned soil. On the other side of the road are rows of crosses marking the graves of German soldiers killed in action. The graves are covered with flowers, each cross is surmounted by a steel helmet and bears the name, rank, and age of the fallen warrior. Wrapped around the cross that marks the grave of an airman is a machine-gun belt (the dead man's Messerschmitt lies in a field of corn, its wings burnt, its fuselage twisted). It is like the serpent, symbol of eternity, which the Ancients depicted on the walls of houses and on the sides of tombs.

There is a presage of death, a sign of dissolution, in the very sumptuousness of the landscape, in the very richness of the ripe grain, in the very opulence of the white clouds stretching above the swelling bosom of the hills. It is the secret essence of summer. Men die, like the seasons. It is a rich death, in the richest season of the year. Then autumn comes, with its sweet purple fruits.

From a distance Beltsy appears to have suffered grievously in the battle that for many days has raged all around it. (I was farther north, at Skuratovoi, when Beltsy fell into the hands of the Germans. From the farm at Skuratovoi one could see the flames tinging the sky with purple over on the right, a little to our rear. And during the last night of the battle the roar of the artillery sounded so near that I was unable to sleep.)

When we reach the suburbs of Beltsy Soviet planes are bombing the airfield. A squadron of German fighters climbs rapidly into the sky and challenges the Soviet Ratas. The battle between the Messerschmitts and the Ratas is brief and violent. The aerial *carrousel* takes place in the centre of a great rose of flak, the shells explode around the Soviet aircraft like red and white flowers opening their petals. The bombers disappear swiftly into the clouds, heading east. I am so intent on following the progress of the battle that at first I do not perceive the frightful state of the town. We are near a level-crossing, at the end of a goods-platform. On the twisted rails lie enormous heaps of iron blackened by the smoke of the explosions, scores of overturned waggons and the remains of a locomotive shattered by a heavy bomb from a Stuka. The locomotive is standing on end, it appears to be emerging from beneath the

ground, like some Plutonic chariot. The fragments of twisted
metal are smoking, a continuous piercing whistle issues from
the interior of the gutted boiler. Dangling from the locomotive's funnel like a flag is a strip of blue cloth, possibly a
remnant of the driver's overalls.

I drive along the main street of the town, which has been
destroyed by bombs, exploding mines, fires, and the ceaseless
pounding of the German artillery. Skeletons of houses tower
precariously into the blue sky. Groups of wretched people
rummage among the ruins, collecting fragments of treasured
possessions, strips of scorched mattresses, empty bottles. (For
the past month the people of Beltsy have been living in the
woods or hiding in cellars; but already the bravest and the
most desperate are venturing from their hiding-places, and they
include women, old men, children, all with the signs of fear,
hunger, and sleeplessness engraved upon their faces.) Gangs
of bearded Jews, supervised by soldiers of the S.S., are busy
pulling down the tottering walls with the help of ropes, steel
hawsers and long poles. Here and there in the dead city one
hears the sound of falling bricks and stones. Troops of starving
dogs and cats scuffle among the ruins. This, then, is Beltsy,
once a prosperous township nestling in an extremely fertile
valley golden with ears of corn. Over towards the airfield, on
the road that leads to Soroki, a number of houses are still
burning. A solitary anti-aircraft machine-gun is firing in the
distance. The tracer-bullets disappear into a snow-white cloud
resembling a cloud of flour. An old Jew, seated in the doorway of a fruit-shop, calls out to me in German : " *Alles gut,
alles gut* !—All's well, all's well !"

The Communist slogan " Workers of the world, unite !" is
inscribed in letters eighteen inches high on the front of Beltsy's
Soviet House, situated in the centre of the town. It is a mansion rather than a house. Set in the midst of a beautiful garden,
it has the appearance of a nineteenth-century villa. A German
sentry is standing at ease beside the entrance, immediately
beneath the huge inscription. Running along one side of the
building, on the first floor, is a long balcony with white-painted

iron railings. In the garden is a statue of Stalin. The Red dictator is represented in his familiar pose : standing, a leather-peaked cap on his head, his big moustache drooping, his right hand inserted between two buttons of his long, ample greatcoat of military cut in the traditional Napoleonic gesture. The statue has fallen from its pedestal and is lying face downwards on the grass; it seems to be biting the dust. It is a chalk statue, dazzlingly white against its green background.

The bridge over the river, just outside the town, is jammed with vehicles. A column of prisoners is waiting for a chance to cross it. The men are sitting on the ground, their backs resting against the walls of a ruined house, their heads drooping from fatigue and heat.

I stop to question them. They are for the most part Ukrainians or Bessarabians. To all my questions they reply unfailingly : " *Da*—yes." They gaze at me with wide-open eyes in which fear kindles a momentary sombre flame. The German soldier who is guarding them tells me they are afraid—afraid they may be shot at any moment. The German soldier laughs. They cannot get used, he says, to the idea that they are still alive. The prisoners look at me, they try to deduce, from the expression on my face, what it is we are discussing. I light a cigarette and throw away the match. A prisoner picks up the dead match and examines it closely.

We reach the outskirts of the town and set off along the road that leads to Soroki. Soon after passing the airfield, which is situated a few miles outside Beltsy, we stop for a snack. Our provisions are meagre in the extreme. All we have is a score of tins of preserved tomatoes and a few bottles of mineral water, together with a canister of tea and a little sugar. Slender resources indeed.

We open a tin of tomatoes, spread them on a slice of bread, and begin to eat. We have eaten practically nothing but tinned tomatoes for the past three days, and I am already sick of them. Having finished our meagre repast, we fling ourselves down in the corn and try to snatch a little sleep. Less than an hour later we are once more on our way.

A dozen miles along the road we encounter some Soviet tanks, gutted by the fire of the German *Pak*. Amid the twisted heap of iron there is one tank that particularly interests us. It is one of those special tanks that are used for the transport of assault-troops. From the front protrudes the barrel of a large-calibre machine-gun. The top is shaped like an inverted *T*. On either side the armour-plating is moulded in the form of a bench. On the two steel benches sit the soldiers. When the battle is on they jump to the ground and fight on foot, supported by fire from the tank. One of these dual-purpose tanks still contains the charred body of the driver. The dead man's spinal column is upright, it is resting against the back of the seat. The bones of his legs and arms lie in a heap between the seat and the instrument-panel.

As we approach the Dniester signs of the fighting become more and more apparent and frequent. They testify to the desperate resistance which the crews of the Russian tanks have offered to the overwhelming forces ranged against them.

When we are within a few miles of Soroki we discern far below us, through the cloud of red dust raised by a column of vehicles, the wreckage of a bridge across the Cainari. In the middle of the bridge, at the junction of the two central spans, which have fallen in such a way that they almost from a *V*, lies a forty-five ton Russian tank. The armoured monster appears to be intact. It is not even scratched. Not one of its steel plates has been displaced. The tank was blown up along with the bridge just as it was preparing to retreat. It was thirty seconds too late, no more. Beneath the bridge, on the gravel bed of the Cainari, is a mound of earth surmounted by a rough cross bearing the words: "*Ein russische Panzer-schützer*". A Russian tank-gunner. This is the first Soviet grave marked by a cross that we have yet encountered.

The sun is already setting when we reach Väntsina. Huge towering masses of red cloud hang above the darkened plain, whose surface is broken by a deep gorge through which a thin grey stream lazily winds its way. Wherever he turns his gaze the onlooker is dazzled by the splendour of the

corn—almost, I would say, by the splendour of the corn at
sundown : for as his eye strays into the distance the superficial
lustre of the vast expanse of wheat seems gradually to fade, it
is dimmed and finally obscured like the radiance of a sunlit
evening sky.

Beyond Väntsina the road climbs a hill, on the other side of
which lies Soroki. The first houses of the little town are
situated on the hilltop. We stop near a large building blackened
by the recent fires. It is the old seminary, built by the Tsar
Nicholas. The building is of very simple neo-classical design
(it is, in fact, an example of that characteristically Russian
brand of neo-classicism which is a belated imitation of the
Empire style). Its column of white stucco, surmounted by Ionic
capitals of the traditional pattern, stand out in shallow relief
from the façade. From close to, it appears to have been completely destroyed. The roof has collapsed, the interior walls
are in ruins. The outer walls are still standing, but they have
been cracked by the heat of the flames. Fragments of scorched
beams litter the vast courtyard which fronts the edifice. The
Bolsheviks had requisitioned the seminary for use as the headquarters of an agrarian syndicate and as a depot for the
agricultural machines which the latter used to hand out to
the various *kolkhozi* in the Soroki district (there was a *kolkhoz*
at Väntsina, another at Zipilova, a third at Kogniski, a fourth
at Valanokulo); and a vast area extending all round the building is strewn with tractors, enormous threshing-machines,
mowers, drills, weeders and ploughs. The place is a graveyard
of agricultural machines.

The road that leads from Väntsina to the top of the hill
overlooking Soroki is likewise flanked by abandoned
machines, many of them damaged, but some in good condition. I go over to inspect three large threshing-machines which
are still intact. They are of Hungarian manufacture, having
come from the Hofherr-Schrantz-Clayton-Suttleworth factory
in Budapest.

By now darkness has fallen, and a *Feldgendarme* tells us
that it would be dangerous to go down to Soroki. The Russian

batteries sited on the left bank of the Dniester are hammering away at the town, raising huge clouds of white dust. From this spot we can hear the characteristic sound of collapsing walls, of falling rubble, that follows each explosion. A great fire is blazing on the horizon, beyond Yampol, over towards Olshanka. Seeking a place of refuge for the night, we knock at the door of a hovel situated a couple of hundred yards from the seminary. It is occupied by a family of poor peasants, consisting of an old couple and a little boy. They receive us kindly; but they have nothing to offer us apart from a large table on which to sleep. No matter. Pellegrini will sleep on the table, I shall sleep in the car. We eat a little bread and some tinned tomatoes, and at the same time we make ourselves a cup of tea. Then I lie down in the car, periodically raising myself on my elbows to gaze at the reflections of the fires that ring the horizon.

Long shadows rise from the corn like black tongues of flame. Squadrons of Soviet planes drone in the starlit sky. A Russian machine-gun fires from the other side of the river, making a sound like a sewing-machine. That *tock-tock-tock* sews up my eyelids, which are swollen from lack of sleep.

X

THE UKRAINE, TOMB OF THE CORN

Before Mogilev (on the Dniester), July 18th.

IT may be that the battle for the Ukraine, which has been raging for several days along the entire Dniester sector, within sight of the Stalin Line, is the battle that will decide the fate of the " Gates of Asia." It may be that the public, hypnotized by the famous names of the cities—Moscow, Leningrad, Smolensk—that constitute the objectives of the German advance in the northern and central sectors of the vast battlefield, have not yet grasped the fact that the issue is really being decided on the southern front, that the decisive theatre of the war is here, in the Ukraine, where the two armies are fighting not only for possession of the Soviet granary but for control of the roads that lead to the industrial and mineral basins of the Dnieper and the Don, to the oil of Baku, to Asia.

But even when I am able to shed my reserve and to describe the vicissitudes of this gigantic battle I shall continue to imbue my despatches with that special character—let us call it a " sociological " character—with which I have sought to imbue them from the beginning. For the interest—indeed, the fundamental importance—of this Russian campaign seems to me to consist not so much in the problems of strategy as in the unprecedented, not to say unique, problems of a social, economic, moral and political character which it presents.

I have a personal experience of Russia and her problems which dates back many years. And the method which I have endeavoured to follow in all my despatches has been, in fact, not merely to report events as they have unfolded before my eyes but to interpret them, and to define with complete objectivity the essential problems arising out of this fearful conflict.

The attentive reader will recall that I have been at pains right from the start not to create in his mind the illusion that the Soviet Army is deficient in fighting spirit. I have never neglected an opportunity of repeating that the Soviet troops defend themselves stubbornly, that they react vigorously, that they fight gallantly. I have tried to determine, by personal observation of the technical proficiency of the Red soldier and of his mode of fighting, the influence which Soviet social and political organization and " industrial morale " may have had on the fighting spirit and on the tactical effectiveness of the Communist troops. And I have not failed to warn the reader that it was not to be expected that at the first impact revolution would break out in Moscow—that, in other words, the collapse of the Bolshevist régime would precede the total defeat of the Army : since, as I have said, the true " social core " of Soviet Russia is the Army, which is the greatest industrial achievement of Communism—far greater than the *kolkhozi,* the great collective farming enterprises, far greater than the gigantic workshops of heavy industry—and the result of twenty-five years of industrial organization and of the technical training of skilled workers in accordance with Stakanovite principles.

Now that I have penetrated so far into Soviet territory, now that I have had an opportunity to observe the great *kolkhozi* of the Ukraine at close quarters, now that I am approaching the industrial regions of the Dnieper, I believe the time has come for me to emphasize the sociological character of my despatches (without, however, neglecting the story of our advance and of the battles at which I happen to be present), so that I may give the reader not merely a picture, but a strictly objective interpretation, of the events of which I am a witness, events that reflect all the aspects—economic, social, political, religious and moral—of the tremendous problem of the Soviet Union.

I will say first of all that the German authorities display a certain caution, though not so much as they should, with regard to Soviet Russia's economic organization, particularly in the sphere of agriculture. In order to understand the reasons for their caution the reader must remember that Communist propaganda seeks, by means of posters and broadcast appeals, to bring pressure to bear on the peasant masses of the Ukraine with the object of inducing them to " bury " their corn. I have seen some of these posters. They read like this: " Peasants! The Fascist occupation spells your ruin. To whom will you sell the products of the land? To the *kolkhozi*? The Fascists will destroy the *kolkhozi*. To the syndicates, the co-operatives, the State clearing-centres? The Fascists will destroy them all. They will seize your corn without paying you for it. In order to save your corn, bury it!"

Among the Ukrainian peasants this practice of " burying " the corn-crop is not new. Even Charles XII of Sweden, when he tried to conquer the Ukraine, came face to face with the problem and was much inconvenienced in consequence. Indeed, it was one of the causes of his ruin—the prelude to Poltava.

In 1918, when they occupied the Ukraine, the Germans did not succeed in getting possession of the harvest. Once again, the peasants had " buried " their corn. As to the method which they adopted little information was obtainable at the time. In the spring of 1920 an official of our Foreign Ministry, Virgili-Amadori, was sent to the Ukraine to get an idea of the conditions prevailing in the region, and he came back with a full report on the various methods by which the peasants contrived to " bury " the corn-crop. Today this report possesses the utmost topicality, and it might with advantage be exhumed from the archives of the Ministry.

In that year—1920—I found myself in Warsaw as a diplomatic attaché at the Italian Legation, and I had an opportunity of reading the report and of discussing it with

Virgili-Amadori. At the time the problem of the "burial" of the corn-crop was also engaging the attention of Monsignor Genocchi, who had been sent to the Ukraine by the Holy See in order to further the interests of the Uniate Church. I met Monsignor Genocchi at the home of the Apostolic Nuncio in Warsaw, the then Monsignor Achille Ratti, and from him I received much information that was of value to me when, shortly after—in June—I accompanied the Polish troops commanded by Marshal Pilsudski as far as Kiev during their Ukrainian campaign. The consequences of the "burial" of the corn were as serious for the Polish Army as they had been two years earlier for the German Army of Occupation; and I was able, on the occasion in question, to study the problem and its economic and social implications at first hand. The knowledge thus gained was subsequently extremely useful in that it helped me to understand the motives underlying the bitter campaign conducted by the Bolsheviks in the Ukraine against agricultural sabotage. Apropos of the "burial" of corn, the agricultural section of the Lenin Library in Moscow contains some most interesting documents and reports in various languages, with which I was able to familiarize myself during my last stay in the U.S.S.R.

Following their dire experience of 1918 the Germans carried out some singularly important researches on this subject; and they have lately indicated their intention of solving the problem by the establishment of clearing-centres.

For the fact is that, if the Ukrainians are to be dissuaded from "burying" their corn, the first necessity is that the system of "Soviet Clearing-centres" should be replaced by an alternative system conceived along similar lines. The possibility of a return to a "liberal" system may be discounted. The Russian peasant has by now accustomed himself to the Soviet system of clearing-centres, and he has even succeeded in turning it to his own advantage. Abolish the *kolkhozi*, abolish the clearing-centres, and the peasant will no longer know what to do with his corn—though if he considers that there is the remotest likelihood of its being requisitioned he will "bury" it.

Just as they are at pains to blow up the bridges, to destroy the railways, to block the roads, to sabotage the machinery of the industrial installations, etc., so the Bolsheviks are concerned to destroy all those features of their economic organization which may make the agricultural exploitation of the Ukraine easier for the Germans. The fact that the Russian troops are accompanied by numerous political agents reflects the Soviet Government's preoccupation with the necessity of exercising a political control over the conduct of the war and of spreading propaganda urging the peasants to resort to " agricultural sabotage " as a weapon against the invaders.

In a number of villages in Podolia the Germans have found pits clearly intended for the storage of the harvest. In the offices of the *kolkhozi* are piles of booklets containing instructions relative to the systematic " burial " of the corn-crop. The Bolsheviks have not had time to distribute these among the peasants. Up to now this propaganda has yielded only meagre results; for the German authorities have hastened to inform the population of the occupied territories that the *kolkhozi* will be replaced immediately by clearing-centres to which the peasants will have to consign the harvest against payment of the new price, which will be considerably higher than the price hitherto paid in roubles. And I myself have been able to establish that in many villages the peasants have hailed this measure with a certain relief, as being the only one that can guarantee the rapid sale of the harvest on the basis of a relatively stable price.

On the other hand, I have often asked myself in recent days why the Bolsheviks did not set fire to the crops before retreating. Such a method of agricultural sabotage would have been far simpler and infinitely quicker. The corn is ripe, the harvest is imminent, a match would suffice to start a tremendous fire blazing all over the Ukraine. But the peasants would undoubtedly have replied to such an attempt to destroy the harvest by rising in revolt. And an insurrection in the Ukraine would have favoured the Germans' plans to such an extent that the Bolsheviks simply dared not provoke it. (I would mention at this point that all the rumours which have been put about to the effect that the Bolsheviks have systematically destroyed the Ukrainian harvest are false.)

Tomorrow, perhaps within a matter of hours, the battle of the Dniester will have reached its end. (As I sit on the back of an anti-aircraft lorry writing these notes the sun is setting, and away in the distance, above the fertile Ukrainian steppe, the crimson clouds are being rent asunder by the blast from exploding shells. Groups of wounded Germans and Rumanians pass by on foot, their faces dripping with sweat, their eyes sparkling with the gaiety of youth. A Soviet officer, gravely wounded in the stomach, is lying on a stretcher beside the field-ambulance. A heavy panzer drives up, stops, the steel hatch is raised, the crew climb out one by one, laughing loudly. Evening falls, damp and heavy with the scent of corn. I cannot yet say anything of the fortunes of the battle. I must content myself with helping the reader to understand the great problems from which this war derives so much of its significance. In a few days, when we move into the region of the great *kolkhozi*, these problems will assume a vital importance; and this fact will serve, if nothing else, to justify the great discomforts and perils which are an integral part of the nomadic and picturesque existence of all those, including myself, who accompany the German motorized columns along the roads of the Ukraine.)

XI

GHOSTS

Soroki (on the Dniester), August 6th.

ALL through the night Soviet planes have been flying over
Soroki, trying to destroy the material which the German
pontoneers are accumulating on the bank of the Dniester,
opposite Yampol. All through the night the din of the
explosions has reverberated down the valley. At daybreak the
aerial bombardment and the anti-aircraft fire became so violent
that I gave up all idea of trying to sleep.

While I am shaving out in the open, in front of a mirror
suspended by a nail from the door of the stable, I start to chat
with an old peasant. When he talks of the *kolkhozi* the old man
shakes his head, looking at me out of the corner of his eye. He
is worried about the harvest. He does not know what to do.
All the able-bodied men are fighting in the ranks of the Red
Army, with the result that there is a shortage of labour. Many
of the agricultural machines are damaged. It will take time
to repair them, and meanwhile the corn is in danger of going
to waste. The old man looks at the sky : black clouds are piling
up on the horizon. It has been a wet summer. It is essential
that the crops should be gathered in without further delay. But
the women cannot do the job unaided. The old man shakes
his head. " What are we to do? " he says.

The sun has barely risen when we resume our journey. We
drive down the hill towards Soroki. It is a small town, Soroki,
beautifully situated in a broad loop of the river, at the foot of
the high cliff that overhangs the valley. As we round a bend in

4   97

the road (a very steep road, jammed with lorries, artillery-trains, and columns of vehicles belonging to the corps of engineers) the town suddenly comes into view. It presents a most beautiful, and at the same time a terrifying, spectacle. On the river-bank stands a fortress, its circular, crenellated towers rising above a black mass of hovels shattered by bombs and gutted by fires. Originally Genoese, it subsequently became first Moldavian, then Turkish, then Russian. We enter the stricken town. For a long time we wander among the ruins passing groups of bare-footed, ragged people with unkempt hair and soot-blackened faces, carrying on their backs mattresses, chairs, and scorched pieces of furniture. A *Feldgendarme,* standing guard at a crossroad, advises us to keep away from the centre of the town, which is still being heavily shelled by the Soviet artillery installed on the far bank of the river. " As you get nearer the outskirts," he tells us, " you will find a few houses still standing." We turn off into a wide street, the car bumps over pieces of masonry, heaps of rubble, charred fragments of beams. Presently we come out into a square flanked by a public park.

With its tall poplars, its leafy limes, its acacias, its box-hedges, its trellises entwined with climbing plants reminiscent of the wild vine, the park stands like a green oasis amid the charred ruins of the stricken town. Chairs, tables, cupboards, beds are strewn in disorder about the green lawns. Arabesques of leaves and branches superimposed on a background of burnished blue are reflected in a basin filled with yellow water, on the surface of which float pieces of wood, sodden leaves, and scraps of paper.

A few women and children are walking in the park. It is one of those provincial parks such as are described in the novels and stories of all the Russian writers, in particular Dostoievsky. Green and damp, full of shady nooks carpeted with soft, spongy turf, it is a romantic place, humble yet dignified in its drab setting of low houses typical of the mean provincial architecture of Tsarist Russia. The sky echoes with the singing of the birds perched in the tree-tops.

A volume of Pushkin is lying on a bench. It is *Eugène Onegin,* printed in Moscow in 1937, the centenary of the poet's death. I open the book and read the first few verses :

> *Moy dyadya samikh chestnikh pravil*
> *kogda nye v shutku sanyemog.*

The mellifluous words move me deeply. (A few years ago I visited the villa near Moscow where Pushkin spent the last months of his short life. I touched, I caressed his familiar possessions—his bed, his pillow, his pen, his inkstand, the locket in which are preserved a few strands of his hair.) My fingers tremble as I turn the leaves of *Eugène Onegin.* Among the pages of the second canto, the one that opens with the quotation from Horace, " *O rus!*", is a filthy, tattered glove that serves as a bookmarker. As I read the lines—

> *Akh, on lyubil, kak v nashi lyeta*
> *uzhe nye lyubyat; kak odna*

—I clasp that glove as if it were a hand.

A blonde woman, still young, decently but poorly dressed, passes along the avenue, leading by the hand a little girl of perhaps three years with fair hair and a very pale complexion. Their faces are filthy, tangled locks of hair hang down over their cheeks, their clothes are thick with dust. As she goes by the woman looks at me curiously, almost shamefacedly. I feel her eyes resting on me as if she were contemplating a painful memory.

Opposite the entrance to the park, a few yards from the *sovietkino,* or Soviet cinema, is a stone-built house of severe aspect. Until recently it was the headquarters of the Soroki Soviet. I push open the door and go inside. The rooms are in a state of indescribable chaos. Overturned tables, smashed cupboards, splintered furniture, piles of papers litter the floor. Portraits of Lenin, Stalin and Molotov still hang from the walls, together with an assortment of posters, propaganda-bills, and maps.

Of these, there is one that interests me particularly. It is a street-plan of the city of Petrograd, with the disposition of the Soviet troops during the rising of October, 1917, shown in red. The revolutionary strategy outlined by Clausewitz in his famous treatise on war, which Lenin had studied, is illustrated on the map in the manner described by John Reed in his diary, published under the title *Ten Days That Shook The World*. The Smolny Institute, headquarters of the Bolshevist revolution, is marked with a little red flag.

On the walls, propaganda-posters urging the public to use the Soviet Savings Bank alternate with charts illustrating the working of a threshing-machine, portraits of the senior people's commissars, statistics relating to elementary education in the various Republics of the Union, agricultural propaganda-bills, and posters urging Communist youths to volunteer for service in the Red Army. There is also a portrait of the celebrated Russian aviator, Chkalok, who flew across the North Pole from Russia to America.

In the drawer of a writing-desk are piles of membership-cards of the Communist Party. Some are all ready to be despatched, and each of these carries a photograph of the new member and is signed by the President of the Soroki Soviet and the Director of the *kolkhoz*. On a table are two empty bottles of *Sovyetskoye Champanskoye*—Soviet bubbly—together with a piece of bread, a pipe, a box of matches with the hammer and sickle printed on the label, and a comb with some of the teeth missing.

The crash of a bomb (it must have fallen very near the building) brings me to the door. Two Soviet planes are fleeing eastwards, pursued by red and white puffs of smoke from the German anti-aircraft shells. A procession of civilians passes down the street, escorted by some Rumanian soldiers, who are taking them to the headquarters of the military police. They are local peasants who have been caught looting. Some are Jews, others are gipsies with dark complexions, brilliant eyes and long hair. I would not give twopence for their lives. German motor-cyclists dash past amid clouds of dust. I ask one of them to direct me to the headquarters of the unit which I am due to join. He tells me it is situated farther north, about six miles from Soroki, opposite Yampol. But for the moment the road is impassable. It is being shelled by the Russians. The motor-cyclist advises me to wait at Soroki until evening.

" *Danke schön*," I reply.

I cross the public park and start to roam the streets of the district that lies beyond it. The houses appear to be undamaged : they are the only houses in Soroki that are still standing. I read the names of the streets : Engels Street, Karl Marx Street, Lassalle Street, Bakunin Street. In Karl Marx Street is the girls' secondary school. Originally a kind of boarding-school for the daughters of well-to-do citizens of Soroki, the Communists have turned it into a school for the daughters of the workers. Tucked away behind the school in Prince Nicholas Street—No. 25—is a house of modest appearance. Its windows are barred and shuttered. We knock at the door. It is opened by an old woman. She says to us in Russian : " *Podozhditye, pozhaluista*—wait, please," and she closes the door behind her. After a few moments another woman, a woman with extremely light hair—I cannot tell if it is blonde or white—appears at a window and asks me in perfect French if I am looking for someone. No, I tell her, I am not looking for anyone : I would merely like to rest for a few hours. " Go round to the back," she says. " Come in by the veranda." On the veranda, neatly arranged about a wicker table, are some rocking chairs, also of wicker—the kind commonly found in country-houses, or on board ship.

The lady with the light hair meets me on the veranda and invites me to sit down. She is a little on the stout side, and I would put her age at something in the region of fifty. Her movements are slow and rather stately. She looks almost as if she were acting a part. She speaks excellent French, with a hint of affectation in her voice. It is the kind of French spoken by governesses who come of good families, the French of the *Bibliothèque Rose* and of the stories of Madame de Ségur. Yes, there are a couple of rooms vacant: they are clean and tidy, but the beds have no mattresses, no sheets or blankets. I thank her: a divan will be good enough for me. The lady makes a deprecating gesture, smiles, goes out on tip-toe. I am about to open a tin of tomatoes when the old woman who had opened the door to me in the first place enters the room.

She is a woman of perhaps seventy years. She has hard features, but her voice, her expression, her gestures radiate benevolence. She proves to be the mistress of the house. She is Russian; her name is Anna Gyeorgyevna Brasul. Her husband, son and daughter-in-law have been deported to Siberia. She is alone in the world. She lives alone.

"What do you expect me to do? *Ya podozhdu*—I wait," she says. She speaks in a low voice, a smile on her lips. She has been waiting more than twenty years. She is poorly dressed; but her clothes, though old and faded, are carefully patched and ironed.

Through the window I can see the rows of trees in the park, a burned-out vehicle at the corner of Karl Marx Street and Engels Street, two children rolling on the pavement, the roof of the girls' boarding-school. The explosions of the bombs dropped by the Soviet planes rock the walls. There is a tinkling of glass as the mirror of a wardrobe in the next room shivers into fragments. It is now past mid-day, a pale light floods the room, a ray of sunshine beats upon the knees of the old woman seated opposite me.

Anna Gyeorgyevna Brasul caresses that ray of sunshine with a hand traversed by a network of thick purple veins. She looks through misty eyes at the lemon which I have taken from my rucksack. "It is such a long time since I saw a lemon," she says. Then she talks to me of the Crimea, of the orange-groves of Yalta, of the happy days of long ago. When she speaks of the Bolsheviks her voice assumes a note of horror which I would call maternal. Yes, that describes it exactly: a note of maternal horror—as if these people who have caused her so much tribulation over the years were naughty boys.

I perceive that she is glad to be able to show off her gentility, to demonstrate her good breeding. She talks in a low voice, a smile on her lips. From time to time she straightens the black kerchief that envelops her hair. She appears incredibly old; I have never seen such an old woman, her age might well be three hundred years. She looks as if she had just stepped from an old cupboard, or from an old picture-frame. While we are talking a sort of butler brings in a tureen filled with *borsh*. He bows to his mistress and her guests. He is an old Ukrainian servant—bare-footed, and wearing a *tolstovka*, a pair of long trousers, poor cotton trousers with frayed turn-ups, supported by a piece of string tied round his waist. After the *borsh* he brings us each a cup of cocoa, together with some white bread and marmalade. And all the while the old woman talks, smiles, periodically straightens the black kerchief above her wrinkled brow. And as she talks she looks at me; she has most beautiful eyes, and a most beautiful smile, and an honest, kindly face which reflects her wonder and delight at the novelty of it all.

She is truly *aux anges,* as the French say. She offers me a little of everything that she has, a little of everything that she has managed to put aside.

After a few minutes the sound of footsteps is heard on the veranda. " Let's go out on the veranda," says the old woman. And so we go out, and one by one there come forward to meet us, as if they were attending a reception, the lady with the light hair, her husband (a man considerably younger than herself, with a ten-days' growth of beard on his chin, though his linen, I notice, is spotlessly clean), another old lady, and finally a tall thin man with a high starched collar. The last-named has a twisted leg, the sleeves of his jacket are patched. He is an ex-Government official of the pre-revolutionary era. Until a few days ago he was working as a clerk in an *Univer-mag,* which is a kind of Soviet Woolworths. The conversation gets under way quickly and easily; we talk in French and

Russian. The lady with the light hair has been to Switzerland, France and Italy as a governess in a Russian noble family. She talks to me of her favourite poets: Coppée, Lermontov, Lamartine, Pushkin. She does not know any of the Bolshevist authors: but Madame Brasul, wife of the former Government official, says she has read the writings of those " hooligans "— the English word has passed into Russian slang—those ruffians, as she contemptuously calls them: but her contempt has a social implication, not a literary one. Time passes pleasantly. I am anxious to leave so that I can get back to the headquarters of my unit before evening; but I dare not break the spell, and I enter into the spirit of that pathetic fiction, that gentle tragi-comedy.

It is a reception *in extremis*. All of a sudden the old lady gets up, hobbles slowly and silently across the room, opens a cupboard, takes down from a hanger an old evening gown with a lace collar and small whalebone stays. That gown would have been fashionable thirty, perhaps even forty years ago. The old lady tells me that she wore it at a party to which she was invited on board a battleship of the Imperial Fleet at Odessa. Then she goes out, holding the dress aloft to prevent it trailing along the floor. I expect to see her return in a few minutes wearing gala dress, like the Baroness de Saint-Auriol in that unforgettable scene at Quartfouche Castle, so vividly described in Gide's *Isabelle*. But she comes back carrying in both hands a tray. On the tray is a boiled chicken, which she insists that we eat. And so we each consume a portion of the chicken. But it is already three o'clock; I am anxious to leave, it is late, I feel ill at ease among these gentle ghosts: but I dare not interrupt that pathetic fiction, I dare not break that nostalgic spell. I would like to kiss the hand of Madame Anna Brasul, but I am repelled by those swollen veins. At last I screw up my courage, close my eyes and kiss her hand. The old woman is enraptured, she looks about her, she looks at her friends with the authentic air of an old noblewoman, she is proud and happy, a tear glistens on her cheek. But her air of social contentment vanishes as soon as I go down the steps of the veranda. It is as if a black curtain were falling on the last scene of a tragi-comedy.

I am about to climb into my car when a woman aged about forty comes running up, panting, weeping. She is Italian, her name is Alice Orlandelli, she comes from Parma, she has been here fourteen years, she came to Soroki in 1927 to join her brother, a contractor: she learned this morning, quite by chance, that there was an Italian officer in Soroki. She has been looking all over the town for him, and now at last she has found us. "Yes," she says, laughing and crying at once, "I am Italian, I come from Parma, I am Italian." At that I go back indoors, I link arms with her, I help her into a wicker armchair. And Signora Orlandelli laughs, cries, and tells us all how happy she is. The other ladies are happy too; they call her "Madame Orlandelle." They talk and talk, I do not understand what they are saying, Signora Orlandelli speaks a mixture of Russian and Rumanian with an occasional word of Italian thrown in. Then suddenly the old Ukrainian servant stumbles and falls to his knees, upsetting a trayful of candied plums on the carpet. "Grigori!" exclaims the mistress of the house in a reproving tone. And she shakes her head, as much as to say: "What times! What people!", while we all hasten to pick up the candied plums.

Signora Orlandelli tells us that she is in charge of the linen at Soroki Hospital. The Bolsheviks always treated her quite well, she says, but they paid her badly; she had to get through an immense amount of work, she was kept busy from morning till night. When they left, the Communists wanted to take her with them, but she refused. "I preferred to stay with my patients," she says, and now she is hoping the hospital will soon start to function again. But the Communists took away all the bed-linen, all the bandages, all the drugs. They even took the surgical instruments. Signora Orlandelli is happy and excited, she gets mixed up while she is talking, she repeats each sentence two or three times, as if I did not understand. She asks me if I know Parma. Yes, I tell her, certainly I know Parma. She asks me for news of this and that family. And I

4*

answer her at random : " They are all well. The daughter has got married, the old man is dead, so-and-so has three children." I don't know one of the people of whom I am speaking, but Signora Orlandelli is consoled by my harmless fabrications. She laughs, she cries, and suddenly she gets up, runs out of the room, comes back after a quarter of an hour with a small jar of honey and a lovely fresh slice of *brintsa,* which is a kind of cheese made from sheep's milk. She insists on my eating some, and I do so, just to make her happy; we all sample the honey and the *brintsa.*

But the time is by now four o'clock, and we are obliged to leave. " Yes, we'll come back this evening," we tell them. " We'll come back to sleep." And with that courteous lie we take our leave of them. They stand watching on the veranda, waving us goodbye. Madame Anna Gyeorgyevna Brasul waves a white veil—yes, believe it or not, a white veil; she waves it wearily, with melancholy grace. And when we turn the corner, and I am confronted once again by the spectacle of the ruined town, by the sight of the rubble-filled streets, it seems to me that I have returned to reality. And I feel a little sad as I think of those ghosts from another age, standing on the threshold of a world that has collapsed in ruins. I think to myself that for them all hope is now dead, that nothing remains to them but a memory, the only thing in this dead city that is still alive and intact.

XII

THE HIPPOPOTAMI OF THE DNIESTER

Before Yampol, August 6th.

FROM the summit of the right bank of the Dniester the eye takes in the whole area of the battle which for some days past has been raging in front of the Stalin Line, along the course of the Dniester and on the plains of Podolia. (Above Yampol, just below Mogilev, the Stalin Line diverges from the river and stretches in a north-north-westerly direction across the Ukraine, covering the approaches to Kiev.)

The gently-rolling steppe is a constant delight to the eye by reason of the golden splendour of the corn, which completely covers the ample folds of the terrain and the sides of the gullies carved by rushing streams in the black earth. Here and there the brilliant green foliage of a wood affords the eye a momentary respite from the glare. For some days now this tranquil countryside, which is perpetually bathed in bright sunshine, has been the scene of one of the bloodiest battles of the campaign. Having forced its way across the Dniester, the spearhead of our column has established on the Ukrainian bank a bridgehead which the Soviet troops, by dint of a continuous succession of furious counter-attacks, are endeavouring to confine and to isolate.

There was a moment yesterday when it seemed that the small Rumanian force which had secured a precarious foothold on the enemy bank was bound to be overwhelmed by the violence of the Soviet reaction. But during the night, following the arrival of German reinforcements, the situation has been

re-established. The Germans were ferried across the river in
Sturmboote or assault-craft (they are in fact small, extremely
fast outboard motor-launches). The battle flared up again this
morning in the marshes that extend around Yampol between
the bank of the Dniester and the advanced posts of the Stalin
Line. The fighting was extremely fierce and bitter, and both
sides sustained heavy losses. This is the critical phase of the
struggle.

" The decisive attack is timed to begin at dawn tomorrow,"
General R——, who is in command of our column, informs us.
The general is sitting at a table out in the open, near a ruined
house. Spread out on the table is a large-scale map (1 : 25,000)
showing the section of the Stalin Line that covers Yampol.
" Our situation is a bit tricky," the general tells us, indicating
on the map the red outline of the Stalin Line, " but the worst
is over."

Away to our left, the troops of the northern column have
succeeded in widening the bridgehead which has been established at Mogilev. To our right, below Soroki, some Rumanian
detachments have crossed the river and are digging in on the
Ukrainian bank. So far they have repelled all the Soviet
counter-attacks. It is a very hard struggle. However, by tomorrow morning the operation will have passed its most
critical stage. " Would you like to take a look at the battlefield?" the general asks us with a smile.

Accompanied by *Sonderführer* Heitel, we set off on foot
towards the edge of the cliff that overlooks the river. The time
is nearly five o'clock. The humid heat of the summer afternoon
broods over the wheat-fields, the air is filled with a gritty dust
that sets our teeth on edge and burns our lungs. In front of
us the Soviet bank rises abruptly, impatiently, revealing the
sharp outline of its steep, clayey slope dotted with white houses
and long sheds with corrugated-iron roofs. Around us the fields
are sprinkled with thick clumps of acacias, whose brilliant
green foliage conceals anti-aircraft guns, munition-dumps,
field-telephones and wireless equipment. Suddenly, in the foreground of that serene landscape of white clouds and golden

ears of corn, I discern a group of dead Russians. One man is sitting on the ground, his back resting against the crumpled body of a comrade. His head is sunk on his chest, his wide-open eyes are turned upwards. It is a classical image of war on the fringe of the drowsy summer afternoon, a Bodonian frieze on the frontispiece of the battle.

Numerous guns of medium calibre are scattered about the fields. Around every gun, as a precaution against fire, the corn has been carefully scythed in a wide circle, like hair around a wound. During the intervals between shell-bursts one hears the voices of the soldiers, the shouted commands of the officers. (The gunfire is rhythmical and violent; from time to time there is a brief lull, during which the roar of the explosions can be heard reverberating along the opposite bank.) A group of artillerymen, stripped to the waist, are digging small trenches for their reserves of ammunition. Others are lying on the ground fast asleep, their faces covered with towels.

In a dip in the ground we come upon five tanks standing in line abreast. The grey steel-plating glints dully beneath its camouflage of acacia-branches and sheaves of corn. The crews sit around their tanks, eating, reading, smoking. One man is mending a tear in his black tunic. He is working not with the intense concentration of a tailor, but with the frantic haste of a cobbler; he looks as if he is stitching a vamp on to a shoe. A lieutenant of the *Panzerschützer* is sitting on a petrol-drum reading a book. He hails me and offers me a cigarette. He is young, fair-haired, with a long scar, a *Mensur,* on his right cheek.

" Would you like a drop of Soviet vodka?" he shouts, trying to make his voice heard above the shell-bursts. He climbs on to his tank, bends over the hatch, puts his arm inside, rummages about, pulls out a bottle. "*Prosit, prosit.*" On the side of the tank is inscribed in green paint a woman's name : " Hilda." The officer rests his hand on the name, covering the first syllable.

I glance at the book that he has been reading. It is a Soviet edition, in the German language, of Stalin's *Problems of Leninism*. Trotsky has written an acute criticism of it which in many respects is highly diverting.

" I found it in the library of the *kolkhoz* at Väntsina," says the officer of the *Panzerschützer*.

We start to discuss the book, with which I am acquainted.

" It is pure Byzantinism," says the officer. " Another drop of vodka?"

I take my leave of the lieutenant of the *Panzerschützer* and make for an artillery observation-post situated close by. The observer officer points to a curtain of smoke, some two miles beyond the Dniester.

" Our chaps are over there," he says. The place indicated is Yampol. It lies in front of us, a little to our right. By now it is no more than a shapeless mass of charred ruins. A group of houses is burning at the edge of the little town. (It is really a large village, containing a few mills, a few tanneries, a few brick-kilns.) Set in the midst of gardens, allotments and clumps of acacias, the houses on the outskirts of Yampol and the long roofs of the barns, granaries and stables of the *kolkhoz*, situated near the banks of the river, appear from this distance to be undamaged.

" What is that low building, the one with the big yard?" I ask the observer officer. " A *kolkhoz*?"

" It's a cavalry barracks," he replies.

Beyond the river-bank, down on the plain, along the road that leads to Olshanka (it is also the road to Balta, Kiev and Odessa), the air is filled with puffs of red and white smoke from bursting shells. The German artillery is hammering away at the road to Olshanka, which is jammed with Russian baggage-waggons. In some places the corn at the side of the road is burning. Farther off, a wood is in flames. The boom of the German assault-batteries on the Ukrainian bank, which are shelling the Soviet bunkers, mingles with that of the Russian guns in a deep, continuous monotone.

Considering the extent of the battlefield and the fierceness of the fighting the second- and third-line artillery, both German and Russian, is numerically insignificant. Modern battles are conducted for the most part at short range. The entire effort of both armies is centred around the front line, where the medium artillery, motorized or drawn by hand, and often the heavy batteries as well, cover, assist and complete the work of " oxy-hydrogenation " which detachments of pioneers are carrying out against the steel-plating of the bunkers and the enemy dispositions. The din in the front-line is terrific. But a little way to the rear, in the second line, the battlefield is silent : a haven of peace, bathed in the ethereal light of a drowsy summer afternoon.

" It will take more than a few oxy-hydrogen blowlamps to break through the Stalin Line," says the observer officer. " To-morrow morning the Stukas will get to work."

I ask him why the Soviet artillery is making no effort to disrupt the German lines of communication.

" It's too busy shelling our front line," he replies. " But every so often a heavy gun lengthens its range and opens fire on our positions this side of the river. Do you see that L.K.W.?"[1]

The vehicle to which he refers has been blown up by a heavy Russian shell which scored a direct hit upon it. For several hundred yards all around the ground is black and littered with boxes of hand-grenades, spent cartridges, and scorched and twisted wads. A score of crosses, each surmounted by a *Stahlhelm,* are ranged amid the corn. The soil above the graves is newly-turned.

We leave the observation-post and walk down towards the river, through woods of acacias interspersed with small clearings where an occasional cow, abandoned to its fate, raises its head from the grass and eyes us curiously but without suspicion. Beneath a tree we see two German soldiers washing their feet in a pool of muddy water. Their great toes are swollen and deformed by long marches and by the heat. Their feet protrude, white and enormous, from their grey-green uniforms like tree-branches from which the bark has been stripped. It occurs to me that the feet of Daphne must have looked like that in the moment of her metamorphosis.

[1] Short for *Last-Kraft-Wagen* (heavy lorry).

In front of us is a battery of heavy howitzers. The gunners are clad only in shorts. Their skin is red, with the redness of white bodies burnt by the sun. It is the colour of the human figures in the encaustic paintings on the walls of Etruscan tombs.

A Herculean gunner comes towards us, carrying on his shoulders a heavy shell. His shorts slip down his thighs, but he is unperturbed. He continues to walk, a pink figure against the background of green grass, stark naked, to the accompaniment of guffaws from his comrades. Those naked men, grouped around the guns, remind me of certain sculptures of Aligi Sassu.

Suddenly a Russian shell bursts alongside a German battery. By the time we reach the scene of the explosion the wounded have already been laid on stretchers. An officer shouts an order into a field-microphone. The metallic voice fills the air, which is still vibrating from the explosion. A hundred yards further on we stop at the edge of a deep gully. From here the battlefield appears in all its vastness, the eye ranges freely along the valley and over the plain.

The clouds of smoke from the fires billow and eddy on the horizon, like enormous balloons straining at their moorings. All along the line of advancing columns there stretches a curtain of red dust and grey-brown fog, a kind of immense screen, on which the sun's declining rays design yellow and purple patterns.

Directly above our heads a squadron of Messerschmitts circles about a formation of Soviet fighter-bombers of the type which the Germans call *Spitzmaus,* or "mouse-face." These new biplanes, which, though made in Russia, are probably of American design, are extremely fast and manoeuvrable. They constitute the most interesting novelty of recent days. (It was barely a week ago that they made their first appearance in the sky above the battlefield.) They present a bold front to the Messerschmitts. The slow, ponderous *tock-tock-tock* of their machine-guns punctuates the frenzied rataplan of the German fighters' cannon. Then they climb rapidly and head eastwards.

In the distance, beyond the Stalin Line, a gigantic column of smoke rises mushroom-like into the sky.

A hundred yards from us, at the bottom of the gully, a detachment of German infantry is advancing in single file across the grass. The soldiers are bowed down by the weight of their haversacks, their tunics are open at the neck, their steel helmets dangle from their belts. Slowly they amble down towards the river, nonchalantly they enter the zone of the fighting. They see me, recognize my uniform, shout: "*Italiener*! *Italiener*!" By now the sun has disappeared beneath the horizon. Here and there in the green twilight one hears the sound of men talking in loud voices, mingled with laughter and the neighing of horses.

Night is falling when, after a long détour, we arrive back at Command headquarters. Darkness descends upon the battle-field like a blanket heavy with dew. Around the headquarters there is a constant coming and going of officers and despatch-riders.

"Got back safely, then!" says Major Werner as he passes me in the gloom. In a few hours our column will cross the river by an emergency bridge and will hasten to the assistance of the troops that have already secured a foothold on the Soviet bank. All is ready now for the great clash of arms which may well decide the issue of this fateful battle of the Ukraine. The cannon thunders without respite, emitting a monotonous booming sound which from time to time grows harsh and sepulchral—a hollow subterranean sound, like the voice of the earth, the voice of the night. A creaking of wheels is heard in the darkness as infantry baggage-waggons, artillery-trains, ambulances and munition lorries pass by on their way to the front. I lie down under a tree, wrap myself in my blanket, and try to sleep.

In a few hours it will be morning. I am dead tired, but sleep will not come. At daybreak a hundred thousand men will hurl themselves against the Stalin Line; they will open a way through the girdle of concrete and steel and pour on to the Ukrainian steppe, on to the road that leads to Kiev and

Odessa. A diffused glimmer appears in the sky above the far bank of the Dniester. It is not the moon. It is the reflection of the shellbursts. The Stalin Line stretches into the distance like a neon tube. Yes, that is the right image : like an endless neon tube, purple in colour. Here and there a searchlight probes the sky above the vast plain. The drone of engines can be heard directly overhead. They are bombing Soroki. Every so often, amid the thunder-claps of the German artillery, I discern the rending crash of a heavy Russian shell. A gun is firing close by. A soldier runs past, shouting : " *Schnell! Schnell!* " I close my eyes, and the creak of wheels, the rattle of tank-tracks, fill the damp air with a subdued medley of sound, like a symphony of Hindemith.

It is still dark when suddenly I am roused by an infernal din, a deafening roar. Soroki, away to our right, is in flames. Yampol too is burning. The whole Soviet bank is ablaze. Here and there huge fountains of earth and immense plumes of smoke can be seen rising into the air. Mala Yaruka is burning. Further off, Tsihivka too is in flames. Squadrons of Stukas dive almost vertically towards the Soviet bunkers to the accompaniment of a fearful whistling sound. The medium artillery is shelling the open spaces between the outworks of the Stalin Line. Already the flame-throwing detachments are melting the steel plates of the redoubts. The long oxy-hydrogen flames are clearly visible amid the smoke of the explosions.

All around me the German soldiers are shouting : " *Schnell! Schnell!* " It is the watchword of all their battles, the secret of all their victories. " *Schnell! Schnell!*—Quick! Quick!* " Already the spearhead of our column has crossed the river, and now the infantry battalions are advancing, one after the other —*schnell, schnell.* In a little while it will be the turn of the unit to which I am attached.

In the uncertain light of dawn we pass along a sunken road screened by a line of acacias and poplars. By now we are within a hundred yards of the river. Ahead of us we can hear the banging of hammers on the planks of the bridge, which the infantry are crossing even before the engineers have finished building it. At this point the river is broad and deep. A beautiful river, the Dniester, so green and smooth in the silky light of early morning.

Presently we hear the crackle of machine-guns, the rat-tat-tat of anti-tank cannon. Above Yampol, a little to our left, two large Russian tanks cleave the waters of the river. They are two of the Red Army's celebrated amphibious tanks—enormous floating monsters of steel which the German soldiers call " hippopotami." The miniature cannon which protrude from their turrets are firing furiously at the bridge. From all along the German bank the *Pak* guns bark furiously at the two " hippopotami " as they slowly advance upstream amid the fountains of water thrown up by the shells. After a while one of the monsters is hit; it continues to swim with difficulty, its bow almost submerged. A moment later the two of them disappear from view round a bend in the river. Shouts of joy go up from the soldiers ranged along the bank, amid the cane-brakes and the clumps of acacias. Meanwhile the *tock-tock-tock* of the Soviet *pulyemot* grows ever fainter and less frequent, the din of the explosions recedes into the distance.

Already the sun is rising, slowly, painfully emerging from the mists that shroud the horizon. Parties of wounded Germans walk down the bridge. Some of them wave their arms in a gesture of greeting and triumph. Or do I misinterpret the gesture? Has it, perhaps, a different meaning? There is always something sad, like a farewell, there is always something nostalgic, something incomplete, about the feeling of triumph that accompanies a victory.

XIII

SOVIET BATTLEFIELD

Kachikovska, August 7th.

WE have just crossed the Dniester by the emergency bridge, built in a few hours by the pioneers beneath a protective umbrella of Stukas, and we are already making our way cautiously through the midst of the houses situated at the south-western end of Yampol, when a frightful stench of burnt flesh catches us by the throat. In the huge yard of a *kolkhoz,* where but lately several squadrons of Red cavalry were quartered, lie the charred remains of hundred of horses. In a neighbouring *kolkhoz* carcases of oxen are piled up in the stables and beneath the roofs of the long open sheds. The corpses of Russian soldiers—sometimes only the legs, some-times the whole trunk—protrude from the steel embrasures of the bunkers built for the defence of Yampol, at the point where a ramification of the Stalin Line insinuates itself between the village and the river.

A heavy Russian tank is lying on its side at the edge of the road, outside an *Univermag,* which is a kind of co-opera-tive store. I walk over to the tank. The driver—a woman—is still inside. She is wearing a grey tunic, the close-cropped hair is scorched and blackened at the back of her neck. Through a tear in her tunic I glimpse a patch of white skin, just below her breast. On her face is an expression of intense concentration; her eyes are half-closed; she has a hard mouth. She is a woman of about thirty. There are a great number of women in the Soviet Army; they fight in the air force and in the tank corps. "Brave girl," I say to myself. I stretch out my hand, gently and reverently caress her brow. "Poor dear," I mutter.

We advance into the village, where a heavy Russian shell still falls from time to time with a furious shriek. The enemy is trying to destroy the bridge, to prevent the passage of reinforcements and supplies. A fearful scene of destruction presents itself to our gaze. Yampol is now no more than a heap of smoking ruins. On the ground near the shattered wall of a house stands an oil-lantern. Its glass windows are broken. Inside, the flame is still burning feebly, almost invisible in the glare from the sun, which is already high. We cover the last few hundred yards to the end of the village almost at a run, seeking refuge from the Soviet bombardment, which grows more intense every minute, as if the Bolsheviks were anxious, before retiring, to use up all their stocks of ammunition.

The road now climbs to the top of the river-bank, and as we approach the last houses of the village the vast Ukrainian plateau opens before us like a fan. The blue vault of heaven is supported by towering columns of smoke which rise at intervals amid the golden splendour of the boundless fields of corn. It is a solemn architecture, a severe, grey Doric colonnade, to which the wind gives an evanescent, magic quality. I look back. Yampol resembles one of those huge steel-yards where the slag from the blast-furnaces is left lying about in heaps. It is a fearful spectacle, that mass of charred ruins set amid the green and gold of the fields.

Not a living soul remains in Yampol. As the tide of battle rolled nearer, the population, of which the vast majority— almost seventy per cent, in fact—is Jewish, fled into the woods to escape the bombardments and the fires. As soon as we are outside Yampol we hear shouts of "*Khlyeb*! *Khlyeb*! —Bread! Bread!" A crowd of about forty women, children and bearded old men are sheltering in one of those wide trenches which are used for the storage of manure. They are all Jews. The children climb on to the edge of the ditch, the old men take off their caps and wave their arms, the women shout: "*Khlyeb*! *Khlyeb*!"

A German officer orders some soldiers to distribute a little bread among those unfortunates. The women seize the small loaves, tear them to pieces, distribute the fragments among the children and the old men. One of the women—in fact, she is no more than a girl—asks me if they can return to their homes. "No, not yet," I tell her. "The Russians are shelling Yampol. Tomorrow, perhaps." They will remain in that manure-trench another day, another two days yet. Then they will go back to their ruined homes. Within a week the stricken village will begin to live again. Human life is a terribly tenacious plant, a plant that nothing can destroy. It is a most beautiful, terrifying force.

We advance slowly along the broad paved road that leads to Olshanka. It is the road to Balta, the road to Odessa and Kiev. The Stalin Line runs parallel to the river on our right. It is not what it seemed from a distance, namely, an unbroken series of miniature forts, redoubts and bunkers, linked by a continuous system of trenches. It is a collection of outworks, separated from one another by vast areas of open ground. And it bears no resemblance, either in extent or from the technical viewpoint, to the Maginot Line or the *Westwall*. It consists merely of a narrow fortified strip, barely two to two-and-a-half miles in depth, no more. It should be thought of as constituting an excellent base for a mobile, elastic resistance rather than a rigid system of defence *à outrance*. And no one can deny that it has fulfilled its function, a simple "covering" function, with the utmost efficiency. The fall of the Stalin Line does not necessarily mean, then, that the Russian Army in the Ukraine has been destroyed. I shall never weary of repeating that the war against Russia is likely to be hard and long. Certain it is that its end has not been brought appreciably nearer as a result of the breaching of the Stalin Line.

The road is littered with overturned tanks, the carcases of

horses, and burnt-out lorries. Soviet corpses are something of a rarity. (It is surprising how few dead one encounters in the wake of the Russian retreat. I shall attempt later on to account for this extraordinary fact, which in the early days of the war greatly impressed the German soldiers, and of which at the beginning contradictory explanations were offered.) Here and there we come upon a dead German, whose body is picked up and reverently laid upon a stretcher.

The shell-holes, the mine-craters, and the enormous funnel-shaped pits dug by the bombs of the Stukas compel us to halt for long periods, sometimes even to leave the road and make our way across the fields. Slowly we advance through a cloud of dust, dense as the mist on a mountain-top. But this is a scorching, blinding mist, a mist that suffocates and makes the head swim, like those acrid clouds of vapour that are thrown off by metals and acids in chemical factories: a poisonous, stifling mist, in which men, horses, and vehicles assume strange forms and fantastic proportions. The reflection of the sun on this cloud of red dust magnifies the images of men and things like a mirage in the desert: I have the illusion that I am walking through a crowd of gigantic shadows, of enormous gesticulating ghosts. Voices, shouts, the roar of wheels and tank-tracks, the tramp of horses, reverberate with frightening loudness through this burning mist, as though reflected from an invisible wall. We feel as if we were being overwhelmed by an avalanche of terrifying sounds.

In order to escape from this haunting mirage of forms and sounds I stray a hundred yards or so from the road. Around me, as far as the eye can reach, stretches a sea of corn, swept by soft, lingering gusts of wind. In the distance, at the edge of the plain, I can distinguish the massive cloud of dust thrown up by the column that is protecting our left flank. Some two miles ahead of us the light detachments of our column maintain contact with the enemy, who is not fleeing in disorder but is retreating slowly, disputing every yard and punctuating his withdrawal with frequent counter-offensive thrusts by strong rearguards. I hear distinctly the chatter of machine-guns, the rending bursts of mortar-fire, the muffled explosions of heavy shells. Undoubtedly the tactics pursued by the Russians are in certain respects very effective. The resistance of their mobile units, their light tanks and infantry detachments, is supported by masses of artillery, much of it consisting of self-propelled batteries of medium guns. It is thanks to the protective curtain of fire thrown up by their artillery that the Russians are able to take everything with them, that they do not abandon on the field even a broken rifle, even the tripod of a machine-gun.

One of the most striking features of these battlefields is the extremely tidy state in which they are left by the retreating Russians: a paradoxical tidiness that fills the German officers and men with open-mouthed astonishment. They take even their boxes of cartridges with them. The care with which they clear the ground almost passes belief. One would say that they were determined to leave behind no trace of their presence—nothing, in short, that might afford the enemy the smallest clue to their methods of warfare, their tactics, the composition of their units, the nature and function of their weapons.

After hours and hours of bitter fighting it is impressive to arrive on the scene of the struggle and to find that the ground is completely clear and almost unmarked, with not a trace anywhere of an abandoned helmet, a haversack, a gas-mask, a machine-gun belt, a box of ammunition, a hand-grenade, or even of those strips of material, those pieces of paper, those gauze bandages, those bloodstained uniforms, which are the inevitable legacy of any normal battle. The Russians leave behind them only a handful of dead, scattered here and there about the plain: those who were the last to fall, those who remained to cover their comrades' retreat. But they are few in number: five, ten, no more. And it is extraordinarily impressive to see those poor corpses, left to rot on the smooth, carefully tidied battlefield. They lie in the green grass as if they had fallen from the sky.

We are greatly surprised, therefore, when, having arrived just outside the village of Kachikovska, we come upon a battlefield strewn with hundreds of Russian corpses and with all the débris that ordinarily remains to mark the scene of a recent battle. Until we are within a few miles of Kachikovska our route leads across a vast, absolutely flat plain, resembling a steppe : indeed, it is the precursor of the steppe that lies farther to the east, beyond the Bug, beyond the Dnieper. But little by little, some twelve miles beyond Yampol, as we approach Kachikovska, the plain slowly rises, to terminate abruptly at the edge of a deep, green valley thick with trees, at the bottom of which, on the banks of a thin stream, lies the village of Kackikovska.

Towards ten o'clock we reach a point situated within a mile or so of the edge of the plain. The Russians, entrenched at the top of the western slope of the valley, are resisting stubbornly. We have to wait outside Kachikovska until the spearhead of our column has succeeded in breaking the fanatical Soviet resistance. This involves a delay of several hours. At midday the battle is still raging. In the meantime the Germans have brought up numerous batteries of medium guns and have installed them in the fields, amid the corn. In the face of heavy fire from the German artillery the Russians resist ferociously. Time and again they counter-attack, forcing the Germans to yield ground. The Soviet artillery supports the desperate efforts of the rearguard, whose total strength is perhaps barely equivalent to that of a battalion, with a terrible counter-barrage which compels the Germans repeatedly to move their own guns and inflicts heavy losses on their infantry. The Germans declare that the Russians have shown themselves to be the best soldiers of all those whom they have hitherto encountered in this war. Better than the Poles, better even than the British. They never surrender. They fight to the last man, with calm, single-minded tenacity.

Around four o'clock in the afternoon we see the first groups of prisoners going down the line. Most of them are wounded. They wear no bandages, their faces are caked with blood and dust, their uniforms are in rags, their hands blackened by smoke. They walk slowly, supporting one another. Their statements confirm what was already suspected, namely, that the bulk of Budenny's army on the Ukrainian Front is not yet fully engaged. The units that are sustaining the German onslaught consist for the most part of young recruits or veteran reservists, called to the colours at the beginning of July: peasants in uniform, not soldiers in the strict sense of the word. Apart from the specialized arms—the air force, the artillery and the tanks—the Red Army proper, by which I mean the professional nucleus of the Soviet military organism, awaits the decisive clash further to the east, perhaps on the banks of the Dnieper, perhaps beyond the Don.

Meanwhile, as we are talking, the *tock-tock-tock* of the Russian *pulyemot* (the Soviet machine-guns have a slow rate of fire, they emit a deep, hollow sound) is receding into the distance, the artillery-fire is growing weaker. " They are going away," says a German N.C.O. who has been wounded in the head, and he looks at his great gnarled hands, oil-stained and black with mud.

When we come to the edge of the plain, to the point where the road descends abruptly into the valley, at the bottom of which lies the village of Kackikovska, cries of amazement burst from our lips. For the first time in this war, for the very first time, there unfolds before our eyes a battlefield littered with Soviet dead, a battlefield which the Russians have not had time to " clean up " before retreating. And it is with a feeling of apprehension, as if I were treading on forbidden ground, that I advance on to the battlefield, into the midst of the enemy dead, who seem to follow with their eyes my every step, my every movement. They stare at me with bewildered, reproachful expressions, as if I had come to probe their secret, to profane the terrible, inviolable chaos of war and death.

XIV

THE FLIGHT OF THE DEAD

Kachikovska, August 8th.

THE retreating Soviet troops do not abandon their dead on the battlefield, nor do they bury them on the spot. They take them away. They bury them twelve, twenty miles further east, in the heart of a wood, or in the depths of a valley. They bury them in huge communal graves : and on the graves they plant no crosses, nor do they leave any marks of identi-fication. They trample down the newly-turned earth and cover it with leaves, grass, branches of trees, sometimes with heaps of manure, so that none may ever be able to violate those secret tombs.

There is something terrible, something mysterious, about this clandestine inhumation, about this surreptitious removal of the dead. " *Eine Totenflucht* " was how a German soldier described it to me this morning. Yes, it is just that : a " flight of the dead "—for all the world as though the dead had struggled to their feet, had slowly walked away, each man helping his neighbour, following unknown paths through the corn-fields and the woods; as though they had fled not because they were afraid, but in order to escape some supreme adven-ture, some unknown, deeply-dreaded fate. It is as though they had fled from the scene of the battle after removing every trace of the ferocious struggle, every object that might recall the bloody clash of arms, or that might by its presence disturb the peace of the woods, of the corn-fields, of the golden expanses of sunflowers. Yes, it seems almost that it is the dead themselves who " clean up " the battlefields. And having done so they slowly drift away, they disappear for ever, leaving behind no physical trace of themselves, not even the imprint of their shoes in the mud, not even the rifles which the splinters from German shells have broken in their hands.

This is a phenomenon which greatly impresses those who happen to cross one of these battlefields immediately after the struggle has ended. In the northern sector too, and in all the other sectors of the front, the retreating Russians take their dead with them. After whole days, after whole weeks of the most bitter fighting, after the ferocious *mêlées*, after the re-peated clashes of formidable arrays of tanks, the German soldiers find on the battlefield not the thousands of Soviet dead that the ferocity of the struggle would have led them to expect, but only a few scattered corpses—forgotten rather than abandoned. This absence of corpses on the battlefield seems no less a piece of human wizardry than a prodigy of nature. It gives the scene of the struggle an eerie aspect. For nothing in the world could be more eerie than a battlefield devoid of corpses. It is like a deathbed after the body has been taken away. There is a nakedness, an unnatural white-ness, about those icy, disarranged sheets, about that pillow with the cold imprint of a head upon it. And, in the same way, there is something icy and naked about the grass, about the stones, about the clods of earth on a battlefield that has been denuded of its dead.

I have been on the Russian Front, with the German troops, since the earliest days of the war. I have followed, step by step, the advance of a motorized column from Stefanesti to Mogilev. More recently, with a column of infantry, I have followed the march from Beltsy to Soroki, and from Soroki, through Yampol, to this village of Kachikovska, situated in the heart of the Ukraine. I now find myself at the easternmost point of the whole vast German battle-line. And I had never yet seen, until this morning, a battlefield littered with Soviet dead. Occasionally I had seen a few corpses, no more—as on that hill near Skuratovoi, or inside those tanks on the road to

Beltsy. But this morning, for the first time, when we reached the edge of the valley, at the bottom of which lies the village of Kachikovska, I saw a battlefield literally covered with Russian corpses—an intact, uncleared battlefield, from which the Russians had been able to carry away nothing, not even their own dead.

The ground that has been the scene of today's bitter fighting, which lasted from ten in the morning until sunset, extends to the very edge of the plain, almost to the top of the steep hill that leads down to Kachikovska. It is flat country, consisting entirely of fields of corn and sunflowers. The upper slopes of the valley are thick with acacias and poplars. Below, a beautiful wood of walnut trees stretches down almost as far as the houses of the village. The Russians had clung desperately to their position at the top of the hill. Although unable to manoeuvre because they had behind them the rugged slopes of the valley, they were none the less extremely well placed for purposes of defence, inasmuch as they were out of range of the German artillery. Until one arrives on the scene of the struggle there is nothing to indicate the extent of the slaughter or the savagery of the fighting. The dead lie partly on the slopes of the valley, partly in the fields of sunflowers or in the corn, partly in the slit-trenches which the Russians have dug along the extreme edge of the plain. Where the Soviet resistance has been fiercest and most prolonged they lie in groups, close to one another, sometimes on top of one another. Elsewhere they lie in twos and threes behind clumps of shrubs, face downwards, still with their rifles clutched in their hands, or on their backs, with arms outspread, surprised by death in that attitude of complete surrender which characterizes the man who has been shot through the chest. Others are doubled up, their cheeks displaying that ghastly pallor which results from stomach wounds.

Some, mortally wounded, sit motionless with their backs resting against the trunks of trees. Others lie on their sides, moaning in low voices, as though secretly ashamed : " *Boge moy! Boge moy!*—My God! My God!" This final invocation, which testifies to the ineffectiveness of so much coercion, of the long repression of so many instincts, of so much indoctrination and propaganda, has, in those poor mouths, a new and unexpected sound, a sound that is pure and true, supremely true. " *Boge moy! Boge moy!*" An officer is lying in the grass, his mouth pressed to the earth, one leg doubled up beneath the other, his right arm clasped to his chest. The ground is strewn with boxes of cartridges, belts of machine-gun bullets, packets of ammunition, all those minute objects which one finds abandoned on a battlefield.

My feet tread on garments stained with mud and blood, on pieces of cartridge-paper, empty milk-tins, mess-bowls, water-bottles, steel helmets, khaki forage-caps, leather belts, broken rifles. A dog tied to a tree-trunk whines miserably, tugging convulsively at the cord in its efforts to break it. One of the creature's eyes hangs from its socket, dripping with blood.

Over a radius of more than a mile the scene is repeated with haunting frequency, clear, precise, identical down to the minutest detail. At points where a heavy shell or a bomb from a Stuka has fallen the bodies of dead Russians and fragments of débris lie in tangled heaps. They look as if they had been dragged there by the current of an invisible river. Many of the corpses are half-naked, stripped by the terrible blast from the explosions. In one place the ground is littered with small loaves from a burst sack. The bread is dark in colour and compact in texture. I try a mouthful. It has an excellent taste, the crust dissolves between my teeth like a biscuit. Sitting almost bolt upright in a shell-hole is a dead Russian soldier, his face splashed with blood. Sprinkled on his knees and all around him are innumerable tiny fragments of that fresh cheese made from sheeps' milk which in these parts goes by the name of *brintsa*. His mouth is still full of food. He was eating when the shell-splinter struck him on the temple.

The German orderlies wander about the battlefield; they move cautiously, stooping slightly. They go through the pockets of the dead, they lay the wounded on stretchers. Meanwhile, a great silence has fallen on the scene. Even the voices of the guns are muffled. (Fighting is still going on in the distance, two or three miles ahead of us, over towards Shuni and Olshanka.) A few houses are burning behind that wood on the far side of the valley. A squad of German soldiers is digging a grave, others are stacking the Russian dead along its edge. Now the grave is ready. One by one the corpses are thrown in. Then the soldiers fill the grave with earth. A guard of honour presents arms. The officer's voice sounds harsh and precise. A few stray rifle-bullets hum through the leafy branches of the trees. A hail of machine-gun bullets passes high above our heads. The sun, now on the point of setting, is warm, the atmosphere thick and heavy.

I sit down in the shade of a tree and look about me. The Soviet detachment that fought here was not large—possibly less than a battalion. It resisted to the last, it sacrificed itself in order to cover the retreat of the main body. A battalion of desperate men, abandoned to their fate. No one has had time to " clean up " the battlefield. Everything is still as it was half an hour ago. This, then, is the first opportunity I have had of studying the essential, secret nature of the Soviet Army, of observing at close quarters its singular composition, of analysing the " chemical formula ", so to say, by which its varied and contrasting elements—political, social, racial, ideological, military, economic—are welded into a corporate whole. No one in this unit has fled, no one, apart from a few badly wounded men, has surrendered. It was therefore a good unit. The officers exercised complete control over their men. They remained, every one of them, at their posts. And even as I begin to look for the factors on which the discipline of this unit and its technical efficiency depended, I note with surprise this blend of the military and the political, the remarkable balance that has been struck between such a variety of elements—social, political, military, human—this extraordinary alliance between military discipline and the Statute of the Communist Party, between the Penal Code of the Red Army and the Manual of the Red soldier.

Lying on the ground near me is a box full of papers—regimental rolls and such-like. On the box is a typewriter, of American design but Soviet manufacture. A copy of *Pravda*, dated June 24th last, all crumpled and mudstained, announces in enormous headlines the outbreak of the war and the first battles in Poland, Galicia, and Bessarabia. On the second page are printed the life-stories of three " agitators ", each of whom has recently addressed a meeting—the first in a factory, the second in the yard of a *kolkhoz,* the third in a military encampment. (These " agitators " are the propagandists of the Communist Party. In time of war they have the task of strengthening the people's will to resist, of explaining the objects of the struggle, of urging the masses of workers and peasants to intensify production in the interests of national defence.) The three men have hard features and prominent jaws; and around them are the usual faces, stern and attentive, of the workers, peasants, and soldiers.

I get up and walk slowly across the battlefield. Presently my foot stumbles against an electric battery, one of the so-called " dry " variety. The two leads from the battery are connected to a lamp, which hangs from a nail driven into the side of a wooden box lined with tinplate. Lying on the box are a broken stylographic pen and an exercise-book filled with notes. Inside is a large album bound in red boards, on which are inscribed in large letters the words " *Tryetya Stalinskaya Pyatlyetka.*" The album illustrates the third Five Year Plan, formulated by Stalin and still in course of realization, with the aid of statistical data relating to the construction of new factories, industrial organization, and production. While I am turning over the pages of the album a German soldier points to something in the branches of a tree. I look up: it is a loudspeaker. Hanging down the trunk of the tree is an electric wire. We follow the course of the wire through the grass.

A few yards from the tree, in a hole in the ground, we come upon the crumpled body of a Russian soldier. The dead man is leaning forward, covering with his chest a large metal box— a radiogram. Scattered all around in the grass are fragments of gramophone records. I try to piece together the fragments, to read the titles on the labels : The *Internationale*, the *March of Budenny*, the *March of the Black Sea Fleet*, the marches of the sailors of Kronstadt and of the Red Air Force. There are also some educational records dealing with social, political and military subjects.

On the red label of one record I read the following words, printed in black letters : " *Na Podmogu Aghitatoru—Vidannaya Ts.K. kp/6/U/N°.* 5—1941." It is a kind of phonographic catechism, a sort of manual of the perfect " agitator ". The articles of this catechism were repeated by the deep, imperious voice of the loudspeaker with the aim of inspiring the soldiers to do their duty to the end. On another record are the words *Poyasnityelni Text*. This is undoubtedly another species of catechism, a kind of vade-mecum of the Communist soldier. A third record bears the inscription " *Teche Ryechka Nyevyelichka*." It is the title of a " factory song ", one of those songs to which the Bolsheviks have given the name *tsavod*.

But my most interesting discovery is an album of twenty-four records, the cover of which bears this title : " *Doclad Tovarishcha Stalina na Chrezvichainom VIII Vsyesoyuzom Syesdye Sovyetov* 25 *Noyabrya* 1936 *G. O Proyektye Konstitutsii Soyuza SSR*." On the forty-eight sides of the twenty-four records is recorded the whole of the marathon speech delivered by Stalin in the Bolshoi Theatre, Moscow, on the occasion of the promulgation of the Soviet Constitution in 1936. The German soldier, who has been helping me to collect the fragments of the records, gazes at me in silence. Then he looks up and sees the loudspeaker hanging from the branches of the tree. He stares at the body of the Russian soldier, slumped over the metal casing of the radiogram. The German soldier's face is serious, almost sad, with the sadness that in simple men is the companion of bewilderment and incomprehension. He is a peasant, this German soldier, not a worker—a Bavarian peasant from the Augsburg district. He does not possess what I would call " industrial morale ", he does not even understand the meaning of " industrial morale ", still

5

less that of its principles, its abstractions, its violent and fanatical realism. (During the fighting, the words of Stalin, magnified to gigantic proportions by the loudspeaker, rain down upon the men kneeling in holes behind the tripods of their machine-guns, din in the ears of the soldiers lying amid the shrubs, of the wounded writhing in agony on the ground. The loudspeaker imbues that voice with a harsh, brutal, metallic quality. There is something diabolical, and at the same time terribly naïve, about these soldiers who fight to the death, spurred on by Stalin's speech on the Soviet Constitution, by the slow, deliberate recital of the moral, social, political, and military precepts of the " agitators "; about these soldiers who never surrender; about these dead, scattered all around me; about the final gestures, the stubborn, violent gestures of these men who died so terribly lonely a death on this battlefield, amid the deafening roar of the cannon and the ceaseless braying of the loudspeaker.)

I lower my eyes, and in the grass at my feet I catch sight of a sort of booklet with a leather cover. It is the paybook of Private Semyon Stolyenko. A Ukrainian name. Beside his service-number, 568352, is written in red ink the word *Byespartiinii,* that is, " without a party ", a-political. Then follow some particulars which I do not understand. Private Stolyenko, I gather, was born at Nemirovski on February 3rd, 1909. He was a machine-gunner. Then I read the word *Traktor.* He was a peasant, then; undoubtedly he used to work on a *kolkhoz* as a mechanic in charge of a farm-tractor. At the top of the third page is written in red ink the word *Byezbozhnik,* literally " without God ". This Ukrainian soldier, this Semyon Stolyenko, aged thirty-two, who professes to be *byezpartiinii,* that is to say, a-political, and *byezbozhnik,* in other words an atheist, this peasant whose martial instincts are stimulated by the imperious voice of the loudspeaker, who does not surrender but fights to the end, this soldier. . . . But he is dead. He has fought to the end. He has not surrendered. He is dead.

The wind rustles the leaves of the tree, sways the branches, many of which are warped and mutilated by the blast from the shells, ruffles the grass where the corpses lie. The blood-stained uniforms, the papers that litter the ground, stir in the breeze. Gradually a murmur spreads through the leaves and the grass. As though by a miracle, the faces of the dead are suddenly illuminated. It is the light of the setting sun that revives those poor faces. The chatter of machine-gun fire is borne on the wind from the village of Shumi. In the distance, the cannon hammers against the green wall of a wood like a battering-ram. A forlorn neighing of horses ascends from the depths of the valley. From time to time the sound of a rifle-shot dies away among the folds of the purple evening, as among the folds of an immense red flag.

XV

THE BLACK BIVOUAC

Shumi, August 9th.

DURING the night-time all fighting ceases. Men, animals, weapons rest. Not a rifle-shot breaks the damp nocturnal silence. Even the voice of the cannon is hushed. As soon as the sun has set, and the first shadows of evening creep across the corn-field, the German columns prepare for their night's halt. It is an interlude of peace, of repose : a suspension of hostilities, a kind of armistice. The two opposing armies fling themselves down in the grass and sleep.

As the officers give the order to stop their harsh voices are muffled by the light mist that rises from the woods. The advanced elements halt and spread out fanwise, forming a shield for the remainder of the column. All the formidable engines of assault move forward and assemble at the head of the column. As a result of this mixed formation, at once both defensive and offensive, the column assumes, for the duration of the night, the shape of a huge nail with its point turned towards the enemy. (These German columns are shaped like a hammer. And their overnight dispositions make it possible for them to strike at the enemy even as he sleeps, to inflict a hammer-blow upon him and to drive the nail into his defences under cover of darkness, to overwhelm him before he has recovered from the first shock of surprise, before he is fully awake.)

Night falls, cold and heavy, on the men curled up in the ditches, in the small slit-trenches which they have hastily dug amid the corn, alongside the light and medium assault-batteries, the anti-tank *Pak* cannon, the heavy anti-aircraft machine-guns, the mortars, and the various other weapons of which the "hammer" is composed. Then the wind rises—a moist, cold wind that fills one's bones with an intense, numbing weariness. (The wind that sweeps this Ukrainian plateau is laden with a thousand scents of herbs and plants.) From the darkness of the fields comes a ceaseless crackle as the moisture of the night causes the sunflowers to droop on their long wrinkled stalks. All about us the corn makes a soft rustling sound, like the rustle of a silk gown. A great murmur arises throughout the dark countryside, which is filled with the sound of slow breathing, of deep sighs. Shielded from sudden attack by the sentries and patrols, the men abandon themselves to sleep. (There in front of us, concealed amid the corn and within the solid dark mass of the woods—over there, beyond the deep, smooth, bleak fold of the valley, the enemy sleeps. We can hear his hoarse breathing, we can discern his strong smell—a smell of oil, petrol, and sweat.)

The Germans call these overnight halts "black bivouacs". They are not characterized by the feverish, nervous vigils of trench warfare. Instead, they afford the weary soldier the opportunity of enjoying a deep sleep, a tranquil repose, at the side of the road, in the corn-fields, in the woods, almost within a stone's throw of the enemy. A kind of bivouac, yes—but a bivouac without fires, without singing, without the murmur of voices: in short, a "black bivouac". A profound silence broods over the sleeping column. Then, at dawn, the struggle flares up again with renewed violence.

But although the sun had set some time before, although the shades of evening were already falling lightly and stealthily from the darkling sky, the order to stop was slow in coming. Already we had reached the first houses of Kachikovska, already the vanguard of the column was making its way up the far side of the valley, in the direction of Olshanka, when a despatch-rider arrived with the news that we were to spend the night at Shumi, a village situated half-way between

Kachikovska and Olshanka. Another six miles to go. Ahead of us, over towards Olshanka, the fighting died a slow, lingering death, like a flame that is constantly revived by the wind. Brief interludes of silence alternated with sudden furious bursts of fire. The immense waves of darkness that descended from the sky above the battlefield did not suffice to smother the flame.

How much better it would have been to stop at Kachikovska! We were dead tired, and in the chill of the evening the smell of the village was warm, like the smell of an oven, or of a stable. " Long Live the First of May !" was inscribed in white letters on an enormous strip of red cloth glued to the front of a *kolkhoz* at the entrance to the village. The horses, scenting the adjacent stream and the wet grass of the valley, neighed impatiently. The soldiers gazed longingly at the white houses (the meanest of these had thatched roofs, those belonging to the more prosperous peasants had roofs of sheet-metal painted green or red). From the village rose the thousand petulant, garrulous sounds which farm animals make at the approach of night. The dogs barked joyously at the entrances to the green gardens gay with sunflowers which surrounded the houses. One heard the subdued grunting of pigs, the muffled lowing of the cows shut up in their stalls, the faint tinkle of their bronze bells.

The village did not seem to have suffered in the battle of a few hours before. A number of medium shells had fallen near the little stone bridge that spans the stream, without, however, inflicting any damage upon it. The local *Univermag* (in all Soviet villages there are one or more branches of the *Univermag,* the co-operative store which has virtually killed private enterprise in the U.S.S.R.) appeared to have been looted. The pavement outside the smashed door was littered with cartridge-paper, cardboard boxes, broken crockery, packing-straw, all the rubbish which looters scatter around gutted buildings. But the village as a whole was intact. Its houses, painted white, green or blue, were surrounded in most cases by a kind of veranda, formed by a jutting roof supported on small wooden pillars with artistic ornamental carvings. Gangs of children rushed up from all sides to watch the column pass. Wounded Germans who had sought refuge in the houses flanking the street while they awaited the arrival of the ambulances which would take them down the line popped their bandaged heads out of the windows and waved arms swollen with dressings. Groups of women and old men stood silently in the doorways of the houses and the stables, still stunned, still uncertain, still fearful. They looked to me a trifle sad—or perhaps they were just embarrassed.

After crossing the little bridge we climb the further slope of the valley, and before long we find ourselves once again on the plateau. The all-pervading scent of the corn assails our nostrils, comfortingly warm by contrast with the breath of the approaching night, which is already keen. And still the order to stop does not reach us. How much farther can it be to the village of Shumi? At this rate we shall be on the road all night. I have left my car at the rear of the column, along with all the rest of the vehicles, and I continue on foot along the road to Olshanka in company with a detachment of infantry.

The village of Shumi, I learn, is situated three miles from here, at the bottom of a shallow valley. Ukrainian villages are always concealed in folds in the ground. At intervals the plain, which in some places is completely flat, in others slightly un-dulating, falls away to form a valley, at the bottom of which a village nestles at the edge of a muddy stream. The result is that from the plateau the Ukraine appears uninhabited : the life of this fertile, densely-populated region is hidden in folds in the ground. It is shy and unobtrusive, like the people them-selves, who are remarkable for their handsome appearance, their gentle ways, their courtesy, and their religious sensibility.

After a few miles the pace of the advance slackens. By now the guns are silent, the crackle of machine-gun fire is becoming less frequent, fainter, more distant, it is like a croaking of frogs along the dark, muddy shores of the horizon. The guns are silent, perhaps we shall soon be able to get the sleep we all long for. It has been a hard day, a day of strenuous exertion and bitter fighting. Tomorrow the battle will flare up again outside Olshanka. "*Halt! Halt! Halt!*" The cry echoes down the column; it is taken up by the despatch-riders, who race along open-mouthed, creating the illusion of a single voice magnified to gigantic proportions by a megaphone. We have reached the edge of the valley. Down below, straight ahead of us, is the little village of Shumi, a patch of white barely discernible in the darkness. Already the leading elements are within sight of the first houses of Olshanka. The cry is repeated again and again : "*Halt! Halt! Halt!*"

I have barely sat down at the side of the road, I have barely started to eat (still the same slices of dry bread, still the same tinned tomatoes), when I hear a voice calling in the darkness :
" Where is the Italian officer?"

" Who wants me?" I answer. " Here I am !"

" Good evening, Captain !" says a cheerful voice, in perfect Italian, with a slight accent which suggests that the speaker comes from Trieste. And there before me, standing at attention, is the squat, bespectacled figure of a German warrant-officer—a *Feldwebel*. He is in his shirt-sleeves, the hair above his low forehead is ruffled, there is a cheery grin on his face.

" Would you accept a cup of tea?" he asks.

" Why not? *Danke schön!*"

" Oh, you can speak Italian," says the *Feldwebel*. " My mother comes from Trieste."

If it were not dark the *Feldwebel* would see me flushing with pleasure at his words.

I follow the *Feldwebel*. He leads me into a little house at the side of the road, just outside the village, near the bridge. The low-ceilinged parlour contains a bed, tucked away in a corner, a table, a quaint iron demijohn and a bench set against the wall. On the bench are a row of small loaves and some tins of meat and marmalade. On the table is a camp-stove, and on the stove is a dixy filled with hot tea. Hanging from the walls are a number of sacred images, some cuttings from newspapers and illustrated reviews, a pendulum clock, a Soviet calendar, and the inevitable portrait of Stalin.

The *Feldwebel* offers me a cup of tea, tells me that he was born at Alexandria, that his mother comes from Trieste, that he is forty-two and joined the Army as a volunteer, that he is a member of the *Verkehrs Aufsicht*, the traffic police. He is happy to meet an Italian officer, an officer in the Alpini— genuinely happy! While he is talking some motor-cyclists, also members of the *Verkehrs Aufsicht,* enter the room. They seat themselves around the table, take off their rubber gauntlets, wipe their faces, which are covered with a film of dust and sweat, drink cups of tea, eat slices of bread spread with lard. They laugh unroariously as they describe incidents and adventures of the past day, their spills and mad dashes through the corn beneath the fire of Russian snipers. They talk to me with that strange familiarity which typifies the relationship existing between the officers and men of the German Army. Some day I would like to discourse at length upon this phenomenon, which seems to me one of the most singular features of life in the *Wehrmacht*, its implications being social far more than political in character.

" And now I am going to offer you a most unusual drink," says the *Feldwebel*, whereupon he picks up the quaint iron demijohn which stands in the middle of the room and fills my glass with a strange-looking red liquid with a most peculiar taste. It is extremely sweet, and it has rather a strong aroma. It is not wine in the true sense of the word. It tastes more like raspberry wine, or currant wine.

" We found it at Yampol, in the cellar of a *kolkhoz*," says the *Feldwebel*.

Soon we are all feeling slightly intoxicated. Our eyes have an unnatural brightness. And the *Feldwebel,* who was born in Egypt, is becoming incoherent. He starts talking in Arabic, then he lapses into Triestine dialect. He mingles German and Italian with the Arabic in a rather attractive manner, reminiscent of certain Syrian characters in the old Provençal *nouvelles.*

5*

But it is late, it is time for me to go and look for somewhere to spend the night.

" I would tell you to sleep in the next room," says the *Feldwebel*, " but we've already given it to the chaplain."

" The chaplain?" I ask in surprise.

" Yes, he arrived here quite by chance," says the *Feldwebel*. " He came up with the ambulances, but he'll be going back again tomorrow morning."

" I should like to have a chat with him," I tell the *Feldwebel*.

" You're sure to find him somewhere near the ambulances," he replies as he accompanies me to the door, adding in his soft Triestine brogue : " Goodbye, *Sior capitano*."

" Goodbye. See you again soon."

I set off in the direction of the ambulances. The German chaplain is not there, he has gone down to the village to pick up the wounded. (There were about a hundred of them sheltering in the houses.) I have to forgo the pleasure of meeting him and having a chat. Never yet, either during the campaign in Jugoslavia or during these first two months of fighting on the Russian Front, have I succeeded in making contact with a German Army chaplain. In the *Wehrmacht* chaplains, whether Catholic or Protestant, are a rarity. Indeed, one of the most interesting things about this army is its secularity. And this is one of the countless aspects of a problem that is far more complex than it might appear at first sight. In the *Wehrmacht* religious feeling exists and is in a sense very strong; but its basic elements, its underlying motives, are different from the normal. In the *Wehrmacht* religion is regarded as a private matter, wholly individual and personal. And German Army chaplains, whose numbers are restricted to a minimum, fulfil a function that bears little relation to the usual one of religious ministration. They affirm a presence, they constitute a living witness, but that is all.

With these thoughts in mind I reach my car, which I have left at the bottom of the valley, right at the edge of the stream. I lie down on the cushions and wrap myself in my blanket. It is cold. Around me the column sleeps : the breathing of men and animals is hoarse and sibilant. The voice of the stream, flowing close beside me, rises and falls rhythmically. The war seems far away, like a distant memory. This is the nocturnal truce, the nightly armistice, the interlude of peace and repose which the Germans have named the " black bivouac ".

XVI

GOD RETURNS TO HIS HOUSE

Olshanka, August 12th.

THIS morning I saw God return to His House after twenty years of exile. A small crowd of old peasants opened the door of a barn filled with oil-seeds and said to Him, very simply : " Enter, Lord : this is Thy Church."

This morning I had the good fortune to witness an extraordinary episode that alone sufficed to compensate me for all the hardships and perils which for more than two months I had accepted as the price I must pay for the privilege of following closely—sometimes too closely !—the course of this Russian campaign. We reached Olshanka about ten o'clock in the morning after a weary march of twelve miles through the suffocating red dust of these Ukrainian roads. And it was here at Olshanka—a small agricultural town situated to the south of Kiev, on the road to Balta and Odessa—that the religious problem in Soviet Russia was revealed to me for the first time in all its complexity and delicacy.

I referred to this problem once before, at the beginning of July, when reporting the advance of a German motorized column on the Mogilev Front. But on that occasion (we were at Zaicani, and I described the chapels without crucifixes, the church devoid of icons, the old peasants who crossed themselves before the bare altar, long since adapted for use as a rostrum for the delivery of lectures on the Communist agrarian system of the *kolkhozi*)—on that occasion, I say, I confined myself to skimming the surface of the problem, without going to the heart of it. A greater experience of the life and character of the people, a more thorough documentation of facts and ideas, carried out on the spot in the course of two months' direct observation, objective inquiry and personal witness, make it possible for me to deal with the question today in greater detail. The religious problem is undoubtedly one of the gravest of all those which the war against Russia obtrudes upon the attention of civilized Europe; and it directly concerns all the nations of the West, not only because of the importance and the complexity of its various aspects, but also because of the repercussions which the anti-religious policy of the Soviets will inevitably have on the life of the Russian people.

Having crossed the vast plateau which separates the village of Kachikovska from Olshanka, we arrived in due course at the edge of the broad green valley at the foot of whose gentle slopes Olshanka is situated. From this vantage-point I was able to pick out the church, perched on a piece of higher ground a little to the left of the township: a white church, vaguely baroque in design with its squat tower (rather than a tower in the strict sense of the word it is a kind of cupola) and its gleaming laminated roof. The church of Olshanka, like those of many other villages in the Ukraine, is not strictly orthodox, but " Uniate "—that is to say, it subscribes to that particular orthodox confession which recognizes the authority of the Supreme Pontiff. (The Uniate churches of the Ukraine are a relic of the former Polish influence. They can be distinguished from other churches both by their architecture and by the three-limbed crosses which surmount their towers.) It is possible that the Uniate Church, which is particularly strongly entrenched in Eastern Galicia, will in the near future increase its influence at the expense of the Russian Orthodox Church (*pravoslavnaya tserkov*) throughout the west and south of the Ukraine, especially in the region known as Zadnyestroye—that is, " the region beyond the Dniester ". But there are many good reasons for doubting this. In any event, the problem of the Uniate Church is a limited and special problem by comparison with the complex and far graver question of the

" void " that has been created in the consciences of the younger generation of Russians by the anti-religious policy of the Soviets and by the fatal decline of orthodoxy.

We enter Olshanka, and stop in the middle of the town at a point where the road widens to form a sort of open space sloping upwards to the foot of the hill on which stands the church. On its longest side this open space is bounded by the massive wall of a large *kolkhoz*. The German spearhead which captured the township passed this way barely half an hour ago. The air is still warm, so to say, from the recent fighting. At the entrance to the village squads of soldiers are dutifully burying the corpses of their comrades who fell in the course of the attack.

Below the open space is a green fountain, from which gushes a stream of clear, ice-cold water. It is the first fountain we have seen since we left Yampol. Around it a group of wounded men are bathing their wounds. They are sitting on large stones, waiting for the ambulances. They laugh and joke among themselves as they unroll their bandages and help one another to dress their wounds.

Suddenly a babel of voices is heard at the top of the hill on which stands the church. I walk up the path, and in the weed-covered churchyard, one corner of which is occupied by an agricultural machine—a brand-new weeder—I come upon a group of women. Most of them are rather elderly, their ages ranging from fifty upwards, though a few, not more than five or six in all, are girls aged from sixteen to twenty. Some are busily engaged in cleaning a number of large, silver-painted wooden candelabras—tall, massive candelabras of the kind that are often to be seen standing on either side of an altar, or on the altar itself. I pause and watch them dusting, rubbing, polishing, scraping off the dirt and the patches of mould with rags and knives. Others are crouching round the doorway, frantically tearing up the weeds that are already threatening to invade the building. A third group are uprooting the briars that have sprung up in the churchyard with the help of spades and hoes.

I walk up to the women and greet them. "Well, well!" I remark. "You've certainly let your church get into a fine state, haven't you?"

The girls, who are wearing short-sleeved white blouses with red trimmings, look at me and laugh, without interrupting the vigorous movements of their sunburnt, muscular arms. One old woman removes her hands from the candelabra which she is cleaning, crosses herself three times, bows, addresses me as *barin* (the old Russian word for "Sir", now replaced by the Bolshevik term *tovarish*), and tells me that it is not their fault, that for twenty years the church at Olshanka has been used as a storehouse for oil-seeds, as a repository for the seeds of soya-beans and sunflowers.

"It isn't our fault," she repeats. "It was the Communists. Oh, Mary, Holy Virgin, it isn't our fault!" And she bursts into tears, clasping her hands to her temples. At that the girls shout :

"Eh, eh—the *babushka* is crying!"

And they laugh, but not unkindly—they laugh for the simple reason that in their eyes it is ridiculous to weep merely because the church has been turned into a storehouse for oil-seeds. Meanwhile, some youths of seventeen or eighteen have joined the group; they too burst out laughing, and one of them says :

"Oh, *babushka,* where did you expect them to put the seeds?"

Another turns to me and explains that at the time when the church was converted into a storehouse for seeds it had already been closed for a year.

But the old women raise their arms menacingly and shout to the youths : "*Poshol! Poshol!*—Be off! Be off!" They tell them that they are young rascals, that they are heathens, sons of Turks, and at the same time they cross themselves three times and spit on the ground. And the youths titter, chewing blades of grass, their caps turned back to front on their heads, which are close-shaven in the Bolshevik fashion. Their manner is not spiteful : they laugh quietly, good-naturedly. And every so often they look at me and at the two German officers who have in the meantime entered the church and are surveying the scene rather nervously, as if they were afraid of committing some gaffe. After a while one of the German officers turns to me and says: " It's a serious problem."

Yes, it is indeed a serious and delicate problem, and it is to be feared that the Orthodox Church will be hard put to it to survive in Russia once the older generation has passed on. The younger generation, those born since 1917, are not interested in religious problems. They know absolutely nothing about religion—in fact, to put it crudely, they don't care two hoots about it. They certainly have no fear of hell.

The old women and the girls continue to polish the wooden candelabras—the old women carefully, respectfully, almost reverently, the young ones with cheerful nonchalance. The girls look as if they were cleaning articles of furniture or cooking utensils.

" When will you be done with the spring-cleaning?" calls a girl from the doorway of the church. " *Syeichas, syeichas!*— In a moment, in a moment!" shout the girls. It is obvious that they do not attribute any special significance to this " spring-clean ", certainly not any ritual significance. They attach no importance to the operation. The homeliness of the phrase used to describe it reflects all the indifference of the younger generation to a problem of which they understand neither the nature nor the importance, and of which they are capable of appreciating neither the delicacy nor the gravity. In their eyes the problem belongs to the past, it is one of the countless problems that concern only the *stariki,* the old.

From inside the church comes a murmur of voices, a banging of hammers, and that light rushing sound which is heard when seeds, peas or beans are poured from a shovel into a sack. I look through the doorway. Between the entrance and the interior of the church is a kind of lobby, a small room with a very high ceiling. Here a group of old peasants are collecting oil-seeds into a heap with shovels and brooms. Inside the church a gang of *stariki* are putting seeds into sacks;

the women hold the mouths of the sacks open while the men wield their shovels. Others are sweeping the floor, others are removing cobwebs from the corners of the ceiling with long poles, others are carrying the full sacks out of the church on their shoulders, others yet are collecting the seeds scattered about the floor into a corner and transferring them into wheelbarrows with spades. There is a constant coming and going, a ceaseless bustling, a continual plying of shovels and brooms amid a grey cloud of dust heavy with the smell of mould and rancid oil. The walls are covered with agricultural propaganda-posters stressing the importance and value of oil-seeds and explaining the operation of agricultural machines, and with large coloured pictures showing the best method of promoting the growth of soya and sunflower plants, of conserving and aerating the seeds and protecting them from parasites, mould, and mice. There is none of that atheistic propaganda which I have noticed in many other churches, long since converted into anti-religious museums or cinemas, into assembly-rooms or theatres for the *rabochie clubi* (working men's clubs), or into peasants' dance-halls, with the platform for the orchestra installed behind the altar: none of those parodies of the *Via Crucis,* none of those posters by means of which the Communists expound to the masses their views on religious problems, seeking to stifle in the minds of the people not merely every glimmer of faith, every gleam of hope, but also every possibility of a return to their old faith, every unconscious aspiration to a future life. Everything that appears on these posters is related to the new function to which the church has been adapted. There is no allusion to its former office, nor to the religion that has been suppressed.

Resting against the wall at the far end of the church are a number of sacred ornaments and some pictures of the Madonna and of various saints. Groups of old peasant women are dusting the sacred images which for twenty years have remained buried beneath heaps of seeds or hidden behind the altar, where the Communists kept the shovels which were used for the periodic aeration of the seeds. I go over and look at the images. Some are genuine "orthodox" icons—saints and Madonnas with black faces, set in the usual custodials of copper, brass or white metal. Others are imitations of Catholic images. One old man, perched on top of a step-ladder, is driving a nail into the wall preparatory to hanging a picture which a girl is about to pass up to him. Two *babushke*, armed with hoes, are giving chase to a family of mice which they have discovered beneath a heap of sunflower seeds. I notice that the old women's faces are covered with a network of dark wrinkles. Meanwhile, the inevitable youths are standing in a group surveying the scene; they are laughing and joking with the girls, but it is impossible to tell whether their words, their gestures, the expressions on their faces denote derision or merely an amiable, amused indifference, tempered with a suggestion of youthful arrogance. Some men of riper years, men of about forty-five (representing the "uncommitted" generation, that of the Great War, the generation which was twenty years old in 1917, when Lenin seized power), are looking on with their hands in their pockets, undecided whether to help the old people or to jeer at them.

"Where shall we put the candelabras?" one of the *stariki* asks the girls, who have finished polishing the ornaments in question and are now bringing them into the church and standing them in a corner between the altar and the wall. They all seem to have forgotten where the candelabras ought to go.

"On the altar steps," says an old woman. "The smaller ones should go·here, actually on the altar."

On the altar-table is a pile of thick ledgers. An old man is turning over the yellow pages with his dirty fingers. Each page is covered with columns of figures and marginal notes. These ledgers are very precious. They contain the accounts of the church over the past few years, or rather the accounts of the storehouse. They contain a record of all the assets and liabilities of the peasants of Olshanka, the dates and amounts of their deliveries of seeds and the sums realized in cash. The old man does not know whether he ought to throw them away or put them in a place of safety. At last he makes up his mind. He seizes the thick ledgers, dusts them carefully and places them in the recess in the middle of the altar—whereupon a *babushka* who has been watching him for some minutes starts waving her arms and shouting in a hoarse voice. All the other *babushke* hurry forward and start yelling. That place is reserved for the sacred books, they declare, not for those filthy ledgers. At this the youths rush to the defence of the ledgers, protesting that they have always been kept there and there they must remain—there is no earthly reason why they should be removed now, they must stay where they belong until the sacred books have been found.

Then, little by little, the tumult dies down, the voices become less shrill, the old women resign themselves to the situation with a bad grace, muttering and shaking their heads. " Here, *babushke*—give us the candelabras," says one of the youths. And he and his colleagues help the *babushke* to arrange the candelabras on the altar.

Meanwhile, the old men are looking perplexed. " Where shall we find the wax candles, the big wax candles that used to be here?" they ask. " If only we had some candles! But it's years since we saw a candle."

Now at last the church has been restored to order. It is no longer cluttered up with heaps of seeds, it has been cleaned and dusted. The Communist agricultural propaganda-posters which until an hour ago covered the walls have been replaced by sacred images. The window-panes have been thoroughly washed and polished. An old woman comes up to me, addresses me as *barin*, asks me if the *pop* of their church will come back soon. He has been in Siberia for twelve years.

" It's possible that he will come back," I reply.

" If our *pop* doesn't come back we shan't be able to reconsecrate the church," says the *babushka*, while all the others listen attentively, pressing round me in a circle.

" It will take him quite a while to get here," says a girl. " From Siberia to Olshanka is a goodish step."

The youths start to laugh, but the old men look at me

in perplexity. They seem to be asking themselves: " What shall we do with our church if our *pop* doesn't come back?" The young men laugh ironically, as much as to say: " Eh, we'll put the seeds in here again if your *pop* doesn't come back."

" It's possible that he's dead," I say. " But if *he* doesn't turn up someone else will come in his place."

All of a sudden an old man says: " What about the bells?" Another repeats his question: " Yes—what about the bells?"

The Russian for " bells " is *kolokolà*. It is a most beautiful word, *kolokolà*—it reproduces exactly the clear, liquid sound of Russian bells echoing through the soft air of the Ukrainian countryside. All around me repeat: " *Kolokolà, kolokolà, kolokolà!*", and in that harmonious onomatopoeia I seem to hear a joyous peal of bells bursting from the church-tower, echoing far and wide across the green and gold of the fields, across the vast expanses of corn. " *Podozhditye*—wait!" says an old man, and he runs outside. We all follow him, we go out into the churchyard, and from there we see the old man hurrying down through the meadow towards some cows that are grazing in the grounds of the adjacent *kolkhoz*. We watch him go up to a cow, detach the heavy bronze bell from its neck, turn back gaily, come back up the path. As he approaches all look at him and say: " *Kolokolà, kolokolà, kolokolà!*" A young man offers to climb to the top of the tower; accordingly, we re-enter the church, the *stariki* fetch a step-ladder and rest it against the inside of the tower, the young man mounts the ladder and disappears from sight. After a little while we hear the bronze bell sending out its grave, sweet note from far above. As the unfamiliar sound echoes, deep, clear and mellow, down the valley, all, even the wounded men seated by the fountain, raise their eyes. It is exactly as if a cow were grazing in the boundless blue meadows of the sky. And even as the image flashes across my mind one of the youths, one of those young rascals, says with a chuckle: " Listen to the *korova*—listen to the cow!" Everyone laughs, but I seize the youth by the arm, shake him roughly, say to him: "Don't laugh!" He looks at me, blushes, is covered with confusion, would like to say something to me, moves his lips but cannot find the words. I would like to say to him: "It is a most beautiful thing, that cowbell up there." But I too am unable to find the words.

(The following lines were suppressed by the Fascist censor.)

While we are listening to the sound of the bell a column of German artillery stops outside the church. An officer dismounts, gives the order to untie the horses, enters the building. He reappears almost at once and calls out in a harsh voice: "Put the horses in the church!"

The old peasant women cross themselves, the old men lower their eyes and walk away in silence. The youths look at me and snigger.

XVII

DUST AND RAIN

Petshanka, September.

AFTER a week of rain, here at last is the fine weather. The dust returns, and the soldiers inhale it with delight. (The choking dust returns, the accursed pall of red dust. Yet we inhale it with pleasure, we greet it with joy, like a dear friend, after all these days of mud, after all these days of weary plodding along the terrible Ukrainian roads, which the rain has made like sheets of glass smeared with vaseline. It takes no more than a shower to cover the surface of these roads —a clayey surface, hard, compact, impervious to water—with a film of sticky, slippery mud, which periodically opens up to reveal a deep fissure, a treacherous crack.) At last we can resume our advance, at last we can continue our march towards the Dnieper. " *Schnell! Schnell!*"—the cry echoes from end to end of the column. The guns have started to bark again on the horizon. Bursts of machine-gun bullets whistle through the deep, waving corn.

The rain began to fall a week ago. These was a moment, just before it started, when I said to myself : " I'm turning back. I've had enough of this." I couldn't stand it any longer. I was already a war-invalid—I was a victim of the last war, the war of 1914-18, during which my lungs were burnt by mustard-gas. And I was unable to breathe in that dense, acrid cloud of dust, which filled my mouth, burst my lungs, made my lips, nostrils and eyelids smart. I prayed for rain. I scrutinized the clear horizon, I looked for a sign of a storm-cloud in the harsh blue sky. I had already stopped two or three times and allowed the column to go on ahead in order to escape from that dense trail of dust. Now the column was miles away, and it was pressing on with all speed so as not to lose contact with the retreating enemy. Even if I hurried I could not have caught it up in less than a couple of hours. I had been left behind, but I did not care. I was tired of coughing and choking in the midst of those clouds of red dust. " If it doesn't rain before evening," I said to myself, " I'm turning back."

It was terribly hot. But there was about the weather an air of uncertainty, an air of unreliability. The sky was clear, yet one felt that something was brewing within the secret folds of the horizon. "This isn't summer weather as they know it in the Ukraine," I thought. I knew from experience what the Ukrainian summer is really like. It is a very hot season, pervaded by the long, slow shudder of an airless wind, which draws from the boundless fields of corn its own characteristic flavour of straw, its own peculiar scent. In 1920, when Marshal Pilsudsky's army invaded the Ukraine and marched on Kiev, I accompanied the Polish troops, in my capacity of official Italian observer, all the way to the Ukrainian capital. It was May, but already a midsummer sun was tinging the vast expanses of corn a deep copper colour. The horses were succumbing in their hundreds to the effects of heat, thirst and fatigue. My knees were raw from days in the saddle. At night we used to fling ourselves down to sleep amid the burning ears of corn. When at last we arrived in Kiev we were in a pitiable condition. I at once took a room at the Hotel Europeiski, threw myself on the bed and slept for two solid days.

I again experienced something of the horror of that terrible summer during the early days of this arduous march. And yet, as we crossed the plateau that extends to Shumi and beyond, there was in the oppressive air a hint of uncertainty, a suggestion of change, almost a presage of a storm. I was following with my eyes the lazy, exceedingly slow flight of one of those reconnaissance aircraft which the Germans call "storks" when suddenly I seemed to see in the distance, immediately above the horizon, a dark brown streak, as it were a line drawn with a pencil on the blue slate of the sky. The "stork" was drifting along just above the ground, very slowly, as if it sensed the approach of rain. And as I watched it I thought to myself : "It *will* rain eventually, and then this confounded dust will be laid once for all!"

As we are driving through the village of Dimitraskovska (the cannon thunders without ceasing two or three miles to our front) a German car overtakes us, the driver leans out and shouts to me in Italian : "Turn back, this road is being shelled by Russian artillery, we've been ordered to divert the traffic down into the valley and across the stream. It's a terrible road—but it's safer!" We park the car under a tree to escape observation from the air and get out. The German driver comes up to us, his face wreathed in smiles. He is a young man aged between twenty and twenty-five, but he looks a mere boy. I ask him where he learned Italian. "In Rome," he replies. "I was a waiter at the Hotel Minerva, behind the Pantheon." Then he adds, with a perfect Roman accent : "Somebody's going to get killed—just hark at the guns!" And he laughs, passing his hand across his face, which is covered with a thin layer of dust.

Pasted up on the wall of the church, one on either side of the entrance, are two coloured film-posters. The church had been turned into a *sovkino,* a Soviet cinema. One of the posters announces a film about love, or so I would judge from the attitudes of the characters : a youth and a girl—he in the usual peaked cap of a mechanic employed on a *kolkhoz,* she with the usual brightly-coloured kerchief knotted under the chin— embracing against a background of corn-fields and agricultural machines beneath a boundless, deep blue sky. The title of the film is *Beyond Love.*

We enter the church, where the Germans have established a *Feldlazaret,* a field hospital. Hanging on the walls are posters advertising the usual Communist propaganda films. Some have as their subject the struggle against illiteracy, alcoholism and tuberculosis, others are concerned with life on the *kolkhozi*, with the organization of the Red Army, with the glories of Soviet aviation, of Soviet engineering, of Soviet industrialization. The principal character in the film about the Red Army is Stalin, who appears in the various panels into which the poster is divided in the guise of a military leader. The film describes a number of episodes of the wars of 1919 and 1920-21 against the Poles, against the "partisans" of Macno and Petliura, against the "Whites" of Wrangel, Kolchak and Denikin. In each picture there appear, along with Stalin, the faithful Voroshilov, the moustachio'd Budenny, and Timoshenko, Kirov, and Chapayev. But I do not see Trotsky, or Tukachevsky, or any of the other revolutionary leaders.

The wounded are lying on improvised palliasses ranged along the walls immediately beneath the film-posters. On the altar are rows of bottles containing disinfectants, together with packets of cotton-wool, rolls of bandages and surgical instruments. Pinned to the white screen that hangs above the altar are the clinical charts. Two medical officers with shaven heads, their eyes myopic and gentle behind the lenses of their gold-framed spectacles, walk slowly from patient to patient, bending over the palliasses and conversing in low voices. Through the broken windows come waves of dust and a medley of sounds, punctuated by the boom of the guns, now near, now far away. A wounded man starts to cough. We go out of the church on tip-toe. Suddenly I notice some enormous pieces of bleeding meat suspended by hooks from the wall of a house situated near the church. They are quarters of beef and pork. The house is the butchery of the little field-hospital. Next to the butchery is the cook-house. A group of walking wounded is gathered round the coppers, waiting for the vegetable-soup to boil.

Outside the church a party of soldiers are digging a grave, while others plant rough crosses of white wood on mounds of newly-turned earth. The churchyard extends all round the building. Part of it has been converted into a kitchen-garden, the remainder into a cemetery. In the kitchen-garden are a number of wounded men. Some are walking about amid the spreading leaves of the potato plants; others, their legs swollen with blood-soaked bandages, are sitting on the ground, silently eating. An exceedingly elegant young officer passes close beside us, flicking his jack-boots with his cane. He has one arm in a sling. He whistles softly as he walks.

Shafts of hot sunlight cut through the dusty air as through a thick mist. At the bottom of the kitchen-garden a wounded man is sitting on a heap of stones, playing an accordion. The tone of the instrument is strident, but the melody is sweet: it is a song of a northern land, a land of mist and damp. (The air above our heads is filled with dust: in the fields a dry wind stirs the dusty ears of corn.) An atmosphere of gentleness and quiet, the serene peace of a monastery courtyard, pervades this kitchen-garden, this cemetery, this churchyard sprinkled with graves, sunflowers, and potato plants. The wounded men talk among themselves in calm voices. Not a cry of pain is heard, not even those feeble groans which delirium forces from lips parched by a feverish thirst. How different are these wounded from those of the other war! I remember. . . . But who does not remember the loud, anguished voices, the ill-suppressed screams, the curses, the desperate appeals to the Almighty, the dull moans of the dying? The wounded of this war give proof of greater virility, of greater steadfastness in their suffering—even, perhaps, of a greater awareness, unless it be that they are more sincere, more serene in their resignation. They seem to me more reserved, more reluctant to reveal the extent of their agony. And this is true not only of the Germans but of the others too—of the Rumanians, and also of the Russians. They do not cry out, they do not groan, they do not curse. (Undoubtedly there is something mysterious, something inscrutable, about their stern, stubborn silence.)

The German soldier who was formerly a waiter at the Hotel Minerva in Rome comes and tells me that we had better get moving—the road is very bad and, moreover, the weather might break at any moment. And he looks up at the sky and points to a cloud, a pitch-black cloud, which is forming rapidly on the horizon. Thank heaven—it's going to rain at last! I can't stand it any longer, I can no longer breathe in this terrible cloud of red dust. But all the German soldiers look up at the sky and shake their heads, hurling imprecations at that distant black cloud, which gradually increases in volume until it extends along the entire length of the horizon. We leave the church and get back into the car. The road descends precipitously in a series of hairpin bends. In fact, it is not a road, it is the dried-up bed of a torrent, littered with large, porous stones. Presently we come to the muddy stream that flows along the bottom of the narrow valley. We pass over some swaying beams fastened together with a steel cable. A number of soldiers are encamped along the banks. They belong to a regiment of medium artillery. Some of their horses are standing knee-deep in the middle of the stream, others are grazing in an adjoining meadow. The road leading up the far side of the valley is blocked by a convoy of ammunition-lorries. Groups of soldiers push with all their might at the wheels, the horses make frantic efforts to secure a foothold, baring their long yellow teeth in mute grins of pain. Two heavy Rumanian lorries—two *Skodas*—lumber with a frantic roar up the dusty slope. The men's faces are covered with thick layers of dust, in which the sweat carves deep furrows.

A small crowd of peasants—mostly women, old men, children, and youths aged from sixteen to eighteen—line the road watching the surging mass of men and animals. They look on seemingly unafraid; they have about them an air of composure tempered with curiosity. The children are cheerful, vivacious, a little shy. The women wear brilliantly-coloured kerchiefs knotted under the chin. Their blouses and skirts are of printed cotton, decorated with gaudy patterns of yellow, green and red flowers. The men, young and old alike, are clad in grey cotton jackets, their trousers are made of the same blue cloth as mechanics' overalls. The *muzhik* of today no longer wears a *tolstovka* buttoned at the side, together with high boots and a fur cap. He looks more like a workman, an artisan, than a peasant. His cycling-cap gives him an air of suburban respectability. Twenty-five years of Bolshevism, twenty-five years of collective farms and agricultural machines, have had a miraculous effect on the Russian peasants, transforming them into a race of heavy workers and mechanics. When, wishing to take advantage of our enforced halt, I open my haversack and start to eat, they all look at me attentively, curiously, talking among themselves and laughing.

" There should still be a packet of caramels under the seat," I say to Pellegrini.

Pellegrini starts to distribute caramels among the children. They approach us timidly, stretch out their hands, deftly remove the paper in which the caramels are wrapped, carefully taste them, and at the sweet flavour open their eyes wide and smile happily. They are, after all, only children, and children are the same the whole world over. It is true that before the war caramels—those small Soviet-type caramels with a faintly salty taste—were available to the people of Dimitraskovska at the various branches of the *Univermag*. But they were expensive—too expensive. I look closely at these Soviet children of 1941, so different from their predecessors of 1920 and 1921. Their hair is ruffled beneath their cycling-caps and their small embroidered skull-caps of Cossack design. The boys wear trousers of blue cloth, mostly either too long or too short, while the little girls are dressed in skirts and aprons, with coloured handkerchiefs on their heads. They talk among themselves in low voices, laughing gaily the while. They follow all my movements with intense curiosity, turning every so often to gaze at the trains of heavy German artillery, at the horses struggling to climb the hill, at the lorries smoking and roaring on the other side of the river. In the meantime, Pellegrini has lit the spirit-stove and is heating a little water for a cup of tea. I produce a lemon from my haversack, and at once the children press round me, gazing at the lemon and sniffing the air. One of them asks: " *Chto eto takoye?*—

What's that?" " It's a lemon," I reply. " A lemon, a lemon," the children repeat to one another. The original speaker tells me that it is the first time they have ever seen a lemon. " It's a bit sour," I tell him, " but it's good. Would you like to taste it?" I let him try a slice. The boy puts the slice of lemon into his mouth, pulls a wry face and spits it out. Another boy bends down quickly and picks it up, sucks it for a moment, grimaces, and passes it to one of his companions. Each in turn tastes it, pulls a face, and spits it out. They have never seen a lemon before.

All of a sudden it starts to rain. At first it is a gentle shower, silent and almost furtive. But soon it develops into a regular hurricane, a veritable cloudburst. Exultantly I submit to the cool caress of the rain, I steep my face and hair in the cool, pure water, greedily I fill my mouth with it. Rain at last! Around me I hear a chorus of yells and oaths. The German soldiers look up at the sky, shouting and cursing. The artillery-trains come to an abrupt halt, the horses slither about in the mud that has formed as if by magic, the lorries skid on the slippery surface. " Oh, b—— the rain!" yell the artillerymen and the drivers, clustering round the guns and lorries, which are soon stuck fast in the mud. A girl appears in the doorway of a nearby cottage and motions us to enter. " *Pozhaluista, pozhaluista*—please, please," she says. We go inside. Seated on a bench are an old man and a youth. Pellegrini busies himself about the spirit-stove, the water for the tea is already starting to boil. I sit down in the corner occupied by the icons (which in Russian homes is the place of honour specially reserved for guests) and proceed to cut a slice of lemon. The youth has a bad leg; it is all red and swollen, he must be suffering from arthritis. He looks at me and moans : " *Mnye bol'no*—it hurts," at the same time gazing at the lemon. The old man and the girl also gaze at the strange fruit, and the old man says : " Why, that's a lemon!" It is more than twenty years since he saw a real lemon. " And yet the Crimea isn't far away," I say to him. " Yes," replies the old man, " but perhaps—who knows?—perhaps the lemon-trees in the

Crimea have all run to seed." (The truth is that almost as soon as they came to power the Communists earmarked the whole of the Crimea's annual yield of citrus-fruits for export, and since then it has been impossible to buy a lemon or an orange anywhere in Russia, except in the big centres like Moscow, Leningrad, Kiev and Odessa.) The older men, those aged forty and upwards, remember what lemons were like. They form part of their memories of the old régime. But the young men have no such memories; they do not even know what lemons are.

We pour the tea into glasses, and in each glass, in each *stakan chaya,* we put a nice slice of lemon. The old man chuckles contentedly as he drinks his tea, and so does the girl. But the youth with the bad leg has an air of sadness and mortification. "During the other war, the *germanskaya voinà* . . . ," begins the old man. (That is what they call it : *germanskaya voinà,* the German war. The old man fought in the Carpathians in 1916.) Then he stretches out his hand towards the bottle of spirit which Pellegrini has left on the table, uncorks it, sniffs the contents, half-closing his eyes in ecstasy as he does so. "With a little water added," he says, "it would make a good drink." Not for three months now—not since the beginning of the war, in fact—has a drop of vodka passed the old man's lips. No—vodka is out. I burst out laughing, the others laugh too, and Pellegrini picks up the bottle and puts it in his pocket, out of harm's way.

We go to the door and look outside. The road is now a river of mud. The rain has ceased, a cold wind is blowing—persistent, dry, and rough as a cat's tongue. "You'll have to spend the night here," says the old man. "The roads won't be dry until the morning." He is perfectly right. It takes only half an hour's rain to turn these Ukrainian roads into quagmires. The war is being fought in the midst of a sea of sticky, clinging mud. The German soldiers run shouting from horse to horse, from lorry to lorry. There is nothing to be done. We shall have to wait for the roads to dry. The cannon thunders in the distance, behind that wood. Such is war on the steppes of the Ukraine: dust, mud, dust, mud. Confound the dust, confound the mud! From the top of the hill comes a confused roar, a blend of human voices and the neighing of horses. More troops are arriving, but they cannot come down into the valley; they·must spend the night up there, the roads will not be dry until the morning.

(Dust and rain, dust and mud. Tomorrow the roads will be dry, the vast fields of sunflowers will crackle in the hot, parching wind. Then the mud will return. This is Russia, this is the Russia of the Tsars, the Holy Russia of the Tsars, and this is also the U.S.S.R.—dust and rain, dust and mud. This is the Russian war, the eternal Russian war, the Russian war of 1941. *Nichts zu machen, nichts zu machen.* Tomorrow the roads will be dry, then the mud will return, and everywhere there will be corpses, gutted houses, hordes of ragged prisoners with the air of sick dogs, everywhere the remains of horses and vehicles, the wreckage of tanks, of aeroplanes, of L.K.W.s, of guns, the corpses of officers, N.C.O.s and men, of women, children, old men and dogs, the remains of houses, villages, towns, rivers and forests. *Nichts zu machen, nichts zu machen.* Farther, ever farther, into the heart of the "Russian Continent": across the Bug, across the Dnieper, across the Donets; towards the Don, towards the Volga, towards the Caspian. *Ja, ja, jawohl. Wir kämpfen um das nackte Leben.* And then the winter will come—the beautiful, beautiful winter. Then more dust and rain, more dust and mud, for as long as the winter lasts—the beautiful, beautiful winter of Holy Russia, the winter of steel and cement of the U.S.S.R. Such is the war against Russia, 1941.)

BOOK TWO

THE WORKERS' FORTRESS

PROLOGUE: THE SIEGE OF LENINGRAD

RETURNING to Italy at the end of September, 1941, I spent the next four months under house-arrest, the punishment being inflicted on me at the Germans' request because of the "inopportune character" of my war-despatches. Then, in February of the following year, I set out for the Northern Front, making my way *via* Poland, Lithuania, Latvia and Estonia to Finland, and finishing up in the trenches outside Leningrad.

My purpose in going so far afield was to obtain a first-hand impression of the reactions of the "working masses" of Leningrad to the moral, political and social problems arising out of the war. At the beginning of the Russian campaign, and throughout the summer of 1941, I had shown in my despatches from the Ukrainian Front how the "peasant masses" of the U.S.S.R., educated and transformed by industrialization, or rather by the mechanization of agriculture, reacted to these same problems, laying special emphasis on the fact that the driving force behind the Russian war-effort consisted above all in the "industrial morale" of the rural proletariat. (A fact that must on no account be forgotten is that, as a result of industrialization, or rather, as I say, of the mechanization of agriculture, the old-time *muzhik* has completely disappeared.) The life of those Russian peasants—both men and women—who are under the age of forty has been profoundly changed by the three successive *Pyatlyetki*, or Five Year Plans. Their implements are no longer the spade, the hoe and the sickle, but agricultural machines in the shape of tractors, mechanical ploughs, drills, etc., etc. (Every *kolkhoz* possesses hundreds and hundreds of agricultural machines.) The transformation has been equally profound as regards dress, manners and customs, and mental outlook. The old life of the Russian village is dead.

Gone is the old fatalism, gone is the old laziness, gone, too, are the high boots, the fur caps, the blouses, the beards. In their place are the blue overalls, the leather jackets, the short-peaked caps and the close-shaven heads and faces of the new generation of agricultural workers. In their place are the violent, active, hard life and the relentless discipline of the collective farms, together with a universal recognition of the absolute primacy of technology. The change is reflected not so much in the peasants' culture, which on the whole is very rudimentary and even, in a sense, naïve, not so much in the standard reached in the field of technical specialization, which is vastly inferior to that attained, for example, by the peasants of Germany or of the United States, as in the matter of industrial discipline and "morale". The *muzhiki* of tradition have developed into a race of mechanics. Moreover, since the outbreak of the war they too have become worker-soldiers, no more and no less than the workers from the great industrial cities.

The subject which I now proposed to study on the Leningrad Front was, by contrast, the reaction of the *working* masses to the moral, political and social problems arising out of the war against the U.S.S.R. In essence, I proposed to assemble, by means of a direct observation of events, the material for a forecast, if possible an objective forecast, of what must inevitably happen when the German Army had penetrated into the heart of the industrial regions of the Don and the Volga —in other words, of what eventually *did* happen at Stalingrad. The compelling interest of this problem, with which the whole fate of the war is bound up, enabled me to ignore the sufferings and perils that awaited me during that terrible winter on the Leningrad-Kronstadt Front.

The Finnish trenches at Byelostrov and Alexandrovka, on the Karelian Isthmus, are situated only ten miles from the heart of Leningrad, at the very edge of the city's outer suburbs. For various reasons—the extreme proximity of the " workers' fortress ", the possibility of gathering first-hand information, the absolutely authentic character of the verbal details that can be obtained from deserters, prisoners, and those extraordinary Karelian informers who ply between the beleaguered city and the Finnish command-posts—they are unrivalled as a base from which to conduct such an inquiry. For a whole year I observed the tragedy of Leningrad in this way, as from the dress-circle of a theatre. For me, however, it was not a " play ", but a sort of examination of conscience, if I may use such a term apropos of a moral, political and social experience of which I was only a spectator—which, in other words, necessarily unfolded " outside " me, independently of me, though its impersonal quality did not prevent me from feeling both compassion and the most profound human sympathy for those directly concerned.

From my observations and reflections on Leningrad the reader will in fact see that the experience of the " workers' fortress " on the Neva, the largest industrial city in the U.S.S.R. and one of the largest in the world, foreshadowed and paved the way for the experience of Stalingrad, the great " workers' fortress " on the Volga. In the midst of this colossal tragedy of European civilization the intellect has perhaps no other task than that of seeking to anticipate the possible surprises of a war that has proved to be as rich in surprises as any in history. To my mind, Leningrad anticipates the terrible " surprise " of Stalingrad.

Outside Leningrad, 1943.

XVIII

IN THE DISTANCE, LENINGRAD IS BURNING

Helsinki, March.

THE steamer, immediately below us, appeared deserted. Not a light showed, not even a navigation-light; there was not a sign of life anywhere. Trapped in the ice a few miles from the coast of Estonia, the vessel resembled a grain of black sand embedded in a lump of amber. And the frozen sea, lit by the lingering fires of the northern sunset, had, in fact, the pink and yellow transparency of amber. The aircraft descended to an altitude of about a hundred and fifty feet, describing wide circles around the ship. We could see a dog running about the deck, looking up at us and barking. A man appeared at a porthole and slowly waved his hand in greeting; then he withdrew and disappeared. (Here and there, along the shores of the Gulf of Finland, many steamers of small tonnage lie trapped in the ice. Always a squad of armed men has been left on board, not to guard the cargo, which has already been taken ashore on sledges, but to defend the ship from attack by Soviet patrols, which sometimes venture across the frozen surface of the sea as far as the Finnish and Estonian coasts.)

Now the aircraft was climbing again, and gradually there unfolded before our eyes the distant blue and white prospect of the Gulf of Finland, which at that point is little more than forty miles wide. Only a pale sapphire streak announced the presence, away to our left, of the Finnish coast. The eye ranged far across the Estonian plain, exploring the vast forests of firs and birches. A little way behind us to our right Reval appeared, veiled by the smoke that belched from the chimneys of its factories. The lofty pointed towers of its mansions, the green copper-plated cupolas of its churches, the masts of the ships embedded in the ice alongside the jetties of its harbour —all now emerged from the dense pall of smoke and seemed to vibrate in the shimmering air. Finally, for as far as the eye could reach the frozen surface of the sea was scattered with long trains of sledges and with patrols of skiers, returning to shore or venturing out into the bay to explore the gathering darkness.

We were in the middle of the Gulf of Finland, at an altitude of perhaps a thousand feet, when the sun sank beneath the horizon. It was a fiery sun, its colour a lovely ruby-red that contrasted harshly and violently with the delicate pastel shades of that surrealist panorama, that cold, virginal landscape. Like the steel disc of a mechanical saw that sinks into a tree-trunk and finally is lost to view, the sun slowly penetrated the hard crust of the ice, vanishing at last with a strident roar. Huge clouds of snow-white steam rose from the horizon. A red streak formed on the sky-line, glowing brightly for a while, then slowly fading into darkness. And all at once the scene changed, became unreal, detached itself from time and space, detached itself, it seemed, from the earth and the sea. Then suddenly I perceived that we were flying inside a crystal globe, a tenuous, transparent crystal globe, and that we were no longer following a straight course but were describing an ample, very gentle curve.

The air within that globe of glass was pink and blue like the interior of a shell. The roar of the engines was exactly like the roar of the sea in a shell—an exquisitely pure sound, an immense, light voice. And whether it was the reflection of that blood-red streak on the sky-line or the strain imposed on the eye by intense vigilance, by long observation, I do not know: but it seemed to me that we were flying in a spiral round a red point suspended in the sky far away to the east, at the head of the Gulf of Finland, over towards Leningrad.

The observer also concentrated his gaze on that red point,

on that dazzling ball of fire. And suddenly he turned, and nodded to me as if in answer to an unspoken question. The smoke of the fire now rose gently in broad spirals, forming castles in the air which the wind continually dissolved and recomposed, creating high up in the sky as it were the inverted image of a city, complete with houses, mansions, streets, and vast squares. And little by little the agony of Leningrad lost all objective reality, all human precision and substance, and became instead an abstract idea, an illusion, a memory. (What is that smoke, what is that glare, away to the east? The smoke of a fire, no more. The glare of a distant fire, no more. The smoke of an immense funeral-pyre, no more. The agony of a city with a mysterious, incomprehensible name: the agony of Leningrad, no more.)

And it really was a thing without substance, that light smoke away to the east, that dazzling ball of fire, that vast ethereal city which the wind gently dissolved and recomposed in the blue evening air. Every so often, from the heart of the Estonian plain behind Oranienbaum, there came a red flash, like the blink of a bloodshot eye. It was the eye of the battle that is raging over there, along the eastern border of Estonia. (An enormous red eye, the eye of Mars in the smoke of the battle.) Meanwhile, night was falling: but the gleaming white carpet of snow, the dazzling reflection of the vast expanse of ice, were transforming the night into a marvellous, resplendent day. A pale, intense light seemed to rise from the depths of the sea, illuminating the crust of ice from below and imbuing it with a magical transparency, which spread to the furthest shores of the gulf—indeed, the land too was suffused with that cold, mysterious light. Inside the crystal globe the roar of the engines rose and fell, then all at once it died down, became a whisper, like the hum of a swarm of bees. And the cause was the mist that was now rising from the frozen surface of the sea and gradually invading the sky. Then, suddenly, we were blinded by a white darkness, and we found ourselves sailing through that soft, silent, opaque cloud of vapour.

Now the aircraft began to climb in an effort to escape from

the mist. And when, a moment later, we emerged into the clear upper air, and the sky appeared once more overhead, infinite and flawless, we saw in front of us a speck of pink, a rose-petal floating in the path of the aircraft. The fires of Leningrad seemed strangely near; as is always the case in a mist, the light, though subdued, had somehow acquired a new strength, being reflected to an incredible distance. The rose-petal moved, curled up, appeared to breathe. We flew thus through the boundless blue for what seemed to me an interminable time. Then at last the aircraft began to descend, and we plunged once more into the mist.

Suddenly, with deceptive speed, the trees leapt towards us, the earth rocked for an instant beneath the plane, then came to meet it like a car launched on to a racing-track at two hundred miles an hour. The wheels of the undercarriage skimmed the tops of the firs, the aircraft reared, thrusting the earth from it like a swimmer who kicks the sea-bed from under him with his heel to shoot straight up to the surface. For a few minutes we flew on, clinging to the ceiling of mist like a fly. We were looking for Helsinki airfield. And suddenly we were on the runway, the aircraft skidded across the ice and came to a stop. In the abrupt silence I heard no voices, no sound of footsteps: only the crunch of a shoe in the snow. Slowly it came nearer; and somehow that light crunching sound gave, as nothing else could have given, the measure of the all-pervading silence, of the immaculate, frozen desert that surrounded us.

XIX

THE VOICES OF THE FOREST

Alexandrovka, March.

HERE I am, then, in the front line, in a wood near the little town of Alexandrovka, ten miles from the old capital of Tsarist Russia. This is the most advanced sector of the whole Leningrad Front: the most sensitive point, the most nervous, restless, exposed section of the ring of steel that surrounds the vast Russian metropolis. I shall speak in the days to come of the character of this siege—of the powerful Soviet defences, of the nature and the various aspects of this struggle without quarter, of the enormous difficulties which the two opposing armies have to face. I shall tell of the agony of this huge city, which shelters within its walls a total of five million human beings, including members of the armed forces. (This is, in fact, the greatest siege the world has ever known.)

Today, still weary from the journey, and still not sufficiently well acquainted with this front to be able to speak of it with authority, I shall confine myself to describing to the reader my first impressions, my first thoughts, the things I saw during my journey from Helsinki to Viipuri, and from Viipuri, by way of the Summa battlefield, Terijoki and Mainila, to this outpost of Alexandrovka.

But first of all I should like to give the reader some idea both of the difficulties of my task and of the hard life that awaits me in the days ahead. Let us begin with the climate. This evening the thermometer registers only 11° F. below zero. That is not much, if one considers the exceptional severity of this winter; but it is too much for me. ("What climes!" exclaimed Leopardi, speaking, in a moral sense, of the northern countries.) In such conditions it is not easy to work. Pending the arrival of Colonel Lukander I am sheltering in a *korsu*— a low-built hut half buried beneath the snow, a kind of Alpine refuge made of tree-trunks, affording adequate protection from shrapnel but not from high-explosive shells. The *korsu* is small, cramped, freezingly cold. The soldiers who occupy it have not yet returned from their daily round of sentry-duty, patrols and fatigues, and in their absence the stove has gone out.

My fingers are frozen, the paper on which I am writing this despatch is covered with a very thin film of ice. I can almost see the page freezing over; it is exactly as if I were writing on a sheet of frosted glass. The film of ice gives my writing a faded appearance, like that of an old letter discovered after many years at the bottom of a drawer. At last a soldier enters with an armful of wood, consisting of sections of the trunk of a birch-tree, light and smooth, with white and yellow patches on the bark. After a little while a pleasant odour of smoke laden with the scent of resin spreads through the *korsu*. The paper on which I am writing unfreezes, the film of ice dissolves, great beads of perspiration trickle down the page.

I have dumped my equipment in a corner of the *korsu*, at the foot of the rough board which serves as a bed. (It really is a board, similar to those found in military prisons. Officers and men sleep on it together: the officers on one side, the men on the other, lying on rough palliasses. The overwhelming impression is one of orderliness, cleanliness, and simplicity. Everything is in its place—mess-tins, rifles, cartridge-cases, hand-grenades, personal effects, snow-boots, white cloaks, skis.)

Although I have not come here to fight, but to observe at close quarters and to describe the conduct and the various aspects of the siege of Leningrad, I have taken care to provide myself with a full range of military equipment, including a sleeping-bag, a wool-lined cloak, an Eskimo-type fur hood, a haversack, and a spare pair of shoes, plus a few bottles of brandy and a stock of tinned food. The reader must remember that in the Finnish Army the officers do not have batmen, and that accordingly I have to carry everything on my back.

I have come here not to fight, but to look into the distance, beyond the parapet of the trench, beyond the barbed-wire entanglements, beyond the Soviet bunkers, beyond the woods and the boundless expanse of snow, beyond the gilded dome of the church of Alexandrovka, at the factory-chimneys, the spires and cupolas of Leningrad. An immense city, Leningrad —flat, angular, without any skyscrapers, without any high towers. Built on the mud, in the marshes of the Neva delta, it seems to sink daily deeper into the slime of its pools and canals. Its buildings are clearly visible in the distance, outlined against the sky, immediately above the horizon. From time to time they are hidden from view by the pale blue haze. Then, suddenly, the haze clears, and you see the city rising before you, so close that if you stretched out your hand you feel you could almost touch it. (That is how it appeared to me a short while ago, when I reached this wood. The mist had cleared temporarily, and for a moment I stood in the middle of the road, my eyes fixed on that spectral, supremely beautiful vision.)

I have been sitting here in the *korsu* for more than an hour, awaiting a summons from Colonel Lukander, the officer commanding this sector of the front. Lieutenant Svardström, who accompanied me all the way from Viipuri, and whom I have asked to go and ascertain the Colonel's whereabouts, comes back to tell me that he has gone out to inspect the lines.

" He'll be here in a little while," he adds.

Svardström is a tall, lean, fair-haired young man with a smile that is at once timid, strangely timid, and ironical. He talks to me in a mixture of Finnish and German, and every so often he laughs apologetically. It is beginning to snow a little. Time passes slowly; the silence has a hypnotic quality.

" I'll go and see if the Colonel is back," says Svardström, and he leaves the hut. I am left alone with the soldier in charge of the stove. He is a dark youth, with rugged features and a benevolent expression. As I write he looks at me furtively, observes my uniform—the Alpine cap, the green flames, the stars. "*Kapteeni?*" he asks me. "Yes, I am a captain," I reply. He smiles, and repeats : "*Kapteeni.*"

I look up from the paper and listen to the voices of the forest, the dark, deep, boundless forest that surrounds us. Are they the voices of men? Of animals? Of plants? Of machines? He who has not been born in these Finnish forests becomes lost in them, as in a labyrinth. Not, to be sure, as in a labyrinth of tree-trunks and branches, but as in a mental labyrinth : a visionary desert, an unreal country, where the spirit loses all contact with reality and everything around is transformed, changes its appearance, in a continuous, fantastic metamorphosis. His senses deceive him, his mind plunges into a bottomless abyss. Voices, sounds, shapes acquire a mysterious significance, a secret, magic meaning. From far away comes the cry of an animal " *Se on koira*—it's a dog," says the soldier. I am grateful to him for translating the voices of the forest into human language. A beautiful word, *koira* : it rings in my ears like a Greek word, it reminds me of the κόραι of the Acropolis. A booming sound is heard in the distance. It comes rapidly nearer, spreads among the trees like the petals of a flower, like the jet of a fountain, like a woman's hair in the wind. " *Se on tykki*—it's a gun," says the soldier. A heavy gun. The sound of the explosion echoes through the wood like the voice of a river. The soldier gazes at me, listening intently. And I am grateful to him for his help, for the voices of these Finnish woods are strange to me, I cannot identify the voices of men, animals, plants, and machines in this boundless, mysterious Finnish forest. " *On tuuli*—it's the wind," says the soldier. " *Se on hevonen*—it's a horse," says the soldier.

A sound of voices approaches the door of the *korsu*. The soldier raises his eyes, looks through the window, says : " *Se on venäläinen*—it's a Soviet prisoner, a deserter." The man is small and skinny, with a thin, exceedingly pale face and tired, shifty eyes. His head is shaven and covered with moles. He stands there in front of a group of soldiers, gripping his pointed Tartar cap convulsively. Great beads of sweat, due perhaps to fear, perhaps to exhaustion, glisten on his brow. Every so often he wipes away the sweat with his cap. " *Ya nye znayu*—I don't know," he says. His voice is timid and slightly hoarse. A Soviet prisoner. I wish he did not interest me, I wish I did not care about him. But the sight of him fills me with pity, and at the same time with a sombre fury. Since yesterday I have seen many of these Soviet prisoners. They are all undersized, skinny, very pale. They all have tired, shifty eyes. They all look infinitely sad and bewildered. Instinctively I wonder how these soldiers, with their timid, harassed air, with their meek, anxious voices, can possibly be the men who have destroyed Viipuri, who have transformed Karelia into a desert, who have reduced Karjalan Kannas, as the Finns call the Karelian Isthmus, to the fearful state in which I found it this morning.

Nothing could be more appalling than the spectacle of Viipuri (the Swedish Vyborg), nothing could be more hideous than the sight of those black ruins half buried beneath the snow. During the " Winter War " of 1939-40 the Russians never captured Viipuri : they occupied it only after the conclusion of peace, in accordance with a provision of the Treaty of Moscow. Last August, when the Soviet troops were compelled to abandon it, the city suffered appalling damage from mines and fires. House by house, palace by palace, the whole of Viipuri was blown up by the ultra-modern method of radio-controlled mines furnished with a minute apparatus which, when attuned to a given wavelength, can be made to explode by the emission of certain musical notes.

This morning, as I wandered through the streets of Viipuri, the wind howled amid the shells of the houses. A grey sky, which looked as if it were made of some hard, opaque substance, lurked behind the gaping holes of the windows. A strong, rich, noble city, Viipuri—eternal bulwark of Scandinavia against Russia. Standing astride the road that leads from Leningrad, Novgorod, and Moscow to Helsinki, Stockholm, Oslo, Copenhagen, and the Atlantic, its very situation is in keeping with its destiny. Clustered about its Swedish castle at the head of a deep, extremely narrow gulf dotted with islands and rocks, it dominates the north-western corner of that massive neck of land, flanked by the Gulf of Finland and Lake Ladoga, which is known as the Karelian Isthmus. Here the sea penetrates far inland, surrounding the city, enveloping it, seeping among its houses, forming a background to its squares, to the courtyards of its palaces. He who is master of Viipuri is master of Finland. It is the key to the lock that is Karjalan Kannas, the Karelian Isthmus. And it is this warlike destiny that from century to century, from siege to siege, has informed the lines of its architecture, the physical manifestations of its grace and strength. Viewed from the sea, or from the edge of the forests that hem it in on three sides, Viipuri resembles one of those castles which Poussin was fond of portraying against a background of damp, shady forests, of green valleys opening on to blue skies flecked with white clouds; or one of those battlemented towns of Latium depicted in the copper-plate engraving that adorn certain eighteenth-century editions of the *Aeneid*.

The Castle stands on a small island, separated from the city by an arm of the sea across which the Russians, during their brief occupation, threw two pontoon-bridges. It is a massive structure, dominated by an extremely high tower, the base of which is surrounded by a circular terrace made of granite. The whole of the fortress proper—barracks, munition-dumps, stores, casemates—is enclosed within the circumference of that terrace. The old city extends in front of the Castle, on the opposite side of the creek. It is a district of winding streets, flanked by buildings of that Swedish military design in which traces of the old Russian influence (I am reminded especially of Novgorod) and of late French pseudo-classicism are still apparent. All around lies the modern city, with its buildings of steel, glass and concrete gleaming white here and there amid the squat *fin de siècle* palaces, perfect examples of that style which in Berlin is called *Jugend*.

I climbed to the top of the Castle tower, making my way up

an iron ladder fixed to the outside of a wall that rose sheer into
the void. From time to time my feet slipped on the ice-coated
rungs. From the summit, from the open gallery dominating the
city, a fearful spectacle presented itself to my eyes : the
monstrous graveyard of houses open to the sky, their gaping
walls blackened by smoke; the harbour, crammed with
truncated masts and funnels, twisted cranes, and holed keels;
and on every side, as far as the eye could reach, mountains of
rubble and charred beams, tragic tableaux of walls poised precariously above the heart-rending desert of squares and streets.
The preternatural whiteness of the snow around the black
ruins, the bluish glitter of the frozen sea, heightened my sense
of grief and dismay, of pity and horror.

After I had descended from the tower the people in the
streets seemed to me stern and self-contained, yet at the same
time they had about them an air of generous humanity. They
were not ghosts, but warm, living presences. Their eyes were
steady, their faces set and alert. Already nearly twelve
thousand of Viipuri's former population of eighty thousand
souls have returned to their ruined homes. They live within the
gaping walls of once-proud mansions at the end of courtyards
littered with débris, in cellars half filled with rubble, in attics
poised precariously on the edge of landings open to the sky, on
the topmost floors of gutted palaces. How splendid is the
vitality of this people—so cold and silent, and yet so constant,
so ardent in the pursuit of their plans, in their passions, in their
resolve ! (That girl whom I saw coming out of a ruined mansion
in the Karjaportinkatu, jumping lightly over the missing steps
like an acrobat descending from a trapeze on a rope-ladder.
That child's face, glimpsed through a window in the front of a
house in the Repolankatu that had been gutted by a heavy
bomb. And that woman, slowly, affectionately laying a table in
a room of a little house in the Linnankatu—a room of which
only two walls remained standing.)

From the railway-station, now no more than a vast heap of
rubble and iron girders twisted by the heat of the flames, came
the shrill, insistent voice of a locomotive. (And the counter of

that haberdashery-stall, standing alone in the middle of the square before the ruins of the market, with the little old woman sitting on a stool behind her pathetic merchandise, which the snow was gradually covering with a white blanket. And the still-intact clock of the Kellotorni, the only tower in the whole of that vast necropolis, apart from that of the Castle, to have escaped damage.)

I left Viipuri this morning, sickened by the sight of so much destruction, appalled by the evidence of so much bestial fury. And now the voice of the Soviet deserter who is chattering away outside the door of the *korsu*—" *Da, pozhaluista—da, da, da*!"—rings in my ears with a sad, meaningless insistence. That voice fills me with compassion and bitterness: I would like not to hear it, I would like to silence it. I go out of the *korsu* and start to walk among the trees outside the little hut in which Colonel Lukander has established his headquarters. In the distance, at the end of the road that leads to Leningrad (it is a magnificent road—broad, straight, paved, like the papal roads of Latium, with cobblestones, which are clearly visible through the crust of ice), there at the end of the road rise the houses of the suburbs, the factory-chimneys, the gilded cupolas of the churches. Slowly the forbidden city sinks into the pale blue mist. Laughing groups of artillerymen, protected only by makeshift screens of fir-branches, man the guns scattered here and there about the woods. Parties of skiers glide softly over the snow; in the freezing air their voices have a warm sound. From the Soviet outposts comes the hoarse stutter of a machine-gun, the sharp crack of a rifle. A distant boom is heard, a dull, muffled boom : the ships of the Russian Fleet imprisoned in the ice off Kronshtadt are shelling the road to Terijoki.

Lieutenant Svardström calls me from the doorway of Sector Headquarters. " Come in," he says. " Colonel Lukander is waiting for you."

XX

CHILDREN IN UNIFORM

Before Leningrad, April.

THEY were passing through the wood on their way down the
line, accompanied by a Finnish soldier. There were about thirty
of them in all, thirty boys, clad in Soviet uniforms, with the
familiar tobacco-coloured greatcoats, tough leather jackboots,
and caps of Tartar design with the twin flaps hanging down
over their ears—each with his mess-bowl suspended from his
belt and his large sheepskin gloves tied together by a piece of
cord. Their faces were filthy and black with smoke. As soon as
they saw the white-clad skiers gliding swiftly and lightly
through the midst of the trees they stopped to look at them.
" *Pois, pois* !—Come on, come on !" cried the soldier who was
escorting them. But he too was only a boy, he too was eager to
stop, and he too *did* stop. At first the prisoners watched the
skiers attentively and with serious expressions. Then they began
to laugh, one could see that they were amused. Some of them
tried to slide over the snow and began to jostle one another in
fun. One gathered up a handful of snow, fashioned it into a
ball, and hurled it at the back of one of his comrades. At that
they all started to laugh, shouting : " *Duràk, duràk* !—Silly
clot !" Again the soldier who was escorting them cried : " *Pois,
pois* !" And so they continued on their way, periodically turning their heads and looking back. In the meantime the group
of Finnish skiers, who were also very young, caught them up
and passed them, gliding swiftly through the midst of the
trees, brushing the trunks of the pines and birches with their

178

white cloaks. It was a day of blue skies, the snow sparkled in the sunshine, in the brilliant, joyous light the ice-encrusted branches of the trees looked as if they were made of silver.

The other day I visited the shell-scarred town of Viipuri. For a long while I wandered among the ruins, among the spectres of the houses. Groups of Soviet prisoners were working in the streets, shovelling away the snow, clearing the rubble from the yards, and pulling down walls that were in danger of collapsing. Against the white background their figures appeared so small and dark that they reminded me of ants. The high Tartar caps above their narrow, infantile brows made their pale, pinched faces appear even thinner, even more wan, even filthier. They were nearly all very young; they could not have been more than seventeen, and they looked like boys of twelve or fourteen. They were short in stature, their bodies were wasted and unformed, they had still a long way to go before they reached the first stage of adolescence. As soon as they saw me they interrupted their work and pursued me with their eyes, gazing curiously at my uniform. If I turned my head in their direction and inspected them they immediately lowered their eyes, looking frightened and confused, just like children who have been caught doing something they know to be wrong.

The officers and men of the Finnish Army are at one in recognizing that these lads fight well, with a steadfast, stubborn courage that is quite different from the courage of a child. But from the technical and military viewpoint they are undoubtedly inefficient. (And one is surprised by the singular and paradoxical fact that, in these boys who are physically so retarded, only the quality of courage is fully developed: in a sense, they already have the courage of grown men.) The thing that particularly strikes the Finnish officers and men is not the retardation of their physical development but that of their moral and intellectual development. Their intelligence is in an embryonic state. One can see that they are still children. They are content to be alive, to feel that they are alive; they are glad to breathe, to have nothing more to fear, to have been delivered at last from the haunting terror of death. Yet I doubt very much whether they appreciate the nature of their own feelings. What I mean is, they have no problems that are not of a purely physical and animal order. At eighteen, any normally-developed youth, whatever his nationality or social status, has his own intellectual and moral problems. But these Soviet prisoners, these boy soldiers, have no problems that are not purely material in character. They cannot answer even the simplest questions. Sometimes, when they are faced with a question which they do not understand, their eyes fill with tears. They are, in short, children in the fullest sense of the word.

One of the characteristic symptoms of their arrested development is the readiness with which they take refuge in tears (a defence-mechanism that is familiar to all students of child-psychology). The other day, in the course of my visit to Viipuri, I had just crossed the square in which stands the municipal library—the building, which is of ultra-modern design, is still intact, as also are its many thousands of books both ancient and modern, among them precious documents relating to the history of Viipuri—and was turning into the street that leads down to the harbour, when I came upon a squad of Soviet prisoners. They were alone, without an escort. (As a rule these working-parties are left almost entirely to themselves, being supervised only by the patrols which tour the streets of the city for that purpose.) They were standing outside a milliner's shop which had been destroyed by a bomb. While they were engaged in clearing away the rubble they had discovered beneath the bricks and mortar a wooden dummy, one of those female figures that are used by dressmakers. They had at once stopped working, and were now standing round the dummy, gazing at it curiously. Their expressions were serious, they did not know what it was or what purpose it could serve. Meanwhile, one of them had picked up off the ground a little red and blue hat—an ordinary little hat with an artificial flower, a kind of yellow rose, stitched on to one side —and had put it on his head; and all his companions were chuckling with glee as they timidly stretched out their hands and touched the rose.

Suddenly they became aware of my presence. And now a singular thing happened. Their first impulse was to run away, to hide, as boys do when someone in authority catches them playing a forbidden game. Then, responding to a contrary impulse, they collected in a group and stood with eyes downcast, looking frightened and embarrassed. The one wearing the hat started to cry and turned his back on me. I confess that at first I was somewhat disconcerted, I felt almost embarrassed myself, and I could find nothing bettter to say than : " *Rabotaitye, rabotaitye* !—Work, work !" But that word, uttered in a harsh voice, had an instantaneous effect. As if by magic all their fear and embarrassment vanished, they seized their picks and shovels and resumed work. A moment later, they had reverted to their former serene, contented state and were looking me up and down, smiling broadly.

In the Finnish Army too, alongside the veterans of the " Winter War " of 1939-40, there are among those recently called up countless soldiers whose ages do not exceed sixteen or seventeen years. But how different they are from the Russians ! They are already men; and, although they have not reached the same stage of physical development as an Italian boy of a similar age—in northern countries people mature much later than they do in the south : with us, a youth of eighteen has already reached a state of complete physical development, whereas, generally speaking, his northern counterpart has still not reached puberty—their faces and eyes reveal those signs of manhood which are a moral rather than a physical fact. They are already men, in the moral, civil, and social sense. They already possess a mature, adult outlook, which makes them not only soldiers, but citizens.

Their serenity when confronted by danger, the gravity and simplicity of their bearing in the face of hardship and suffering, the objectivity of their judgment, and the austerity of their mode of life all testify to a profound sense of duty—and I mean of their duty not only as soldiers but also, and above all, as citizens : in other words, to their sense of what they owe to their country in a moment so decisive for the existence and the future of Finland.

From what these soldiers, especially the younger among them, tell me, as well as from remarks which I happen to overhear when they are talking among themselves—remarks that are translated for me by Captain Leppo, Lieutenant Svardström and the officers of the infantry battalion which is holding this section of the line, extending from Valkeasaari to Alexandrovka—I am becoming more and more convinced each day that Finland's soldiers, from the hoariest veteran to the youngest recruit, are not only among the most valiant in the world, but also among the most civilized. All their words, all their actions—even those that are most spontaneous and unguarded—bespeak the presence of a singularly alert and sensitive moral consciousness. They are all of them, even the youngest, perfectly *au fait* with the political and military situation of their country, with the nature and objectives of the war that is being fought in Europe and elsewhere in the world; and they discuss these matters with an earnestness and a sense of responsibility that are truly admirable in soldiers who are for the most part of humble origin—peasants, workers, woodmen, fishermen, reindeer-herds, accustomed to the hard, austere, lonely life of the forests, lakes, and vast deserts of the North. They are " civilized " soldiers, in the loftiest and noblest sense of the word. And it is precisely because of their alert and sensitive moral consciousness that I am tempted to describe Finland's war—this pre-eminently " national " war—as disinterested, almost gratuitous.

This morning a Finnish soldier, alluding to these young Soviet prisoners, remarked : " They are degenerate children." This vivid, melancholy phrase came from the lips not of a veteran of the " Winter War," but of a boy of seventeen, one of those countless boys clad in the familiar ski-ing uniform with the green badges beneath the white cloak and the dagger—the *puukko*—suspended from the belt; one of those countless boy soldiers with beardless faces and timid expressions (there is, none the less, a suggestion of toughness and resolution in the depths of those eyes) who for months and months have been fighting in the front line, which extends from the pine-forests at the western edge of the White Sea to the trenches facing Leningrad. " Degenerate children." This phrase alone gives the measure of the enlightenment and the sense of responsibility (and perhaps I might add of the extreme bitterness) with which the generous youth of Finland judges the physical and moral state of the youth of Soviet Russia, which from the historical and social viewpoint has been far more severely tested and is, in a sense, less fortunate.

Whenever I happen to meet these beardless Finnish soldiers in the trenches, or in the approaches that have been dug in the snow, or in the *korsut,* their appearance, their smiling faces, their simplicity, their gay indifference to danger, the humanity of their discipline—all these things make me intensely conscious of the chivalry, the moral purity, of this Finnish war. It is a bitter, inexorable, exceedingly hard war; but it is cleanly contested. Here even death has a chivalrous quality. I would say that its presence illuminates only the purest aspect of things. (Down there in the wood, opposite the *korsu* where I am writing this despatch, stands a *Lottala,* a recreation-hut of the " Lotta-Svärd." Near the entrance two girls in grey and white caps are doing the washing in a tub full of hot water. Every so often they pop their heads out of the cloud of steam and look about them, laughing merrily. Some soldiers are loading on to a sledge three Russian corpses imprisoned in a lump of ice as in a lump of crystal. They found them by chance this morning, while they were digging a pit for storing ammunition. A runaway horse gallops through the midst of the trees, pursued by a shouting, gesticulating gunner. The girls laugh, the soldiers who are loading the corpses on to the sledge turn and laugh too. The postures of those petrified corpses, imprisoned in the transparent lump of crystal, have a limpid, precise, luminous quality.)

In the same way, the rat-tat-tat of the Soviet machine-guns, that furious, insistent crackle, and the roar of the heavy guns of the Russian ships stationed at Kronshtadt which at this moment are enfilading our lines, and that stretcher which four men are carrying on their shoulders through the wood, and the wounded soldier lying on the stretcher, his face hidden by bandages, and the laughter of those girls—all these sights and sounds appear to me instinct with chivalry, with a pure, intense humanity, like incidents and voices from a life exalted beyond reality by a sublime moral consciousness.

XXI

FORBIDDEN CITY

Before Leningrad, April.

FROM the trenches of the sector covering Valkeasaari, the Byelostrov of the Russians, situated on the outskirts of the Soviet township of Alexandrovka, the beleaguered city resembles one of those chalk models which are to be seen at exhibitions of urban architecture. (The very whiteness of the snow suggests the idea of chalk.) This section of the front occupies a somewhat prominent position, being situated slightly above the level of the plain on which stands Leningrad. From the trenches the Finnish soldiers look out on to the former capital of the Tsars as from a balcony. The monotony of the terrain is varied by a series of parallel undulations, no more than a few feet in depth. But even those few feet are sufficient to afford relief to the eye and to give breadth and depth to the view.

As the crow flies the distance from here to the outskirts of Leningrad is only eleven miles. And from over yonder, from the Finnish outposts situated north of Alexandrovka, to which we shall shortly proceed, it is rather less than ten miles. A few of the ridges are covered with a thin sprinkling of trees, but the majority are completely bare. At a depth of about three feet, beneath the superstratum of barren soil, the pick encounters granite, which at some points is exposed, forming steps thirteen to sixteen feet high. Behind these steps nestle the *korsut*, the Finnish Army huts, which are made of tree-trunks. In between the ridges the ground falls away in a series of ample, gentle curves. At the bottom of each hollow is a stream, which at this time of year is covered with a crust of ice, or a pool, or a marshy meadow from whose frozen surface protrude the sharp points of unusually slender rushes. In some places there are groups of trees. But generally speaking the ground is bare, and the observer is confronted with a succession of inclined planes white with snow.

From our present vantage-point, that is to say from the top of one of the granite steps, situated half-way between the wood in which Sector Headquarters have been established and the line of outposts, the eye ranges over a vast open space. The immense forests of Karjalon Kannas, the Karelian Isthmus, which become progressively sparser and less frequent as one approaches the suburbs of Leningrad, terminate a little way to our rear, between the villages of Mainila and Valkeasaari. They consist of trees of moderate height, among them numerous birches with light foliage and silvery trunks which contrast vividly with the dark blue of the firs. As I have already said, beyond Valkeasaari and Alexandrovka, over towards Leningrad, the forests give way to open country, the monotony of which is relieved in places by thin clumps of trees. At the same time, the villages become more and more frequent and less and less rural, and gradually the scene assumes the familiar aspect of the environs of a great city.

In between the villages one encounters in ever-increasing numbers those small rustic villas known in Russian as *dache,* where in former days the *bourgeoisie* of St. Petersburg were wont to pass the summer months. These *dache* are small houses built of birch-wood and painted blue, soft green, and pale pink. They now belong to the Soviet State trusts, the trade associations and the public assistance institutes, whose members, both workers and officials, are sent to them in batches with their families to enjoy their annual holidays or to convalesce. Some years ago I happened to witness the return of a group of workers from a brief holiday in the country near Alexandrovka sponsored by a Leningrad industrial trust. I was walking one evening beside the Neva, accompanied by some friends, when we saw approaching us from the bridge that spans the river in the vicinity of the Peter and Paul Fortress a convoy of coaches filled with working-class youths and girls. The coaches stopped just behind the Winter Palace, and from them emerged a singing, laughing throng—the girls carrying in their arms bunches of wild flowers parched by sun and dust (it was early spring, and the sticky heat which characterizes the Leningrad summer was already beginning to make itself felt), the men leafy branches of birches and freshly-cut sticks with ornamental handles fashioned with knives. We asked them where they had been, and they replied that they were just back from Alexandrovka, in Karelia. They particularly mentioned Alexandrovka. I remember the incident because at the time I was writing a biography of Lenin, and I had asked the Soviet authorities for permission to go to Alexandrovka in order to visit the places where Lenin had hidden on the eve of the rising of October, 1917. Permission was refused owing to the fact that Alexandrovka was situated near the Finnish frontier and therefore in a zone of military importance from which foreigners were excluded.

That party of workers, then, was returning from this same district, perhaps from these same meadows and forests of silver birches where now the lines of Soviet barbed-wire entanglements sparkle against the dazzling background of the snow. I look through an embrasure and survey the plain which slopes gently down towards Leningrad. The zone of the *dache* gives way to an expanse of uncultivated land, a kind of wilderness littered with refuse and industrial waste such as characterizes the immediate vicinity of any large modern city. To the naked eye the varied details of the landscape appear foreshortened : they are concealed as it were within the folds of the bellows of a camera. But as soon as I look through the telescope mounted inside the front-line observation-post the bellows open out, the various features of the landscape are separated one from another, the eye probes the spaces between the folds of the imaginary bellows and is able to explore the terrain and observe its every detail.

Ahead of me, at a distance of perhaps two hundred yards—

but apparently so close that I feel I could touch them with my hand—are the enemy's barbed-wire entanglements, his front line, interrupted at intervals so as to leave a clear field for the guns embedded in the concrete bunkers, and the zigzag pattern of his communication trenches. Anyone who fought in the first World War would recognize this as a typical scene of trench warfare viewed through a loophole in a parapet. Here, the war has clung to the ground, it has reverted to the methods and forms of the war of 1914-18—the war of positions. I feel as if I had gone back twenty-five years in time, as if I had shed twenty-five years of my life. Even the persistent sniping of the Soviet vedettes ("I feel a little nervous today," Colonel Lukander says to me with a smile) has a familiar sound, is like a friendly voice. And those dead men lying among the barbed-wire entanglements, those frozen corpses, fixed for ever in their final postures, and that Soviet soldier over there, kneeling amid the strands of barbed wire with his face turned towards us, his brow shaded by a sheepskin hood covered with a layer of snow—how many times have I seen them before, how many years have I known them? Nothing has changed in these twenty-five years. The *décor* is the same, the routine is the same, the sounds, even the smells are the same.

But the thing that gives this familiar scene of trench-warfare a singular importance, an extraordinarily new and unexpected meaning, is the background against which it is set. No longer, as in the other war, is it a background of rugged, broken hills, of trees reduced to skeletons by gunfire, of shell-torn plains traversed in all directions by a maze of trenches, of ruined houses, standing alone amid meadows and bare fields littered with steel helmets, smashed rifles, haversacks, machine-gun belts: the usual dreary, miserable scene which opened up behind the trenches on every front in the first World War. This, by contrast, is a background of factories, houses, and suburban streets, a background which, viewed through the telescope, assumes the likeness of a gigantic wall of white glass-and-concrete façades, the likeness of an immense barrier—it is the plain buried beneath a carpet of snow that suggests the image—an immense barrier of ice that blocks the horizon. Ahead of us, forming a backcloth to this battlefield, is one of the largest and most populous cities in the world, one of the greatest of modern metropolises. It is a scene in which the essential elements are not those created by nature—fields, woods, meadows, rivers, lakes—but those created by men : the high grey walls of the workers' houses, pierced by innumerable windows, the factory-chimneys, the bare, rectilinear blocks of glass and concrete, the iron bridges, the colossal cranes of the steelworks, the bells of the gasometers, the gigantic trapezoidal frames of the high-tension electric pylons : a scene which seems to reflect, with the precision of an X-ray photograph, the true nature, the essential, secret nature, of this war, in all its technical, industrial, and social aspects, in all its modern significance of a war of machines, of a technical and social war : an austere scene, smooth and compact as a wall, as the boundary-wall of an immense factory. Nor will such an image appear arbitrary to anyone who considers that Leningrad, this former capital of the Russia of the Tsars, this capital of the Communist revolution of October, 1917, is the greatest industrial city in the U.S.S.R., and one of the greatest in the world.

Today Leningrad is in its death-agony. Its factories are empty, deserted, its machines are silent, its blast-furnaces are extinguished. The arms of its powerful steam-hammers, their great steel fists poised aloft in the sinister silence, are broken. Of its eight hundred thousand workers some have been transferred to the industrial centres of the East, beyond the Volga, beyond the Urals, some have been drafted into the " technical " commandos of specialized workers and Party activists (*spyetsi* and Stakanovites), specially constituted with a view to a desperate, last-ditch defence of the city.

The eye, dazzled by this almost terrifying backcloth of glass and concrete, by this vast ice-barrier of smooth, compact walls, seeks relief at the edges of the austere scene, where the woods and snow-covered fields once again dominate the landscape. To the north of the city one discerns a dark patch, a wood, which, gradually broadening as it escapes from the stranglehold of the houses, extends to the edge of the sea. Through the trees are clearly visible the broad frozen veins of the Neva, which at this point divides to form a delta. That wood is Leningrad's park, known as The Islands. Except, perhaps, for the area around Hay Square, which is one of the oldest quarters of Leningrad, no part of the city is more closely associated with the former romantic life of St. Petersburg. It was there, on The Islands, that the smart set of the capital liked to spend the hot summer nights—the " white nights "— sitting about in the innumerable cafés and restaurants which made of that green maze of canals, groves, footpaths, avenues, and kiosks buried amid the trees a kind of Luna Park, at once aristocratic and rustic, at once refined and countrified.

It is there, on The Islands, that some of the most unforgettable scenes of Dostoievsky's *Idiot* are set. It was along those avenues that Natasha Filipovna used to pass in her carriage, amid the murmurs of the people and the strains of the miniature orchestras, under the fierce gaze of Ragoyin and the pallid gaze of Prince Muishkin. Who among the great names of Russian literature has not left footprints, some light, some deep, in those dusty avenues, on those grassy paths? Gogol is still there, among those trees. Pushkin walks there, sadly, with Engène Onegin. Some years ago I returned to Leningrad in midsummer, and one evening towards the end of my stay, I boarded a tram with the intention of visiting The Islands. I alighted at the end of a broad suburban street and, setting off on foot along an avenue, made my way to the end of the park and sat down on a wooden bench separated from the edge of the sea by a curved marble balustrade, which at that point forms a kind of belvedere, well known to *habitués* of The Islands. There was about the place and the hour an air of unutterable sadness. I do not remember clearly if it was a Sunday, but I think it must have been, because silent groups of workers, girls, soldiers and sailors were wandering amid the trees or sitting on the other benches of the belvedere. The sun had just sunk beneath the horizon, but, as happens at this season of the year, the pink reflection of the sunset still lingered in the western sky, and at the same time the sky to the east was already assuming a rosy hue. It was still sunset, and it was already dawn.

The sea was smooth, calm, and the colour of milk; it was scarcely breathing. There in front of me lay the island of Kronshtadt, enveloped in a light pall of smoke. The shore of the Karelian Isthmus (where I am writing these lines) curved gently away to my right, the meadows around Alexandrovka and the woods of Valkeasaari (the same meadows and woods that confront me at this moment) were gradually being swallowed up in the luminous twilight. That bench is only a few miles from where I am now. From it I had been able to see this vast, undulating plain, now a battlefield.

The park known as The Islands had lost its character of former days, when it was sacred to the *beau monde* of St. Petersburg. The restaurants and cafés were closed, the kiosks were deserted, the villas had been turned into *rabochie klubi*. The park too was a reflection of the new Soviet order : forbidding, drab and in a sense austere, but full of sadness and solitude. And yet—how sweet it appears to me in memory, when I think of the agony of Leningrad, of those five million souls imprisoned within that huge cage of concrete, steel, barbed wire, and minefields. (If you remove the bolt from your rifle and look down the barrel, that huge cage appears at the far end of the weapon, framed in the aperture of the muzzle; but the image is small, minute, no greater in diameter than a .303 bullet.) The city's agony has lasted now for six months. It would be distasteful to me, and it would be useless too, to dwell on the details of this colossal tragedy—a tragedy that can only be comprehended (and then only in part) by those who are personally acquainted with the characteristic features of Soviet life, by those who have experienced, if only as spectators, the life of the masses in a Communist society, by those who have mingled, in the streets, trams, theatres, cinemas, trains, museums, and public parks, in the *rabochie klubi* of the factories, in the popular *stolovie*, with those anonymous, drab, uniform, silent crowds of the cities of the

U.S.S.R. : with the crowds of Leningrad, with those throngs of people who before the war strolled aimlessly, silently, day and night, along the asphalt pavements of October 25th Prospect, formerly Nevsky Prospect; who day and night milled silently around the stations, the army barracks, the factories, the hospitals; who day and night streamed silently into the boundless spaces of Admiralty Square; who day and night silently filled the streets and alleys around Hay Square.

Of all the peoples of Europe the Russian people is the one that accepts privation and hunger with most indifference, it is the people that dies most readily. This is not stoicism. It is something else—something deeper, perhaps, something mysterious. And the story that many tell of five million starving men and women, already a prey to despair, already ripe for revolt, of five million human beings cursing and blaspheming in a dark, frozen desert of houses without heat, without water, without light, without bread, is merely a myth, a ghastly myth. The reality is perhaps even harsher. Informers, prisoners and deserters are at one in describing the siege of Leningrad as a silent, stubborn agony, a slow, grey death. (The people die in their thousands every day, from hunger, privation, and disease.) The secret of this huge city's resistance consists not so much in the number and quality of its weapons, not so much in the courage of its soldiers, as in its incredible capacity for suffering. Behind its steel-and-concrete defences Leningrad endures its martyrdom amid the ceaseless braying of the wireless loudspeakers which from the corner of every street din words of fire, words of steel, into the ears of those five million silent, stubborn, dying men and women.

XXII

THE WORKERS' ACROPOLIS

Outside Leningrad, April.

TO reach the picket-post in front of Alexandrovka one has to negotiate a long stretch, perhaps half a mile, of open ground, at the constant risk of being fired on from three sides by Soviet snipers. (The picket post is situated at the end of a salient which protrudes deep into the Russian lines.) At first one walks along a kind of path, which in fact is nothing more or less than a narrow causeway of ice, or rather, one might say, a ribbon of ice resting on the surface of the deep, powdery snow. The man who takes a false step to right or left of the ribbon of ice will sink into the snow up to his waist. It is well to pray that one may be spared such an accident; for the Soviet snipers, whose rifles are equipped with telescopic sights, lie in ambush along the edges of the salient at a distance of two or three hundred yards, and only await a suitable moment to send a bullet (if you are lucky) singing past your ear.

Fortunately, the air is a little misty, and we proceed without mishap as far as the entrance to a communication-trench. Here, in a sort of cave dug in the snow, we find a guard-post, of a kind that in the other war would have been called a liaison-post. It is in this cave that soldiers whose duties take them to the picket-post leave their skis, continuing their journey along the trench on foot, and collecting the skis on their return, so that they may the more quickly cross the open space which separates the guard-post from the front line.

When we reach the guard-post, which is manned by a

corporal—a *korpraali*—and two soldiers, we find there two runners who have just returned from the picket-post and are singling out their skis from the heap stacked against the wall.

We pause for a moment to rest (we have had to cross the danger-zone at a smart pace, for fear that a gust of wind, sweeping aside the snow, should suddenly reveal our presence), then we proceed to make our way along the trench. It is a narrow, shallow affair, and we are forced to bend down so as not to show our heads. At last we reach the picket-post, which consists of a hole dug in the ground at the foot of one of those granite steps of which I spoke when I was describing the battle-field around Leningrad. We clamber up a short ladder and peep over the top of the parapet of snow. There in front of us, a little below eye-level, are the enemy lines, and there in the distance is the city, so clearly outlined in the suddenly limpid air that from here it really does resemble one of those chalk models which are to be seen at exhibitions of urban architecture. From this elevated spot we can distinguish clearly, in the midst of the huge, compact mass of buildings, the faint green-ish shadows that mark the positions of streets and squares.

That large patch of shadow over on the left, beyond the region of The Islands and the delicate blue vein of the Neva, is Admiralty Square, the square in which stand the Winter Palace and the Hermitage Museum. That straight furrow which cuts diagonally across the city from north-east to south-west, from one elbow of the Neva to the other, is October 25th Prospect, formerly Nevsky Prospect. That low cloud over there, at the other end of Leningrad, is suspended immediately above the site of the Putilov Steelworks, one of the largest steelworks in the world and the most awe-inspiring colossus of the Soviet metallurgical industry. (It is a cloud of smoke, the cloud of smoke from a fire.) And if, going back along October 25th Prospect, at a certain point I turn to the left, I presently encounter a great sepia-coloured curve resembling a pencil-mark, which I recognize as the Fontanka, the canal that cuts across what used to be one of the aristocratic quarters, perhaps the most aristocratic quarter, of old St. Petersburg.

I scrutinize the chalk model intently in an effort to locate the neo-classical pediment of the Smolny Institute, the one-time aristocratic convent-school which during the "Ten Days" of October, 1917, was the headquarters of the Bolshevist insurrection, the meeting-place of the revolutionary Committee. Yes, that must be it, over on the right. How close it seems, from here! And how the events of this terrible winter of siege remind one of the events of October, 1917!

For the defence of Leningrad, capital of the Communist revolution, is entrusted to those same elements which played the leading part in the October rising. The defensive tactics adopted by the military and political authorities in Leningrad are in many respects, and particularly in their basic principles, the same as those employed by the revolutionary Committee in 1917 against the Cossacks of the *Dikaya Diviziya*, the "Savage Division," and later against the "Whites" of General Yudenich. The nerve and sinew of Leningrad's resistance are provided, now as then, by the workers in the metallurgical industry and the sailors of the Baltic Fleet.

Last summer, hanging on a wall in the assembly-room of the Soviet House at Soroki, on the Dniester, alongside the usual maps of the U.S.S.R., the usual coloured charts containing agricultural and industrial propaganda, the usual posters issued by the *Ossoaviakhim* (the propaganda-organization for chemical warfare and aviation), alongside the inevitable portraits of Lenin, Stalin, Voroshilov and Budenny, I found the original topographical plan of the October insurrection, comprising an ordnance-map of Leningrad with the dispositions of all the revolutionary forces (distribution of Commands, deployment of shock-troops, workers' brigades, etc.) shown in red in the minutest detail.

Bright red arrows indicated the directions of attack. The dates of occupation of the centres of enemy resistance were printed in black characters framed in red circles. Three scarlet flags, of differing shapes and sizes, marked the headquarters of the three principal revolutionary Commands, representing the shock-brigade of the Putilov Steelworks, the naval detachments from

Kronshtadt, and the rebel elements of the Baltic Fleet whose leaders had established themselves aboard the cruiser *Aurora*. (The latter had sailed up the Neva and, after anchoring in the middle of the river at a point level with the Peter and Paul Fortress, had, at the crucial moment, supported the action of the detachments of workers and sailors, opening fire on the Winter Palace, the Admiralty and the various resistance-groups of Kerensky's forces.) The Smolny Institute, headquarters of the revolution, was covered by a large red flag with the name " Lenin " inscribed upon it in white letters.

That topographical plan of the October rising might very well serve to illustrate the basic features of the current defence of Leningrad. It is probable—indeed, it is quite certain—that the purely tactical dispositions—the distribution of Commands, etc.—are different from those of 1917, and that the headquarters of the Soviet Military Command are not located in the Smolny Institute. (I should not wonder, however, if that building were now the headquarters of the political Command.) But from all the news and information that reaches the Finnish General Staff from inside the beleaguered city it emerges clearly and unmistakably that Leningrad's resistance is far more political than military in its inspiration. It is, in fact, to the exceptional importance of Leningrad as capital of the October revolution and as the citadel of Communist extremism that the resistance in question owes its special political and social character.

I have already had occasion to refer to the deplorable physical condition of the latest Red Army recruits. And I have described my astonishment at finding that the defence of Leningrad (which, " from the political viewpoint," has a decisive bearing on the general economy of the war) has been entrusted not to fully trained and seasoned troops specially chosen for their physical fitness but to recently formed detachments of infantry consisting largely of extremely youthful elements, badly trained and therefore inefficient, albeit excellently armed and equipped. (It is known, as a result of checks carried out in the sectors of Lake Ilmen, Smolensk and the

Don, in other words in the sectors where during these last few weeks the Soviets have put forth their maximum counter-offensive effort, that the best units of the Red Army are deployed at these key-points of the front.) But what is there, on the Leningrad Front, behind these scratch formations of peasants and boys who, for all their courage and tenacity, are technically inefficient? The answer, today as in 1917, is the sailors of the Baltic Fleet and the metal-workers of Leningrad itself.

If I were asked to sum up the political and military situation of Leningrad I could not do better than point to that poster, still the most characteristic example of the iconography of the Communist revolution, in which are represented, against a background of smoking factory-chimneys, a sailor from Kronshtadt and a worker from the Putilov Steelworks, armed with rifles and in the act of fighting. The sailor, in his blue-and-white striped vest and with the two long ribbons at the back of his cap hanging down on to his shoulders (the name of the cruiser *Aurora* is inscribed on his cap-band), is looking back and shouting words of encouragement to invisible masses of workers, his rifle in his left hand, his right arm outstretched and pointing in the direction of the enemy. The worker stands at his side, half facing him, gripping his rifle tightly with both hands, his face grim, his brow dark and contracted. As in October, 1917, so today, this poster is the symbol of Leningrad's resistance. And nothing could give a clearer idea of the factors—in particular, the political and social factors—on which the defence of the city depends than this pungently expressive pictorial representation.

In judging the position, we must not lose sight of a fundamental fact—namely, that for five months Leningrad has been virtually isolated from the rest of Russia, without any possibility of obtaining fresh supplies of men, food and ammunition, except by way of the track which crosses the vast frozen expanse of Lake Ladoga, the largest lake in Europe. It is this impossibility of obtaining reinforcements and supplies, together with the industrial character and the special political significance of the city, that has induced the Soviet military Command to adopt, for the defence of Leningrad, the typically Communist expedient of employing shock-brigades of workers and sailors. The enormous mass of workers—some hundreds of thousands of men capable of bearing arms—who were not evacuated in time to the industrial regions of Eastern Russia have been formed into special commando units which contain all the characteristic elements of the revolutionary organization planned and created by Trotsky in October, 1917 : bands of technicians, squads of mechanics from the tank and artillery regiments, detachments of sailors from the Baltic Fleet. These commando brigades, to which must be added the squads of specialists responsible for the laying of mines, are deployed at the most vulnerable points not only of the military, but of the political front. The scratch formations of infantry which man the front line, where they are called upon to bear the main burden of the siege, form part of a typically Communist warmachine which discharges above all a political function, and in the military field conforms to a tactic which has nothing in common with that employed in a war of positions : that is to say, to a typically revolutionary tactic, the tactic of the civil war.

In a sense, this siege marks the return of the proletariat of Leningrad (which from the Marxist viewpoint is the most advanced and the most intransigent in the whole of the U.S.S.R.) to the Communistic spirit, as well as to the tactics of the civil war. The squads of armed workers, lacking military training but technically very efficient and animated by the most violent fanaticism, retain the characteristics of those shock-brigades of *spyetsi, udarniki* and *stakanovtsi* which were formed in the course of fifteen years of total industrialization and of *Pyatlyetki* or Five Year Plans. Undoubtedly they represent, together with the sailors of the Baltic Fleet, the best and most reliable elements of the Communist Party. Where, then, is the weak point in this workers' military organization, which keeps not only the civilian population of Leningrad but the military authorities themselves under its thumb, maintaining strict control of all the nerve-centres of the city's defence?

Its weakness lies in its very origin, in its very political nature, in its fanaticism and, at the same time, in the peculiar character of siege warfare. Let it be noted, in the first place, that the considerable losses resulting not so much from the actual fighting as from hunger, privation and disease (in Leningrad petechial typhus alone kills off about two thousand people each day) are gradually thinning the ranks of these skilled workers. In other words, the passive defence of the city is depriving the Communist Party of its best elements, of those of its members who, technically and politically, are most experienced and most reliable. The Party is losing its " proletarian aristocracy." The huge body politic of Russia is losing its backbone.

In order to reduce this daily decimation of its best elements to a minimum the Soviet military Command tries so far as possible to protect the working men's units. (Hitherto, it transpires, the commando brigades of workers have been employed only on the Oranienbaum Front and in the Schlüsselburg and Tsarkoye Selo sectors.) On the battlefield these units have once again given indisputable proof of their courage and technical efficiency. But their morale appears now to have been seriously impaired by five months of inactivity and domestic controversy.

It is a well-known fact that for any body of troops inactivity spells danger—the danger of moral disintegration—and that this danger is all the greater when the military formations in question have a political character. In the last few weeks this process of disintegration, taking the characteristic form of a struggle of rival factions, has inevitably made considerable headway among the working masses of Leningrad. First-hand news has been received of serious discontent, of bitter party strife, of a growing tendency to subordinate wholly military problems to those of a purely political nature. The Left Wing of the Communist Party, with which the overwhelming majority of the proletariat of Leningrad identifies itself, grows daily more outspoken in its criticism of the political and military authorities in Moscow, whom it accuses of having failed to adopt, in their conduct of the war, what the extremists call " Communist strategy."

Exactly what, from the military viewpoint, this " Communist strategy " entails is not clear, though it is evident that the expression refers to the purely political rather than to the military conduct of the war. Undoubtedly the criticism has its origin in some internal, Party conflict—in one of those familiar internal conflicts which, born of the innumerable, and inevitable, corruptions of and deviations from Marxist ideology and of the countless interpretations of Leninism, have made the Communist extremism of Leningrad, traditionally a restless, turbulent city, the gravest threat to good order in the whole of the Soviet Union. (Many will recall the ferocious policy of repression carried out by Lenin in 1920 against the workers of Leningrad and the sailors of Kronshtadt, in other words against the " old guard " of the Revolution, which was accused of menacing the solidarity of the Party and of endangering the future of the dictatorship of the proletariat. The memory of these massacres is still alive in the minds of the working masses of the revolutionary capital and of the sailors of the Baltic Fleet, and this will certainly not make for a conciliatory attitude on the part of Leningrad and Kronshtadt in the event of a political rift with Moscow.)

Hunger, inaction, and the terrible daily spectacle of the sufferings which the siege imposes on the civilian population, in other words on the families, on the women and children, of the working class itself, undoubtedly tend on the one hand to favour the formation of desperate plans, on the other to encourage the working masses to seek a solution, a way of escape, by political means—that is, through party strife and domestic violence. The proletariat of Leningrad is in an extremely sensitive and dangerous frame of mind; and this is a matter of grave concern to the political and military authorities in Moscow, who are powerless, because of the siege, to try to improve the military and alimentary situation in the city. Moscow is perfectly well aware that such a state of things could in the long run weaken the military efficiency of the workers' battalions.

Before leaving the picket-post I again look over the top of the parapet and survey the beleaguered city. A light veil of mist is rising from the frozen waters of the Gulf of Finland, between Kronshtadt and the mouth of the Neva. Little by little, amid the uniform whiteness of the landscape, Leningrad takes on a sinister appearance. It becomes an insubstantial, spectral city, a mirage in the shining white desert of snow. (As a result of the ceaseless pounding of the German heavy artillery a dense cloud of smoke is rising from the industrial quarter, from the Putilov Steelworks.) After exchanging farewells with the picket we make our way back along the trench, pause for a moment at the guard-post, then set off at a smart pace across the narrow ribbon of ice, trying to take advantage of the mist to keep out of the Russian snipers' sights.

It is late, and by the time we reach the front line dusk is already falling. Major Junqvist, who with his battalion controls the Alexandrovka sector, asks us into the *korsu* which serves as his headquarters and offers us a cup of tea. After a few minutes we take our leave of Major Junqvist and his officers, and as we emerge from the *korsu* my attention is attracted by a spectacle with which I am by now familiar, but which never fails to astonish me : two completely naked men come running out of a *sauna*, their bodies dripping with sweat, and proceed to roll over and over in the snow.

(No doubt the reader will already know what a *sauna* is. In point of fact, it is a Turkish bath—one of those distinctive Turkish baths which the Finns regard as indispensable even in the front line. This trench-*sauna* consists of a small hut containing a stove—a kind of oven open at the top and covered with a stout iron grid, on which are heaped a number of large stones. The stove is lit, and gradually, through contact with the flames, the stones become red-hot. Buckets of water are then poured over them to produce steam. After sweating profusely the bathers run out into the open, passing abruptly from a temperature of 140° F. into one of up to twenty degrees below zero. They then proceed to roll about in the snow.)

It is at this precise moment that the shell descends upon us with a raucous shriek, arriving so suddenly and unexpectedly that we do not even have time to throw ourselves to the ground. It bursts some twenty yards away, covering us with a shower of ice-splinters and lumps of snow and frozen mud. Captain Leppo, who is next to me, is struck on the arm by one of those hard, frozen clods. I am conscious of having received a terrific blow in the ribs which takes my breath away. Luckily it is caused by an ice-splinter, not by a piece of shrapnel. Anyone hurt? No, no one is hurt. We burst out laughing, and the two soldiers, seated amid the snow, are also highly amused. They are as naked as new-born babes, and dripping with sweat. It seems to me that in the circumstances anyone might be expected to break into a sweat: a *cold* sweat.

XXIII

THE RED FLAG OF THE *AURORA*

Before Kronshtadt, April.

THERE in front of me is Kronshtadt, the island of Kron-shtadt, refuge and prison of the Soviet Baltic Fleet. From the cliffs of Terijoki the island of Kronshtadt appears in outline —flat, grey-blue, like the silhouette of a ship trapped in the frozen waters of the Gulf of Finland. It is a bright morning, the air is flooded with an extraordinarily clear and brilliant light. Already one discerns a first, timid sign of spring in the lengthening days. But the cold persists : this morning, when we set out from the Alexandrovka Front, the thermometer registered forty-five degrees of frost. (And in Italy the grass is already green, the trees are already in flower !)

It is only a few miles from the trenches of Alexandrovka and Byelostrov to Terijoki. But in that short distance the outward and visible signs of the war, the countless aspects of this siege of Leningrad, undergo such a transformation that I feel as if I had travelled hundreds of miles. The Terijoki Front, which faces Kronshtadt, is undoubtedly the most singular, and the most picturesque, of all the fronts that I have had occasion to visit in the course of this strange war. Apart from its political character, apart from its outstanding political significance (Kronshtadt, as the reader already knows, is only a part of the Leningrad Front; but from the political viewpoint it is the nerve-centre, I would almost say the acropolis, of the Red citadel of Leningrad), the Kronshtadt sector is undoubtedly the most interesting, and in a military sense the most complex, sector of the whole vast battle-line extending from Murmansk in the north to Sebastopol in the south. And the reason is that it confronts the strategist with the task of finding, not more or less new solutions to old problems, as is the case with other sectors of the Eastern Front, but entirely new solutions to absolutely new problems, with which students of the art of war have never had to grapple until today.

The Terijoki Front follows the coastline—a low coastline, more or less regular in its conformation. The Finnish trenches run along the shore, and there in front of us, a hundred yards from the muzzles of the machine-guns, are the lines of barbed-wire entanglements, stretching across the frozen surface of the sea, interrupted at intervals by the gaps that have been left for the passage of patrols. Parallel with the shore, immediately behind the trenches, runs the street: a wide street flanked by little wooden houses and villas, serene and charming in this exquisitely bare, austere landscape of snow and forests. The birches, firs, and Arctic pines stretch down to the sea, here crowded together, there more thinly scattered, in places as dense and wild as in the depths of the Karelian forests, elsewhere so widely spaced as to form what is in fact almost a public park, complete with wooden benches, bandstands, and little avenues winding their way among the mossy tree-trunks.

In the time of the Tsars, Terijoki was one of the pleasantest and most elegant holiday-resorts in the whole of the Gulf of Finland—the aristocratic " lung " of the capital. Yet it should not be thought of as a luxurious society playground. Rather was it a peaceful, unspoiled village sprawling amid the woods at the edge of a sea as pale and warm as a lake.

This was the age, the golden age—an age now faded in memory, a faded oleograph hanging on the white wall of memory—when the upper-class families of St. Petersburg used to come to Terijoki to pass the hot summer months in the fragrant shade of the birches. Evening after evening they would sit on the wooden verandas with the little ornamental pillars inlaid with historical scenes picked out in green, red and blue, chatting over their glass of *chai*. In my imagination I seem to hear the soft, high-pitched voices of those old Russians as they sat there amid the limpid splendour of the "white nights", talking incessantly, ever returning to their original theme, ever tackling it anew from a more difficult angle. They would linger for hours discussing things that do not exist, or that hardly exist. They had a charming way of repeating themselves, a delightful weakness for inconsequential chatter, a felicitous habit of forgetting completely what they were talking about. And as the evening wore on they would become oblivious of time and space, oblivious even of the green, red and yellow signal-lights of the warships anchored off Kronshtadt, which in the clear night air could be seen twinkling in the distance.

Now those happy days are gone for ever. Now the streets of Terijoki are full of soldiers, the grey steel of the cannon glistens here and there amid the trees, and behind the charred ruins of the church the Finnish dead sleep peacefully bene th the simple Lutheran cross. Groups of machine-gunners sit on crates of ammunition at the edge of the street, clustered around the tripods of their weapons. From time to time a sledge passes, drawn by one of those beautiful Finnish horses with long, soft, light-coloured manes and liquid, almost feminine eyes.

This peaceful scene, this serene and somnolent tableau, here in the front line, here in this village nestling beside a sea covered with a shining crust of ice, a village that is periodically shelled by the heavy long-range artillery of the Soviet Navy, is the strangest, and the most delectable, that I have so far encountered in this bitter war. Whether it is the faint suggestion of spring, already discernible on this sharp, clear morning in the different colour of the light, in the less piercingly cold air, in the reflection of the snow and ice, which is already less white, already less blue; whether it is this scent of burnt wood (a scent of pines, a scent of birches, a scent of those green branches that are used in the *sauna* for the therapeutic castigation of the bathers); or whether it is this warm smell of smoke, I do not know : but the fact is that the war is not present to me today as a living, cruel reality, it is present only as a memory—a kind of photographic image conjured up from the remotest depths of my consciousness.

And now this peace and serenity (I should say : this memory, this image) are suddenly shattered by the harsh voice of a gun —the 381 of a ship anchored off Kronshtadt. It is a tremendous voice, a prolonged roar that curves like a rainbow into the sky between Kronshtadt and Terijoki. The 381 shell bursts in the wood to our rear. The air shivers into a thousand fragments, the blast from the explosion spreads in waves across the countryside, which rocks like a stage-set buffeted by the wind. " They're starting again," says Lieutenant Svardström with a smile.

For several days now something unusual has been happening on Kronshtadt. The heavy German batteries installed on the opposite shore of the gulf ceaselessly bombard the Soviet columns that pass to and fro across the frozen surface of the sea between Leningrad and the island. It is a strange operation, an orderly, methodical coming and going repeated at fixed interval as though it were a military exercise. What on earth can the Russians be transporting to Kronshtadt? And what on earth can they be taking *from* the island? Air reconnaissance is illuminating on this point. It shows that at certain hours of the day and night there is a continuous movement of lorries and infantry between Leningrad and Kronshtadt. (The nights are beginning to grow shorter, and ever lighter.) The theory, advanced at the outset, that with spring imminent the Soviet military Command is intent on strengthening the defences of the naval base by sending food and munitions to the island does not hold water. There is an equally grave shortage of food and munitions in the old capital. The need is greatest among the defenders of Leningrad. The Baltic Fleet, on the other hand, has its own reserves, which remain abundant. If anything, therefore, it would be more logical to suppose that Kronshtadt was sending munitions and food to Leningrad. But the siege of Kronshtadt will assuredly last longer than the siege of Leningrad; and it is unthinkable that the naval base is disposing of its reserves just as winter gives way to spring. Can it be, then, that the island's garrison is being strengthened? This second theory is no more feasible than the first. Kronshtadt has no need of men : it has too many as it is. The count is quickly made : all the sailors of the Baltic Fleet, plus all the crews of the coastal batteries deployed around the perimeter of the island, plus the detachments of naval engineers, plus the garrisons of the artificial islets of steel and concrete, of which the largest is called Totleben, dotted around the island of Kronshtadt, plus the skilled workers, numbering some tens of thousands, employed in the arsenal.

The theory which, on the evidence of various concordant items of information, seems to be the correct one is that which takes account of the peculiar political character of Kronshtadt. For nearly a year now—ever since the earliest days of this war against Soviet Russia—I have been saying that the political criterion is one we can ignore only at the risk of grave error when we come to judge the U.S.S.R.—its mind, its power of resistance, its possibilities of retaliation, its fanatical resolve—and, more particularly, to determine the basic, decisive factors in the defence of Leningrad. (The reader must forgive me if I repeat once again—and by no means for the last time—that the key to the political situation in the U.S.S.R. is Leningrad, stronghold of Communist extremism and intransigence. By constantly bearing this point in mind he will come to understand many things whose importance and significance would otherwise escape him.)

The theory, then, which seems to be most feasible is that the Russians are summoning a large proportion of the crews of the Baltic Fleet to Leningrad with the intention of transforming them into new commando brigades, designed to reinforce their front-line troops and at the same time to support the work of surveillance and of revolutionary propaganda carried out by the political authorities both among the industrial masses and among the military leaders. Many of these crews are by now unemployable in a strictly naval sense, the reason being that is is impossible for the Fleet (today immobilized by the ice and soon, when the thaw comes, to be immobilized by the minefields which block the Gulf of Finland) to come out and give battle, with the result that Kronshtadt has necessarily assumed the character more of a maritime fortress than of a naval base.

If this theory is correct, the movements of the columns of lorries and infantry which for the last two or three days have been shuttling to and fro between Leningrad and Kronshtadt are no more than a Soviet manoeuvre designed to deceive the enemy as to the real direction of this one-way traffic, in other words to camouflage the transference to Leningrad of some of the crews of the Baltic Fleet. In the last analysis it is always the political character of Kronshtadt, its function—and hence its destiny—as the " acropolis " of the capital of the October Revolution, that determines the methods adopted for the defence of Leningrad, the tactical use to which the regular troops and the commando brigades of workers and sailors are put. It will not be long before the political function of the crews of the Baltic Fleet and of the workers of Leningrad is revealed with all its nation-wide implications.

Meanwhile, the time is ripe for me to take a closer look at Kronshtadt, to attempt, from this advanced position, to review the different elements of this stupendous siege in all their variety and singularity. From my present vantage-point (I am standing at the top of one of those fifty-foot wooden towers which the Russians have built here and there to enable them to watch the roads and the woods in the vital frontier zones and in the vicinity of the towns) the eye takes in the whole breadth of the gulf from shore to shore. The sun is shining brightly but obliquely (in these latitudes it never climbs very far above the horizon) on that boundless expanse of frozen water, which emits a blue radiance, as if it were illuminated not from above but from below. In the distance, on the opposite shore of the gulf, near the bridgehead at Oranienbaum, which the Russians are defending with incredible fanaticism against the German pincers, the glare of fires is visible against the background of a pitch-black cloud with sharp and precise contours. Away to my left Leningrad also is burning. The German heavy artillery is subjecting the industrial area of Uritski, the district in which the Putilov Steelworks are situated, to a continuous bombardment.

And there, in the middle of the gulf, is Kronshtadt, enveloped in a light, opaque mist reminiscent of the silvery haze of a " white night ". From this spot one can distinguish with the utmost clarity the red, yellow, green and blue stars of the rockets that ascend at intervals from the ships and from Kronshtadt's defensive ring of artificial islets. They have an unreal, ghostly air, those winking stars, hovering like will-o'-the-wisps amid the light silvery haze of early morning. They resemble wings of butterflies which, suddenly illuminated as they pass through a sunbeam, are at once obscured, only to light up again a moment later as they pass through another sunbeam. That haze reminds me of a clear summer night, a limpid night when the moon is full, a night illuminated by the delicate brilliance of glow-worms and fireflies. A tall column of grey smoke rises like an enormous tree from either end of the island of Kronshtadt. From time to time the crust of ice separating the eastern tip of the island from the mainland is cleft by an orange flash from the German heavy batteries which are shelling the Russian columns as they pass to and fro between Kronshtadt and Leningrad.

Captain Leppo hands me a pair of binoculars. And now, through the aura of blue light reflected from the frozen surface of the sea, the forest of factory-chimneys and the steel turrets of the ships anchored in the harbour of Kronshtadt appear before me with startling clarity. They make an impressive sight, those ships—an entire fleet, the most powerful in the Soviet Union, imprisoned in the ice as in a huge block of concrete. They cannot move, they cannot fight. " They have lost their legs," say the Finnish soldiers. An entire fleet as it were turned to stone. On another tower I see something dark moving.

" What's that?" I ask Captain Leppo. " A flag?"

"Yes," replies Captain Leppo. "Moscow Radio announces that it's the flag of the famous cruiser *Aurora*. It's flying from the tower of the Admiralty building."

It is not a naval flag, it is a red flag: the flag which the sailors of the *Aurora* hoisted above the Palace of the Tsars in October, 1917. (The red colouring of the flag cannot be distinguished from here. One's impression is rather of something dark, something funereal. This is a fitting moment to recall, for the benefit of any who may be unaware of the degree of political tension existing between the extreme Communists of Leningrad and Kronshtadt and the rulers in the Kremlin, that there was a time during the decisive hours of October, 1917, when the red flag of the *Aurora* sent a chill of fear down the spine of Lenin himself.)

XXIV

PRISON OF SHIPS

Before Kronshtadt, April.

IT is a strange battle that has been unfolding for several months now around the island of Kronshtadt : a most singular battle, in which the protagonists are a fleet embedded in the frozen sea as in a block of concrete, unable to move, unable to manoeuvre, and the seasoned land-armies that besiege it from every side. I would describe it as a naval battle fought on dry land.

For the extraordinary thing about this paradoxical situation is that the Soviet Baltic Fleet is separated from its adversaries not by the green waves of the sea, but by a huge expanse of smooth, ice-cold marble, on to which the Finnish infantry, equipped with skis, periodically venture out for the purpose of boarding, so to say, the Russian battleships.

Imagine a fleet immobilized, paralysed, imprisoned in ice that hems it in on every side. Imagine then an assault by skiers on these captive ships, and you will have a clear enough idea (albeit very far from the reality, which is infinitely more tragic, infinitely more paradoxical) of this contest of men against battleships, of this struggle of infantry, armed with rifles and hand-grenades, against heavy naval artillery. On moonless nights lit by the blue reflection from the ice (the ice has a transparency all its own, a luminosity that rises from the utmost depths of the sea), the ski-patrols pour through the gaps in the barbed wire and venture out into the middle of the gulf.

The other evening I witnessed the departure of one of these assault-columns (to be truthful, the term " column " is inappropriate, for as soon as they have emerged from behind the barbed-wire entanglements the patrols spread out fanwise, dividing into groups of two or three skiers, who scatter over the boundless expanse of petrified waves). Nothing could have been more impressive, nothing could have been more thrilling, than the spectacle of those skiers setting out for the open sea.

The most profound silence reigned along the edge of the frozen waters. The departure of those patrols, which were sallying forth to attack one of the most strongly-fortified naval bases in the world, reminded me strangely of the departure of a fleet of lateen craft from a fishing-port. The women, children and old men on the jetty silently wave farewell to the boats as, propelled by the oars, they move away from the shore. And now the sails spread, catch the wind, and the vessels recede into the distance, gliding swiftly over the surface of the sea.

It was exactly like a departure of sailing-boats, and in the freezing air, redolent of ice and birch trees (that cold, naked smell of ice, that warm, deep scent of birches) I caught the tang of seaweed, of salt water, of fishes' scales.

After about an hour we heard the first rifle shots. They came from far away on the horizon, which could just be discerned amid the encircling gloom. Red and green rockets ascended from the boundless expanse of ice like jets of water from a fountain. The Finnish patrols had made contact with the Russian patrols, which are not composed—as on the Eastern Karelian Front, or in the Aunus sector, between Lake Ladoga and Lake Onega—of Siberian skiers, but of sailors of the Baltic Fleet. The strangeness of this war! The sailors descend from the ice-bound battleships equipped with skis and proceed to fight on the sea. Sometimes they venture as far as the Finnish shore, even as far as Terijoki. From time to time furious skirmishes break out around the island of Hogland, situated to the west of Kronshtadt, which the Finns have lately

wrested from the Russian sailors. It is a war of derring-do:
a struggle, I repeat, of men against battleships, of skiers armed
with rifles against the steel turrets of the 381's.

The Finnish skiers fly across the ice, dragging behind them
small sledges laden with heavy machine-guns and boxes of ammunition. It is on these same sledges that they bring back the
dead and wounded to their lines. (There is one thing which
the Russian sailors and the Finnish *sissit* have in common:
they do not abandon their dead. Sea-going folk—and the
Finnish skiers are nearly all sea-going folk—fishermen to be
precise, plying their trade in the Gulf of Finland and the Gulf
of Bothnia—are jealous of their dead. They know that the sea
is greedy: it eats the dead, it devours them. There is a folk-
song current among the Finnish fishermen of Turku and the
surrounding region in which the sea, trapped beneath the crust
of ice, shouts and curses, beating its head against the hard,
transparent blue roof, what time a party of fishermen walk
along the frozen surface, carrying a dead comrade on their
shoulders.)

It should not be thought, however, that the battle for Leningrad is limited to these incidents of the war of patrols. The
struggle now taking place around Kronshtadt is only one of
the countless episodes of this stupendous siege. (I shall speak
of the others when I come to visit the Ladoga and Aunus
Fronts, situated to the north-east of Leningrad.) It is an
enormous ring of steel that is now tightening round the be-
leagured capital of the Communist Revolution. And to explore
the area completely, to get to know it in all its aspects, in all
its details, one has to travel hundreds of miles, visiting every
sector, every salient, every outpost. It is impossible, for example,
to go from the Karelian Isthmus (where I am at present) to
the Aunus Isthmus by way of Lake Ladoga. It is necessary
instead to return to Helsinki, strike north into the interior of
Finland, then head south-east—a total journey of more than
six hundred miles. This example must suffice for the moment
to illustrate the difficulties of a siege conducted on such a vast
scale, against such an enormous city, on territory rendered

impassable in the winter by ice, and in the summer months by lakes and marshes.

I have already tried many times to describe the appearance of the siege-front, the configuration of this immense ring of trenches. It is a kind of enormous quadrilateral, extending from the Aunus Isthmus, situated between Lakes Ladoga and Onega, to the Karelian Isthmus, and from Schlüsselburg to Peterhof. The defensive system of Leningrad is the most formidable that could possibly be imagined : a system of specially-constructed outworks and permanent fortifications—some of which date back to the time of Peter the Great—completed and reinforced by some mighty specimens of the art of military engineering, by a double line of concrete bunkers and steel cupolas, and by all the most modern inventions, all the latest devices of a defensive order. Its topographical design is distinctly reminiscent of Vauban; and, as an example of the art (in which the Communists excel) of transforming a modern city into a fortress, it shows unmistakable signs of having been based on the experience of Madrid. (In the matter of siege-warfare the experience of Madrid is still topical today. And a chapter apart could well be devoted to discussion of the indisputable fact that the Communists have shown, alike in the Spanish Civil War and in the present campaign in Russia, a supreme mastery of the technique of defending a city even against an army equipped with powerful modern weapons and armour. It would certainly make most interesting reading. For the fact must have an explanation; and it can hardly be a purely military one.)

The defensive system of Leningrad would not be complete without Kronshtadt. The naval base of Kronshtadt has undergone no radical change since it was first designed, with the help of French military engineers, by Peter the Great, on the model of the great naval bases of France and of those English bases which the Emperor himself had inspected in the course of his famous visit to England. But the technical novelty of the fortress of Kronshtadt, which is already formidable by its very nature, consists in the two islands, Totleben and Krasnoarmyeski, and the seven artificial islets of steel and concrete that encircle it. These seven artificial rocks rise from the depths of the sea like lofty towers, like slender Dolomitic pinnacles. Only their tops protrude above the water, and from a distance they resemble turtles—an image suggested not only by their appearance, which is precisely that of turtles, but by the fact that the island of Kronshtadt itself has the form of an enormous turtle's head, ringed by Totleben, Krasnoarmyeski and the seven other little concrete turtles. The whole defensive system of Leningrad can in fact be likened to a gigantic turtle sprawling along the eastern end of the Gulf of Finland. The head, represented, as I say, by Kronshtadt, is barely visible above the surface of the sea and is joined to the rest of the body by a long neck, consisting of the channel by which the ships of the Baltic Fleet are able to reach the port of Leningrad even at low tide.

Flat and grey in the midst of its ring of fortified rocks, the island of Kronshtadt gives me the impression, as I study it through the binoculars, of a smooth mass, without indentations or cavities, without any landmarks that catch the eye. But little by little I begin to discern the yellow patches of its fortifications, the white expanses of its two airfields, situated at opposite ends of the island, and the dark blur of the town, enclosed within the steel ring of its defences, some ancient, some modern. From time to time I see glinting in the sunlight the green cupola of the cathedral, the laminated roofs of the military stores and the hangars, the immense glass walls of the arsenal, the oil-tanks, and the armoured turrets of the vast underground bunkers that extend all round the circumference of the island. The tall, trapeze-shaped steel mast of the radio station points like a slender spider's web into the pale sky. And there, beyond a long line of low roofs, are the captive ships, the ships of the Baltic Fleet, the most powerful fleet the Soviet Union possesses.

An entire fleet—totalling some seventy units both large and small, plus about sixty submarines—assembled in such a limited space, would at first sight seem inevitably to offer an easy target to the Stukas and to the heavy guns installed on either shore of the Gulf of Finland. Yet the experience of last autumn, coupled with the experience of this winter, has demonstrated that the very fact of being confined in a narrow space may well constitute a fleet's best defence. True, it has been a perilous experience, from which the Soviet Admiralty has been unable to save itself. But consider what the naval base of Kronshtadt comprises: an immense steel fortress, a formidable assembly of armoured gun-turrets and steel-plated decks, bristling with artillery and anti-aircraft machine-guns. The number of muzzles pointing skywards from the ships of the Fleet, from the island's fortifications, from Totleben, Krasnoarmyeski and the seven concrete islets must be reckoned in tens of thousands.

No aircraft could face so formidable a concentration of fire without exposing itself to mortal danger. To which must be added the fact that the Soviet winter offensive, though strategically abortive, has obliged the German Military Command to withdraw its line of heavy artillery, thus reducing the effectiveness of the heavy guns directed against the fortress of Kronshtadt.

Although I should be failing in my task if I did not stress the purely military factor in the situation, I would not wish the reader to allow the military aspects of the siege of Leningrad to blind him to the extraordinary importance of this siege both from the political and from the sociological viewpoint. For it is a fact that every Russian problem of today has a political and sociological, as well as a military significance. Indeed, I would go so far as to say that the military problem posed by the siege of Leningrad is merely an aspect of the political and sociological problem.

This characteristic of the struggle which for several months past has been raging around the capital of the October Revolution has not escaped the notice of the Finnish soldiers, who in a sociological sense are undoubtedly among the most enlightened in the whole of Europe and so are the best able to appreciate the sociological aspects of the most widely-varied problems. Whenever I am in the company of one of them I am struck by the refinement and sensitivity of this people, by its perfect sense of justice, and still more by its attitude—a wholly Christian attitude—to social relationships and its acceptance even of wrong-doing as a social fact. So far as I am aware, no one has yet pointed out that on the Leningrad Front we are witnessing a clash of two philosophies, among the most uncompromising and the most extreme in Europe. If Leningrad is the stronghold of Leninist intransigence, of Communist extremism, Finland is, in a sense, the stronghold of that Lutheranism which is perceived more as an affair of the conscience than as a historical fact, in other words as a subjective rather than as an objective reality, and in which accordingly sociological problems assume a fundamental importance.

I was talking only this morning to one of these Finnish soldiers. The man in question had just returned from a patrol-action. He was calm and smiling. From the seaside resort of Terijoki to Totleben is not much more than four miles—an insignificant distance to these indefatigable skiers, who are capable of covering sixty miles in twenty-four hours. We were sitting in a *Lottala,* a recreation-hut of the " Lotta-Svärd ", hidden away in a wood on the outskirts of Terijoki. The *Lottala* was crowded with soldiers, sitting in silence round the tables, before them glasses filled with a pink beverage, a kind of hot syrup with an agreeable taste. The *Lotta,* clad in their grey uniforms, were going round the tables carrying trays and glasses. Next to us a soldier was mending a tear in the sleeve of his tunic. Many of his colleagues were writing, many others were reading. Suddenly an artilleryman came in with an accordeon. He began to play a popular air, a kind of lover's lament, instinct with a desolate, virile sadness. One by one the soldiers began to provide a vocal accompaniment to the music of the instrument, singing very softly, as if reluctant to disturb the tranquillity of the hour and the place; and somehow that subdued chorus of manly voices made the sad music sound even sweeter and more tender. Every so often the window-panes vibrated. The heavy guns of the ships trapped in the ice off Kronshtadt were in action, and the shells were bursting not far from the village, in the depths of the wood. The acrid smoke from the explosions entered the room in clouds every time the door opened. It was a bright, simple scene, an " interior " full of serenity and grace. And we were twenty yards from the front line (we only had to cross the road to find ourselves in the trenches), exposed to the fire of the heavy guns of the Baltic Fleet.

The soldier talked to me placidly, smilingly, in halting German mingled with incomprehensible Finnish words. He told me that the artificial islets, when seen at close quarters, really do resemble turtles. At the slightest sound they raise their heads from the crust of ice and look about them with the piercing eyes of their searchlights, sweeping the frozen surface of the sea with furious bursts of machine-gun fire. He told me also that the Russian sailors are courageous, but too " pre-occupied " with technicalities. (He meant embarrassed by their very technical specialization. That Finnish soldier was a worker, and his interest was naturally aroused by questions of a technical order, such as that of the embarrassment produced by his own specialization in a worker who is compelled to perform unfamiliar tasks.) They move about the ice, about that limitless expanse of ice, as if they were still on the deck of a battleship. They seem concerned lest they should interfere with the operation of the guns and of all the complicated machinery of their ship. They are too much a part of their ship to be able to wage a war of patrols on the surface of the sea. Such a war puts a premium on personal initiative. Not only is it, in the fullest sense, a war of movement, a war of manoeuvre, but at the same time it calls for team-work of the highest order.

The soldier with whom I talked was a young man of about thirty. Before the war he had worked in a cellulose factory at Hämeenlinna, in the interior of Finland. (I discerned in his speech, in his gestures, in his calm, severe expression, in his honest, direct gaze, that special quality which characterizes all Finns, to whatever class of society they belong : a quality that is the reflection of a shining tradition of self-government, social organization and technical progress.) When he spoke of the workers and the soldiers of the U.S.S.R. his voice trembled with a kind of bitter, virile regret, as if he despised his adversaries for proclaiming themselves Communists, for blindly accepting the doctrines of Marx and Lenin, and at the same time for failing utterly to appreciate the benefits which the Finnish people has secured for itself through its social organization.

" Finland," he said, " is not a nation of capitalists. It is a nation of workers." As always, as for every Finnish worker, the problem was for him a problem of conscience—of social conscience. And, as I talked with that soldier in the *Lottala* at Terijoki, I became aware for the first time of what lies at the root of Finland's war against the U.S.S.R. : her people's consciousness that they are fighting to defend not only their national territory, but their social achievements, their labour organizations, their dignity and freedom as workers.

After a little while we left the hut and began walking along the shore. A few hundred yards beyond the barbed-wire entanglements there occurred the other night a clash of patrols. We set off towards the scene of the encounter, picking our way carefully between the wooden stakes that mark the limits of the minefields. The ice was littered with weapons and broken skis, with caps, hoods, and fur-gauntlets—all that remained of a patrol of twenty sailors from Kronshtadt, who, perhaps, had lost themselves in the storm, or else had deluded themselves that they could take the Finnish sentries by surprise. I picked up the cap of a Russian sailor with the two blue ribbons still dangling from the back. The band showing the name of the ship had been removed, undoubtedly by the sailor himself before he went out on patrol. How pathetic they are, those miserable remains that one finds abandoned on the frozen surface of the sea. They are like relics of the shipwreck of an Arctic expedition, thrown up after many years on to the polar ice-bank : unexpected, tragic evidence of a disaster of long ago.

While we were on our way back it started to snow. Soon the landscape was obscured. In the soft light reflected from the snow the smallest details, the minutest objects, even the cracks in the ice, were revealed with extraordinary precision, as if magnified by a lens. (The abandoned shoe, the broken ski, the match-box with the hammer and sickle on the label, the imprint of a Lappish boot, the clotted mass of bandages black with blood entangled in the barbed wire; and, on the shore, beside his weapon, the machine-gunner, smoking placidly, his eyes half-closed, his teeth clenched, his mouth contorted.) Groups of skiers—*sissit*—smilingly saluted us as they passed us on the road. The muffled voice of the heavy naval guns of Kronshtadt reached us from across the gulf. Gradually the tempo of the bombardment quickened, gradually the sound of the explosions came nearer. The shells dropped now here, now there in the wood that surrounds Terijoki. And the air trembled, as if the mouths of the guns of Kronshtadt were uttering secret, mysterious words of infinite delicacy and purity.

XXV

THE BLOOD OF THE WORKERS

Byelostrov, April.

FROM Terijoki I had returned in the late evening to Alexandrovka, and I was sleeping in the *korsu* that constitutes Sector Headquarters when suddenly the dull roar of a violent artillery bombardment arose from the direction of Leningrad. It was two in the morning. I jumped out of my camp-bed and went outside.

The storm had ceased, the sky was clear again, a first glimmer of moonlight gilded the vast expanse of the forests of Karelia and the shining white carpet of snow. The whole of the sky above the south-western suburbs of the city was brilliantly illuminated by fires. The bombardment was heaviest in the Uritski district, in the region of the Putilov Steelworks, the Kirov Foundries, the October 25th Metallurgical Institute and the Voroshilov Smelting Works. From the trenches outside Alexandrovka the water-front of Terijoki, situated away to our right, directly opposite Kronshtadt (from here it is only a few miles as the crow flies to Terijoki), is not visible, being concealed from view by the slight rise in the ground on which stands the residential quarter of Alexandrovka. But the sky above the city was a rich copper colour, traversed by long black vertical streaks—undoubtedly columns of smoke.

The long-range artillery of the Baltic Fleet (amid the formidable chorus one distinguished clearly the voices of the heavy guns of the two biggest Soviet battleships, the *Marat* and the *October Revolution*) replied to the German mortar-fire with a violent counter-bombardment, which became more intense and more furious every minute. The cupola of Alexandrovka's church stood out in sharp, clear outline against that sky of molten copper. It was an impressive sight, of a wild, naked, violent beauty, to which the profound silence that brooded over the Finnish trenches afforded a striking contrast.

The soldiers moved about me noiselessly, talking among themselves in low voices. I heard only the light hissing sound of skis on the snow, the snorting of the horses tethered in the woods, the sharp creak of the breech-blocks as the artillerymen loaded their guns so that they might be ready to put up a barrage at a moment's notice in the event of an enemy attack. But the Soviet positions, a few hundred yards to our front, were also plunged in the most profound silence.

Not a voice, not a rifle shot broke the stillness—not even that vague hubbub, that medley of sharp, metallic sounds (the banging of rifle-butts against mess-tins, boxes of ammunition and corrugated iron), which tells of uneasiness, of uncertainty, of anxious waiting, of last-minute preparations. No doubt the Soviet infantry too were at that moment peering over the back of their trenches at the city, gazing at the fearful spectacle of the bombardment. At intervals clouds of red sparks rose from the Uritski district like huge swarms of fireflies, while from time to time columns of smoke would suddenly shoot high into the air, to fall back upon themselves a moment later like enormous water-spouts.

The bombardment of a city is not even remotely comparable, in its terrible effects, to that of a line of trenches. Although the houses consist of dead, inert matter, the bombardment seems to imbue them with a violent life, with a formidable vitality. The roar of the explosions, within the walls of the houses and mansions, in the streets and the deserted squares, echoes like a hoarse, continuous, terrifying scream. One has the impression that the houses themselves are screaming with terror, dancing up and down and writhing amid the flames, before finally collapsing in a heap of blazing ruins.

In a passage listing the alleged characteristics of Castruccio

Castracane, Seigneur of Lucca, which occurs near the end of Machiavelli's *Life of Castruccio,* there is an image subsequently appropriated by Pirandello. It is an image of " houses that would rush in terror out of their own doors if they felt that an earthquake was imminent ". In my still drowsy mind, pervaded by the horror of that scene, the image of the houses and factories of the Uritski district rushing with panic-stricken yells out of their own doors—half-naked, hair streaming in the whirlwind of smoke and cinders, eyes staring, mouths gaping, hands clasped to their temples—amid the roar of the explosions, amid the purple reflections of the fires, superimposed itself on the no less striking image of the Russian soldiers, standing motionless in their trenches a few hundred yards to our front, their faces turned towards the martyred city.

For us who are not imprisoned within the vast cage of the siege, for those who, like us, are able to watch the tragedy from afar, the agony of Leningrad can no longer be anything but a terrible spectacle. A spectacle, and nothing more. The tragedy of this city is so enormous, it has attained such superhuman proportions, that one feels incapable of participating in it at all, save with one's eyes. There is no Christian emotion, no pity, no compassion great and deep enough to comprehend this tragedy. It partakes of the nature of certain scenes in Aeschylus and Shakespeare: the mind of the spectator reels before so much appalling violence as before a spectacle that is not human, that is outside the realm of nature and humanity, that is extraneous to the very history of human affairs.

And it is extraordinary how the Communists, who are directly involved in this tragedy, who are actually living through it, contrive to regard it as a normal human experience, as an expression of their doctrine, of their logic, of their life. For there emerges from the statements of all the prisoners and all the deserters (among them a score of Spanish Communists who fled to Russia after the collapse of Red Spain and were captured some days ago on this front) one definite and indisputable fact: that the tragedy of Leningrad is to the

Communist mind a wholly natural and logical episode in the class-struggle, in which all play their parts with inflexible determination, and without the slightest feeling of revulsion.

The human type created by Communism has always interested me greatly. What has impressed me most during my visits to Soviet Russia has been not so much the social and technical achievements, not so much the outward form, as it were, of this collective society, as its internal, spiritual elements, as the type " man," the " man-machine " evolved in the course of some twenty years of Marxist discipline, of Stakanovism, of Leninist intransigence. I have been struck by the moral violence of the Communists, by their preoccupation with theory, by their indifference to pain and death. (I refer, of course, to the out-and-out Communists, the true-blue Communists, not to that numberless class of officials of the Party and of the trade-union organizations, of employees of the State and of the industrial and agricultural trusts, who keep alive in Russia, under the cloak of new names and new methods, the weaknesses, the egoism, the chicanery—in a word, the characteristic *Oblomovchina*—of the old petty *bourgeoisie*.)

" My mission in life is to combat Oblomov," wrote Lenin. Oblomov is the hero of the famous novel of Goncharov who epitomizes the laziness, the indolence, the fatalism of the Russian *bourgeoisie*—in short, all those qualities which are summed up in the word *Oblomovchina*. The Communists who are defending Leningrad are made of very different stuff from the countless Oblomovs of the Party and the State. They are the extremists, the fanatics, the hard core. The people of Europe have only the vaguest notion of the lengths to which the inexorable fanaticism of the true-blue Communist can go.

For some days now the commando brigades of workers and sailors have been bleeding themselves white in a series of furious assaults on the sector of the German battle-line which extends from Schlüsselburg to Peterhof. The bombardment that is turning the sky above the city the colour of copper is the result of a German standing barrage designed to cut off the shock-detachments of workers from their base. It is a very hard struggle, and the Soviet losses are appalling. The commando brigades are trying to break the ring of steel, or at any rate are hoping to disrupt the German formations and so to delay the spring offensive. The main body of the attacking infantry is composed of elements of the regular forces, of the Red Army : but the nerve and sinew of the commando units consist of workers and sailors. It is a massacre of specialists, of *Stakanovtsi,* of technicians—the cream of the labour force of Soviet Russia.

When one considers the back-breaking effort, the perseverance, the sacrifices, the years and years of technical selection that are required to turn a simple peasant, a builder's labourer, a navvy, in fact a worker of any kind, into a skilled craftsman, a specialist, a " technician " in the true sense, in the modern sense of the word, one is horrified at the thought of this wholesale slaughter of workers, of the best workers in the U.S.S.R. The capital of the Revolution, the Soviet " Mountain," the international " Commune," is not Moscow but Leningrad. And it is here in Leningrad, more than on any other sector of the vast Russian Front, that the workers are fighting and dying in defence of the Revolution.

XXVI

A GRAVE IN THE SUBURBS OF LENINGRAD

Kuokkala, opposite Kronshtadt, April.

LAST year, during the Jugoslav campaign, I spent Easter among the Turkish residents of the island of Ada Kale, situated in the middle of the Danube, whither I had gone in order to witness the forcing of the Iron Gates. The German shock-troops had crossed the river, taking the Serbian bank by storm; and I had remained on the island, waiting for a boat to ferry me across to the Rumanian shore. It was a warm, bright Sunday, but my heart was filled with sadness as I wandered through the midst of those crowds of honest Turks, along streets heavy with the greasy smell of the *rahat-lokum* displayed in the windows of the hundred squalid little confectioners' shops and with the delicious aroma of that light-coloured tobacco which in Eastern countries is known as Sultan's Beard. There was little food to be had on Ada Kale during those war-time days; and I was forced to content myself with two tins of *rahat-lokum* and a few cups of coffee.

This year, by contrast, I spent a happy Easter among the Finnish troops stationed in the trenches of Terijoki, Kellomäki and Kuokkala, in the Kronshtadt sector. And for the first time since my arrival on the Leningrad Front the sky was absolutely clear. Not a single cloud, not the lightest veil of mist obscured that infinite expanse of burnished blue.

I had passed the night in the villa which is now the head-quarters of the Kellomäki Sector Command, and which before the Revolution belonged to a noble family from St. Petersburg.

Unlike most of the villas that grace this elegant " lung " of the Tsarist capital, this one is built not of the wood of birch-trees and Arctic pines but of bricks and stone. The interior is decorated in that luxurious, bizarre, frivolous, and withal comical bad taste which characterizes Russian houses of the second half of the last century, a taste which, unlike that of Italy, France and Germany, underwent no radical change at the beginning of the twentieth century, but remained unaltered, stopping in its tracks, as it were, on the threshold of our own age, and making hardly the smallest concession to the grace and coquetry of the newly-invented " floral " style. The walls of imitation marble, the stucco columns with the gilded capitals, the large, extremely high stoves of white majolica with the neo-classical bas-reliefs (Minervas with golden helmets, two-headed eagles, coronets bearing strange monograms, green and blue enamel coats of arms, and naked angels, of the kind that I would call, in Russian, *byespartinye,* that is, " politically neutral "), had combined to procure for me the sweetest sleep I had enjoyed since the end of February.

I had been dead tired that night, after a gruelling day on the Alexandrovka Front, whither I had accompanied my friend Count de Foxá, Spanish Minister in Helsinki, who had come up here to interview a group of Spanish Reds captured by the Finns. They had prepared a makeshift bed for us on the green baize top of an immense billiard-table with enormous spiral legs like the cupolas of Vasili Blayenni in the Red Square in Moscow. Stretched out beside the Spanish Minister, I had allowed my thoughts to dwell on those Minervas, on those eagles, on those coats of arms, on those gilded capitals, and on the happy, tragic life of the Tsarist nobility.

The villa that is the headquarters of the Kellomäki Sector Command is barely two hundred yards from the front line. All night long the machine-guns had sung the chorus of the frogs in Aristophanes; the Soviet patrols had vainly probed the Finnish lines at a number of points; the guns of Totleben had periodically shelled the road to Kuokkala. But neither the stutter of the machine-guns nor the roar of the medium artillery had succeeded in rousing us from our slumbers. At about seven in the morning we had been awakened by the joyous shouts of " *Hyvää Pääsiäistä*!—Happy Easter!" which the Finnish Staff-officers were exchanging among themselves. Major L— (whom everyone calls by his nickname " Vippa ") had come to offer us his good wishes, at the same time bringing us two large glasses brimful of cognac. And our heads were swimming when, accompanied by Captain Leppo and Lieutenants Svardström and Kurjensaari, we set out for Kuokkala, to " wish old Repin a happy Easter." (Count de Foxá is a poet of the most refined modern taste, a man of exquisite culture; and he knew very well what I meant by the phrase " to wish old Repin a happy Easter.")

And so we set off on foot along the sea-shore, following the line of the trenches. Near the *korsut* carved out of the ice soldiers stripped to the waist were shaving in front of small mirrors suspended from the tree-trunks or resting in the breeches of the anti-tank guns, and as we passed they raised their lathered faces and courteously wished us " *Hyvää Pääsiäistä*!" Packs of dogs with unkempt grey coats, the dogs of the *sissit* and the artillerymen, ran along the ice beside the barbed wire, barking; and already Corinthian columns of white smoke were rising from the chimney-pots of the *Lottalat*, announcing to the soldiers that their tea was ready. It was Easter Day—a day of glorious sunshine and radiant happiness. And the happiness was universal, the sunlight sparkled on the armour-plating of ice that covered the sea, on the copper boxes filled with anti-aircraft shells, on the barrels of the machine-guns. A distant hum was audible in the clear blue sky, the white puffs of smoke from the A.A. shells marked the course of three Soviet planes whose wings glittered like silver in the sunshine. Even the sense of danger, even the atmosphere of war, were dispelled by the warmth of the spring sun.

After an hour and a half's walk we reached Kuokkala, the favourite seaside resort of Russian artists of the generation of Turgeniev, of Chaikovsky, of Chekhov, of Andreyev. They had told me that Repin, the greatest of Russian painters, lay buried at Kuokkala, in the grounds of his villa. Captain Leppo, who knew Repin when he was alive, had promised to take me there to wish the good old Ilya Efimovich " a happy Easter." From time to time it is well to open a window in the smooth, solid wall of war, and to gaze through it at the secret country, at the serene, pure world that each one of us carries within him. It is well to open that window even if it overlooks a tomb, even if it gives on the world of the dead. In the midst of this hard, inexorable social war I felt that by spending an hour in the company of Repin, of the grand old man stretched out in his grave within range of the guns of Kronshtadt, I should be discharging a duty not to Repin only, but to myself.

Repin's villa stands a few yards from the sea-shore, in the middle of a large park thick with black firs, copper-coloured pines and silver birches. It is a wooden structure, conforming to that strange Russian style of the earliest years of this century which adumbrates Bakst's settings for the ballets of Diaghilev : a great house, full of friezes and fluted pillars, of recesses and sharp corners, of large, horseshoe windows, of balconies let into its outer walls. The roof is surmounted not by the usual dome, but by a lofty pyramid of tree-trunks. An " orthodox " design, I would call it, in the sense in which Russians use the word *pravoslavnaya*. And it is the house of a rare and whimsical spirit, the house of an artist—but of a Russian artist, indissolubly linked to his age and to the destiny of his generation. During their brief occupation of Kuokkala in 1940-41 the Bolsheviks fixed a wooden tablet to the façade, with the following epigraph inscribed upon it in letters of fire : " In this house lived Ilya Efimovich Repin, the great Russian painter : born 1844, died 1930."

We go inside. And at once, as soon as we enter the hall, a strange " interior " greets us, unfolding its intimate perspectives before our eyes, displaying the grace of its whimsical, elegant *décor,* of the carved wooden frames that surround its windows and doors, of its massive stove of white majolica. From the hall we pass into a room lit by spacious windows, where, beneath a brass chandelier with painted porcelain lamp-globes, we find a table with enormous feet, fashioned in the likeness of a lion's feet complete with claws : a sad, solemn sight. The faded, tattered curtains still hang from the windows, the dusty remnants of frayed, discoloured Persian carpets still cover the floor. In a corner of the room sleeps a chair with rounded legs and dainty little feet. The feet are human in form; they look like women's feet. (It is extraordinary what an impression this bizarre furniture makes upon me. Despite its age, it is astonishingly reminiscent of the surrealist furniture of Salvador Dali, of the sculptures of Giacometti, of the plastic creations of Archipenko, of the tables and chairs with women's legs, the chair-backs embellished with carvings of young breasts, and the armchairs resembling seated girls, which characterize—I will not say adorn—Hugo's settings for Cocteau's *Orphée,* the interiors of the surrealist painters, the photographs of Max Ernst. Those features which surrealism has borrowed from the taste of the *fin de siècle* Europe of the last years of Queen Victoria, and from that of the precious, bourgeois age of Fallières, D'Annunzio, and Jean Lorrain, represent an inheritance which not even Salvador Dali can ignore : and it is singularly gratifying to find in the house of Repin, situated in this suburb of Leningrad, within range of the guns of Kronshtadt, these archetypes of the most bizarre and Freudian forms of modern surrealist furniture.)

Ilya Efimovich Repin was undoubtedly the greatest Russian painter yet born. It is true that, in comparison with Western painting, that of Repin possesses a traditional rather than an artistic significance. Yet it still belongs to the age of Tolstoy, Dostoievsky, and Mussorgsky, and it evokes—even in its most Parisian extravagances, even in its imitations of Goya, even in its sophisticated elegance—the essential spirit and temper of that age, with its undertone of bitter, cruel sadness. I recall that when I stood before his pictures in the art-galleries of Moscow and Leningrad I was surprised, almost saddened, by his exclusive preoccupation with his own age, with the destiny of his own generation and of his own countrymen. It seemed to me that in him the tragedy of Russia was " discounted " in advance, that he had in his painting already solved, perhaps with excessive ease, the most complex and most dramatic problems of his own age and of the age that followed. I would describe him, in a phrase, as a sort of Keyserling, a sort of Berdyaev of painting.

It is possible that his greatness, the most genuine manifestation of his character and his art, consists in fact in this apparent moral facility. (And yet, to him—as to so many others, among them Leonid Andreyev himself—the Communist revolution of October, 1917, and the collapse of the Empire, and the great suffering of his countrymen, came as a most grievous shock, as a sudden rude awakening. It seemed that until then Repin had understood nothing of the destiny of his generation. He fled from St. Petersburg, he took refuge at Kuokkala, situated in Finnish territory, hardly more than a mile or two from the new Russian frontier, where two months before Lenin had sought shelter when he was on the run from Kerensky's police. He would never again return into the midst of his own people; nor could he find it in his heart to cut himself off from them completely. Eventually he died here, in his wooden house; and now he sleeps in the shade of the trees that grow in his park, within range of the Soviet batteries of Totleben.)

We enter a great hall, and pause in front of a tall, dusty mirror. Nothing could be more impressive than that dead mirror standing intact in the great ice-cold hall. Painted on the glass, whose surface has become blurred and corroded with the passage of the years, are a number of delicate, pale flowers, pink, yellow, green and purple in colour. Those spectral flowers (it is natural that I should think of *The Spectre of the Rose*) are the handiwork of Repin himself; and they have, in this hour, in this place, in these circumstances, a magically evocative quality that is quite extraordinary.

If I take up a position alongside the mirror—sitting on the low, spacious divan with no back and no arm-rests that stands beneath the mirror, close to the stairs—I can see the image of the room reflected obliquely in the blurred glass, behind the pale, spectral shadows of the flowers; I can see the oil-lamp hanging from the ceiling, the great majolica stove adorned with green and blue enamel plaques showing scenes from history, the *tsakuski* table designed and constructed by Repin himself (it is a circular table with a wheel in the centre which rotates at the slightest touch), the furniture decorated with bizarre floral designs, the frayed and faded tapestries, and, through the windows, the trees of the park, the yellow patches of sunlight gleaming amid the transparent whiteness of the snow, the pale sky of delicate blue parchment. From the far end of the room, from a wall half in shadow, I see slowly emerging, as from the blue dust of an antique night, the head of Aesop painted by Velasquez, the original of which hangs in the Muso del Prado in Madrid.

Next we climb a wooden staircase to the upper floor and enter Repin's studio. In the cold, clear, zenithal light that pours down through the *abat-jour* I see two chalk death-masks, resting on brackets set half-way up the wall. One I recognize as the mask of Peter the Great, with his bovine eyes, his arrogant moustache, his thick lips, his vulgar nose, his hard, obstinate brow. The other I am unable to identify; and I should perhaps be wrong if I were to say that it was Gogol's. Almost hidden behind the massive majolica stove, wedged between the stove and the wall, is a chalk statue. It is a likeness of a young woman, by Paul Trubetskoy. In the full sleeves, the ornate hair-style, the gesture of the hand pressed to the cheek, the set of the shoulders, the noble, scarcely furrowed brow, there is all the Milanese grace of the earlier Trubetskoy. That magical feminine presence, in the empty house poised precariously on the edge of the war as on a window-sill, moves me strangely. ('It is an inscrutable presence—the image of a woman with a mysterious, unpronounceable name.)

I remain alone for a few minutes in the painter's studio. In that clear, cold light I try to walk with slow, deliberate steps, as if my eyes were blindfolded. (The war taps with soft fingers on the window-panes; the sound is like a distant drumming, like the mutter of distant thunder.) A serene orderliness, a precise harmony still prevails within these bare walls : it is a reflection of the spirit of a great artist, stamped indelibly on these inanimate objects, on this tableau of man-made things. From time to time a sound, a voice, a creak imbues the dead silence with a living quality.

After a while I begin to find this strange silence disturbing, oppressive. It is a stealthy, almost menacing silence. I press my forehead against a window-pane and gaze at the coastline of Kronshtadt, high and white as the cliffs of Dover, at the great green cupola of the cathedral, at the oil-tanks, at the smoke rising from the arsenal. Totleben is there—very close, a little to my left, its steep sides riddled with the embrasures of its casemates. Ever and again a brief whistle, sharp as a razor, cuts the shafts of sunlight reflected from the sea's armour-plating of ice. The shells fall in the depths of the wood that rises on the outskirts of Kuokkala; the sound of the explosions spreads softly, like a wave, among the tree-trunks. Convoys of sledges, groups of skiers, pass along the road. A piece of plaster comes away from the cornice of the white majolica stove. It lands on the wooden floor with a thud. Repin's house is dying, little by little, piece by piece.

I almost run out of the studio, and before I realize it I am looking out on to the *terrazza* where Repin used to sleep. This was the painter's " bedroom " : an open veranda, surrounded by a balustrade of carved wooden pillars. In all his life, in all his eighty-six years of existence, Repin never slept indoors. Even when he travelled—to Paris, to Berlin, to Vienna—he used to drag his bed out on to the balcony. In the depths of the Russian winter, with the temperature anything from twenty to forty degrees below zero, he would sleep in the open on his rough couch : not a bed in the proper sense of the word, but a kind of divan. He slept, one might say, stretched out on the edge of the horizon. He had a horror of confinement, a hysterical fear of being shut in. (This, incidentally, is a typically Russian phobia. The people of Russia are like a bird that has swallowed its cage. Their characteristic craving to escape, their horror of confinement, is merely the inverse of their love for their prison : it is a craving to spew up the prison

8*

that is within them, not to escape from it. It is of this conflict that the *shirokaya natura,* or soul, of the Russian people is compounded.)

I hear the voice of Count de Foxá calling me from the park. " Let's go and look for Repin's grave !" he shouts. We set off into the midst of the trees, sinking knee-deep into the snow. The grave will be somewhere here, surmounted, probably, by a large, plain cross. For several minutes we wander about the wood without finding any trace of it. Then, at last, in a kind of clearing, right at the end of the park, I catch sight of something that looks like a mound. That, surely, is the grave. The cross is no longer there; the Bolsheviks have removed it and, in accordance with their custom, have erected on the mound a wooden pillar, on which are inscribed, in letters of fire, the name of Repin, his date of birth—1844—and the year of his death—1930. It seems as though he had been dead a hundred years, so legendary is his world, so remote his age. He was a contemporary of the Russian master-spirits of the nineteenth century. He survived Tolstoy, Dostoievsky, Turgeniev, Mussorgsky. He even survived himself. He died in a foreign land, an exile not so much from his country as from his age, from his world. (His true grave is not here, amid the trees of his park, beneath the wooden pillar erected by the Bolsheviks. He is buried in the mirror, in that magic mirror, blurred and corroded by the years, beneath the pale, spectral shadows of the flowers which he painted as a young man, beneath the spectres of those spring flowers.)

We stand before the snow-covered mound with bowed heads, and I call aloud to Repin, I give him the Easter greeting of the Russians : " *Khristos voskryesye !*—Christ is risen !" De Foxá responds in a low voice : " *Voistinu voskryesye !*—Verily He is risen !" The cannon thunders beyond the trees, from somewhere behind the last houses of Kuokkala comes the muffled rataplan of a machine-gun. And yet there is no human voice capable of dispelling the silence of this grave.

We turn back, and once again I enter the deserted house, once again I climb those winding staircases, open ten, maybe twenty doors, lose myself in that labyrinth of bare rooms and corridors. All the madness (all the hesitancy, all the inquietude) of the Russian soul is in this house, which is like a *boîte à surprises*. I feel that at any moment, as I push open a door, some hidden spring will set off a peal of bells. The house seems specially made for magical evocations, for the diversion of ghosts and invisible presences.

I sit down for a moment on the divan that stands beneath the mirror; and suddenly, on the floor, between the divan and the wall, I catch sight of a heap of small rolls of some glossy black material. They are old photographic negatives. I unwind the small, dusty rolls one by one. And now Repin is before me in the flesh, I see him emerge—tall, thin, elegant—from the narrow, gleaming black mirror of the film. There he is in St. Petersburg, in Paris, at Kuokkala. There he is outside the Trocadero. There he is, standing beside a Greek amphora in a park designed by Le Nôtre. There he is, riding on a sledge through the streets of Kuokkala. There he is in the doorway of his house. And that gracious figure of a woman at his side is without a doubt the dear companion of his life, of his exile. Those images from a past age, those spectral images, disturb me profoundly, inspire me with a kind of affectionate fear. It is as if I were actually witnessing Repin's resurrection from the dead. As I gaze at those photographs his presence, until now invisible, becomes alive and concrete, assumes a human form.

I close my eyes, and even as I do so I hear a footstep in the house. It is a light, soft, almost airy step—as soft and light as a caress. Even thus do the dead walk in deserted houses.

XXVII

ANGELS, MEN AND BEASTS IN THE FORESTS OF LAKE LADOGA

Raikkola Forest, East of Leningrad, April.

EVER since my arrival on these southern shores of Lake Ladoga, situated at the north-eastern tip of the Karelian Isthmus, which is to say at the extreme left of the siege-front, I have felt as if I had come here for the purpose of attacking the defenders of Leningrad in the rear.

For the end of the long line of trenches that extends from mighty Lake Ladoga, greatest of European lakes (the Russians call it " the Caspian of Europe "), westwards to Alexandrovka and Terijoki, terminating at a point directly opposite Kronshtadt, is situated much farther forward, much farther east than the rest of the front, with the result that it can truly be said to threaten the beleaguered city in the rear.

In fact, the trenches of Byelostrov, Alexandrovka and Terijoki overlook the western suburbs of Leningrad—that is to say, the district of The Islands, which the Russians call *Ostrova,* the suburbs of Vassilyostrovski and Kirov, the edge of the suburb of Petrovski (which forms part of the original city founded by Peter the Great), the Decembrist quarter, and the port of Leningrad, which stands at the mouth of the Bolshaya Neva, the largest and southernmost of the three arms of the great river. From here, from the trenches of Lake Ladoga and from Raikkola Forest, one looks out on to the suburb of Viborgski (that same suburb where Lenin lay in hiding during the days that immediately preceded the October Revolution) and on to

that vast expanse of waste land which adjoins the suburbs of
Krasnovgardyeiski, or " Quarter of the Red Guards," Pisca-
revka, Ribalskaya, situated on the banks of the Bolshaya Okta,
Nargolov, and Shuvalovo, merging imperceptibly into the
forests and marshes that lie to the east of the city.

Whereas the industrial suburbs of the south-west, which contain some of the largest and most important smelting works in
the entire Soviet Union, are inhabited by the great mass of the
workers, the northern suburbs have a mixed population, comprising perhaps the poorest section of the community—for the
most part labourers, market-gardeners, fishermen and artisans.
I know these northern districts well, having visited them
several times when I was engaged in writing the early
chapters of my *Technique du coup d'État* and in making notes
for my *Bonhomme Lénine*.

The little house in the suburb of Viborgski where Lenin
lived in hiding for several days in October, 1917, right on the
eve of the Communist insurrection (he had recently returned
from Finland, from Kuokkala and Rasliv, where, following the
arrest of Trotsky and the other leaders of the abortive rising
of July, he had spent the summer months with Zinoviev in a
hut hidden away in the woods that rise near the shore of
Rasliv's little lake), is a modest structure of wood and grey
bricks, a working-class cottage surrounded by a little garden
overrun by weeds. It contains only a few rooms—poor, bare
rooms, with whitewashed walls. It was, I recall, in this house
that I saw for the first time, hanging from the wall in a rough
wooden frame, the photograph of Lenin disguised as a workman. In this truly impressive portrait, which figures among the
illustrations of my book *Bonhomme Lénine,* Lenin appears
dressed as a mechanic : he has shaved off his moustache and
beard, he has a cap with a leather peak jammed down over
his forehead, he is wearing a shirt without a collar and a
patched jacket. In that clumsy disguise, the sight of which
made Trotsky laugh and Dan and Skobelyev turn pale when
he appeared in it at the Smolny Institute on the evening of
October 25th, 1917—the evening of the insurrection—Lenin

succeeded in evading the clutches of Kerensky's police and in remaining undisturbed in his hide-out in the suburb of Viborgski, where he drafted his famous " points " on the impending revolution.

All these things were in my mind the other day, as I drove from the Terijoki Front, on the shores of the Gulf of Finland, all the way across the Karelian Isthmus to the Raikkola Front, on the shores of Lake Ladoga. In the course of my journey I passed through the vast forest of Tappari—a wild, impenetrable region, unspeakably dreary, solemn and severe, extending from the banks of the River Vuoksi, through the woods of Raikkola, down to the tree-covered marshes of Lumisuo. It was snowing at the time, and in my imagination the trees on either side of the road formed as it were the two high walls of a prison-corridor. Flocks of crows flew cawing overhead, skimming the tops of the firs and the Arctic pines, whose trunks were covered with a copper-coloured rind. Enormous lumps of red granite, the famous granite of Karelia, glittered here and there amid the dense undergrowth of the forest; they were exactly like heliographs, transmitting signals against the chequered background of the trees and snow. For the first time in my life —far more than in the jungle of Jimma, in Ethiopia—I " felt " all the horror of the forest.

How different is this Ladoga Front from that of Alexandrovka and Terijoki! From the trenches of Alexandrovka and Terijoki one can already smell the suburbs of Leningrad : the houses, the roads, the post-and-rail fences that surround the gardens of the villas, the telegraph-poles, the pillar-boxes painted light blue, the shop-signs, the very air itself are already impregnated with the odour of smoke, gas, coal, and asphalt, they already have the colour of the city, they already have the typical atmosphere of the outskirts of a great metropolis. It is a human smell that assails the nostrils at Kuokkala, at Alexandrovka, at Byelostrov.

But here, on the Ladoga Front, the contrast is complete. Hidden from view as it is by the vast forests of Karelia, which extend to the very edge of its north-eastern suburbs, the city's

presence is not so much felt as divined. It is, none the less, a
living presence: a mute presence lurking behind the high,
compact wall of the forest. One seems almost to hear the
laboured breathing of the martyred city. But the protagonist
of the drama on this front is the forest. Savage and ruthless, it
dominates, devours, crushes everything. Here the smell of man
gives way to the much stronger smell, at once pungent and
sweet, the thin, cold smell of the foliage, of the inextricably
tangled branches, of the colonnades of red, white, and black
tree-trunks.

Ever since our arrival in the vicinity of the River Vuoksi the
harsh, violent breath of the immense forest of Raikkola, rushing
to meet me beneath a canopy of low clouds (the storm was
raising whirlwinds of snow on the horizon), had filled me with
dismay. It was a sombre greeting, an ominous warning. I felt
somehow bewildered, I was seized with a terror which at first
I could not explain. And now, to jerk me out of my bewilderment, three Soviet aircraft, piercing the low ceiling of dense
grey clouds, suddenly appeared away to my right, almost
behind me, from the direction of the village of Sakkola. Their
metallic hum, the opaque silvery reflections of their aluminium
wings, were a harsh and unexpected reminder of human
realities that brought me back to earth with a jolt, giving me
back the consciousness, the measure of my mortality.

Confronted with the hostile force of nature, confronted with
that violence and cruelty which the forest—far more than the
sea or the highest mountain—expresses with an agonizing
intensity, men, even when they are at war one with another,
can find no help, no peace, no security save in the realization
of their common humanity. Sometimes this may prove to be a
tragic illusion. Now, in fact, it was a snare, an ambush laid for
me by my own bewilderment: for when, some hours later, I
plunged into the heart of the great forest, it was borne in upon
me that nothing makes men so mutually hostile, nothing has
such a power to arouse them and to bring them into conflict,
nothing renders them so callous and inexorable, as the preternatural violence of the forest. In the forest man rediscovers his

primordial instincts. His most primitive animal impulses return to the surface, break through the delicate tracery of his nerves, reappear outside his veneer of civilized conventions and inhibitions in all their exquisite and squalid virginity.

The unexpected appearance of the Soviet aircraft (that gentle hum above the bleak landscape, that solitary voice in the sky) made me look around instinctively for some sign of my fellow men, for those evidences of humanity, those manifestations of human life, which would set a term or limit to my inward perturbation.

The first human image that emerged from that cold, bare, elemental scene was extraordinary beyond belief. Like two demons lying in ambush, like two " black angels " expelled from heaven by an irate Divinity, like two miserable, pitiful Lucifers, the bodies of two Soviet parachutists dangled side by side from the branches of two fir-trees. A party of Finnish soldiers was bringing up ladders and various implements with which to take down the bodies and bury them.

The two miserable corpses hung from the trees like twin sacks. (There was, however, nothing in the least macabre about the spectacle.) The bodies of the dead Russians could be sensed rather than seen through the rents in their heavy flying-suits —padded suits that looked almost like quilts made in the form of men. Through the tears in those padded quilts, which reminded me of the costume worn by baseball players, there showed not the khaki of Soviet battledress but the steel-grey of Finnish uniforms, torn in many places. Within those shapeless sacks the bodies of two men hung limply, arms dangling, heads slumped on their shoulders. Their frozen faces were of that livid colour which characterizes the faces of men numbed by cold. There they were, suspended from the branches : the bullets of the Finnish *sissit,* who search the woods night and day for parachutists, had struck them even as they descended from the sky. (Nearly every day Soviet aircraft drop groups of parachutists on to the Finnish lines of communication, many of them wearing Finnish uniforms to deceive the enemy.) There was, I repeat, nothing repulsive about the spectacle. It resembled one of those scenes portrayed by the Italian primitives, in which the figurations of "black angels," of demons, were calculated to inspire the beholder with a feeling of religious horror. And, indeed, it was a feeling of religious horror that I experienced now: as if there had appeared before my eyes concrete evidence of the wrath of God, the last scene of a drama enacted in some exalted, superhuman realm, the epilogue to a tragedy of pride, to a betrayal, to a revolt of "black angels." I think that William Blake, in his visions of hell, never saw anything so grandiosely terrible, so purely biblical as this: not even when he depicted his angels roosting in the branches of a tree, as in that drawing for *The Marriage of Heaven and Hell* which is in the Tate Gallery in London.

One of the poor corpses had shed a shoe, which lay in the snow at the foot of the tree. It was extraordinarily alive and real, that solitary shoe at the foot of the tree, that empty shoe of stiff, frozen leather, that sad, bewildered, terrified shoe, which could no longer walk, which could not escape. A shoe— I would say after the manner of Poe—which "looked up" with a terrified air, with something animal in its expression: like a dog that looks up at its master, imploring his help or protection.

I walked across to the two trees. The "fallen angels" were too far off the ground for me to be able to touch them. One of them was clutching something bright in his hand. It was a large pistol of a well-known Russian make—a *nagan*. Scattered all around in the snow were a number of cartridge-cases. The soldiers told me that as he descended from the sky the man had fired continuously, at the same time uttering ferocious yells. At the top of the two fir-trees the white umbrellas of the parachutes enveloped the great branches like two huge dead wings. A squirrel hopped about on the snow a few yards from me, fixing me with its small bright eyes. Crows flew cawing above the tops of the fir-trees; every so often I heard a rushing sound in the distance as they dived to earth. All around a stern silence reigned, cold and transparent as a block of crystal. Meanwhile, the soldiers had propped the ladders against the two trees and were already starting to climb them. (A sinister, pitiful " deposition from the Cross.")

As I approach the bank of the River Vuoksi the signs of humanity become more frequent, more specific, amid the immense, impassive violence of the forest. I encounter traces of the furious battle that has raged for many months in these boundless woods : broken rifles, abandoned machine-guns, steel helmets, Soviet forage-caps of Tartar design, Finnish caps of silver-grey lambs'-wool, cartridge-cases, loading-clips, rolls of barbed wire—all the trappings of war, all the miserable yet splendid trappings of war. I continue to come across them until I reach the river. Here, the forest has a moment of hesitation, a moment of remorse : it meekly allows itself to be interrupted by the river, which flows through a broad depression with gently-sloping sides. But over on the far bank the forest begins all over again, only now it is even denser, crueller, more violent than before. In the distance I can hear the stutter of machine-guns, the sharp crack of rifles, the dull thud of explosions among the trees. And at the end of that panorama of sounds and colours, through a gap in the forest, I discern a glint of blue, like the shimmer of an ethereal sea. It is Lake Ladoga, the vast frozen expanse of Lake Ladoga.

Although Leningrad is but a few miles away the war seems, in these forests, to renounce its political and sociological character. No longer is is oppressed by the violence of the Soviet " industrial ethic." Instead, it is oppressed by a violence that is even more savage : the primitive ferocity of nature and of man. It assumes a simpler, more concrete, and hence more terrible character, without ideological or moral overtones. It is war in its most absolute form : wholly physical, wholly instinctive, wholly ruthless.

The Soviet units that are defending this sector of the front do not consist of shock-brigades of workers as on the Alexandrovka and Byelostrov Fronts. They are units from the north of Russia—Siberians from the *taiga,* soldiers from the Urals, men born and bred in the woods. And the Finns who oppose them are likewise men born and bred in the forests—woodmen, peasants, and shepherds. All, Finns and Russians alike, are men in the simplest and truest sense of the word. But, without wishing to belittle Soviet military prowess, I am bound to say that when it comes to this type of warfare the Russians are distinctly inferior to the Finns. Not in courage, not in their spirit of sacrifice, nor even in their basic human qualities: but in personal initiative, in technical efficiency.

In forest warfare, which, in addition to natural aptitude, calls for the utmost speed of decision and action, the Finns always have the advantage of their adversaries, who are slower, less sure of themselves, less active, and, what is of even greater importance, more numerous—I should say too numerous, for in fact the Russians suffer from an excess of numbers, which in forest warfare is a serious handicap. Their patrols consist of thirty, fifty, sometimes a hundred men. The Finnish patrols, on the other hand, comprise small, isolated groups, very mobile and fast-moving. The Finnish *sissit* fly along on their skis, swoop down on their adversaries from every side, surround them, annihilate them with the accurate fire of their *konepistoolit*. By contrast, the Russians, unequipped with skis and snow-shoes, move about on foot, frequently sinking into the snow up to their waists. They fight furiously, but they always have to admit defeat in the end. In my judgment, this Finnish superiority springs not only from a more acute sense of the requirements of forest warfare, not only from a keener instinct, a more delicate, almost animal sensibility, but from the fact that every Finn, be he woodman, peasant, fisherman, or reindeer-herd, is helped, comparatively speaking, by the extremely high degree of technical development attained in a country where the dominant " ethic " is an " industrial ethic " socially more advanced, determined to a more appreciable extent by technical factors, by technology, and, finally, more individualistic than the " industrial ethic " of Soviet Russia. (It must, moreover, be borne in mind that, despite the widespread industrialization of agriculture, and indeed of Soviet life in general, despite the *Pyatlyetki,* despite the Stakanovism of the *kolkhozi,* the mines, the sawmills, the fishing trusts, etc., the resultant benefits have not yet extended to the extreme northern regions of European and Asiatic Russia, in other words to those regions from which the Soviet troops engaged on this sector of the front originate.)

In this sense, one may say that Finland, like Sweden and Norway, is not only a nation of woodmen, peasants, shepherds, and fishermen, but also a nation of "workers." The Finnish people possesses an "industrial ethic," not an "agricultural ethic." It reveals promptness of decision and action, individual initiative, etc. (qualities which the workers of every country in the world indubitably possess in far greater measure than the peasants). Its superiority to the Russian people lies not only in its intuition but in its moral qualities. (And, of course, by "moral" qualities I do not mean those which are associated with personal conduct, with the notion of good and evil. I use the word in a sociological and technical sense, not merely in a human sense.)

Here, as I have already said, man appears in his most absolute and most essential form. Man, in the forest, is pure : his strength lies wholly in his reliance on instinct, in his surrender to the mysterious power of that unexplored wood which stirs in the depths of the human soul. His extraordinary vitality alone serves to demonstrate that in him the simplicity of natural man is accompanied by an almost unnatural detachment from the physical world. He is like a block of stone, like the trunk of a tree : indifferent to fatigue, to privation, to wounds, to physical pain. He accepts death with a philosophy that is surprising, almost terrifying.

Colonel Merikallio, who controls the Raikkola sector, speaks to me of his men with an affectionate understanding that springs from their life in common and from the serenity with which all, officers and men alike, face up to war in the forest, to death in the forest. (Colonel Merikallio is a man of about forty-two, with a youthful face and deep, clear eyes. He talks, laughs, moves with a simple, unsophisticated elegance. He is a Northerner : he comes from Oulu, in Ostrobothnia.) We are sitting in his *korsu,* which stands in the middle of a wood, near a ruined village. Outside we can hear the placid voices of the soldiers, the hissing of skis on the snow, the sharp clump of a hatchet on a tree-trunk, the creak of a sledge.

Already the sun is setting. The limpid sky is like a dome of ice. The blue reflection from the surface of Lake Ladoga is gradually merging into the twilight. We go outside the door of the *korsu*. A hundred yards from us are the stables. We can hear the horses neighing softly as they wait for their meal of cellulose. (In the absence of forage cellulose is the staple diet of the Finnish horses.) Four *Lotta* armed with sharp *puukot* are standing round a rough table gutting some large fish caught by the *sissit* in holes dug in the ice of the lake. The strong smell of the fish is carried towards us in waves by the light wind that is blowing from the forest. A group of soldiers is gathered outside the small hut which serves as a field-hospital.

" What's up?" Colonel Merikallio asks an artilleryman. " Somebody wounded, by the look of it," replies the artilleryman.

We walk across to the field-hospital. Inside, a *Lotta* nurse, a fair-haired girl with a beautiful, shy smile, is offering a glass of cognac to a soldier.

" Look at that man," says Colonel Merikallio, gripping me by the arm.

He is a tall young man—strong, dark-haired, very pale. He is capless, and there is a red patch in the middle of his forehead—a small red patch, just above the junction of his eyebrows.

The soldier takes the glass with a steady hand, raises it to his lips, drains it at a single draught. He is smiling. As he turns to give back the glass to the *Lotta* we see the nape of his neck. There is a hole right in the middle of it, from which a thin stream of blood is slowly trickling. That hole was made by a bullet. The missile passed through his skull, how I don't know, without touching any vital spot. The wounded man is talking and laughing: he has walked through the forest all the way from the outpost to the field-hospital. Someone offers him a cigarette. He takes it, starts to smoke, and I am half afraid I shall see the smoke coming out of the hole in the middle of his forehead. (I relate this episode with some diffidence, knowing full well that the reader must be suspicious, that his credulity must be strained to the limit by such a fantastic story. Yet it happens to be true. And I can add only one detail: the wounded man's name is Pentti—Linnala Putteli Johannes Pentti.) He stands there, outside the door of the field-hospital, talking and laughing as though nothing had happened. He says: "I felt a heavy blow in the middle of my forehead, as if I had been hit by a stone. I sat down with a bump." All around him are laughing. He is as pale as a marble statue. He is not just a man: he is a stone, a plant, a tree.

"They're all like that," the colonel tells me with a smile. "They are a part of the forest, they are fragments of the forest." We start to walk along the narrow path leading into the midst of the trees. The field-guns are dotted about the wood, half-buried beneath their rustic camouflage of branches. Around us the forest is alive with noises, with faint cries and almost imperceptible cracking sounds. Colonel Merikallio tells me that the Finnish patrols keep in touch with one another by imitating the voices of nature: bird-calls, the movement of squirrels among the leaves and branches, most frequently of all the song of the cuckoo, which is the sacred bird of Karelia. The *sissit* walk along carrying dry twigs, which they periodically break between their fingers, skilfully regulating and modulating the resultant snapping sound. The *sissit* of the neighbouring patrol decipher the crack of the breaking twig and reply to it; and by imitating the voices of nature in this way the two patrols are able to carry on a conversation. To warn distant patrols of danger a *sissi* clambers up the trunk of a birch tree and gently shakes its topmost branches, just as a squirrel would do. The top of another birch-tree replies in the distance.

The cannon thunders on the shores of Lake Ladoga. The crash of the explosions echoes from tree to tree like a whirring of wings, like a rustling of leaves and branches. And high above that living silence, which the solitary crack of a rifle, the distant

roar of the cannon, accentuate with an almost dreamy fitful-
ness, rises the song of the cuckoo. Cu-ckoo, cu-ckoo, cu-ckoo,
cu-ckoo!—insistent, monotonous, crystal-clear, that cry seems
little by little to take on a human quality. Colonel Merikallio
starts to hum the song of the Karelian woodmen, *Reppurin
laulu* :

> *Siell' mie mierolaisna lauloin*
> *kun ees oll' mieron piha*
> *Karjalan maill Kuldakäköset kukkuu.*

A cold shiver runs down my spine. And it is not fear, it is
something deeper, something more primitive. It is horror :
horror of the forest, of the cold, impassive violence of the
forest.

XXVIII

WITH THE "DEAD MAN" IN THE GREAT FOREST

Lumisuo Forest, East of Leningrad, April.

SOME years ago I was sitting in the orchestra stalls of Moscow's Bolshoi Theatre—formerly the Imperial Opera House and still the largest theatre in the U.S.S.R.—watching a performance of a famous ballet, *Krasnii Mak* (*The Red Poppy*), which at that time was sending the working masses of the Soviet capital into raptures. The ballet is inspired by the first Chinese Communist Revolution, the one led by Chiang Kai-Shek and the Soviet Commissar Karakan, the Red dictator of China. (I was sitting next to the playright Bulgakov, author of *The Days of the Turbin Family*.)

At one point the stage is invaded by a multitude of dancers dressed in red, symbolizing the Chinese Communists, and by a vast array of dancers dressed in yellow, representing the anti-revolutionary forces. The battle between those two armies of flowers, the army of the Red Poppies and the army of the Lotus Flowers, rises to a crescendo of fury, conforming to a choreographical pattern rich in volutes, arches and spirals, the effect of which is extraordinary, not to say astonishing. The exquisitely refined art of the Ballet School of the old Imperial Theatre, which has been revived by the Soviet Government, that gigantic choreography (it is estimated that at the climax of the battle some twelve hundred dancers burst on to the stage), all that phantasmagoric, absurd, and yet lucid symbolism, the tapping of those light, incredibly rapid feet, the opening and closing of those thousands of arms, the flying leaps of those hundreds of dancers, created a singularly tense atmosphere in the vast theatre, where a packed audience of workers sat in silent rows, hardly breathing—their eyes glued to the stage, their hands gripping the arms of their seats, their bodies straining forward eagerly, fearfully. The heavy, lingering scent of the poppies seemed to invade the auditorium in a warm, dense wave that enveloped the multitude of spectators, plunging them into a strange, narcotic stupor. Dazzled by those contrasting reds and yellows, they watched spellbound as corollas, pistils, petals, as flowers, flowers, and yet more flowers of flesh whirled round and round in an enormous wheel of light. And that narcotic stupor somehow induced in them a kind of terror, a genuine feeling of agonized suspense.

Suddenly the music rose to a deafening crescendo. Then, with equal suddenness, it fell silent, the whirlwind of poppies and lotus flowers ceased abruptly, and beneath the palpitating wing of the petals, gently stirred by the hurried breathing of the *corps de ballet,* there appeared hundreds of human faces, all of them contorted by the effort of dancing.

It was the signal for an outburst of pent-up emotion. For a few seconds the crowd of spectators sat in stunned silence. Then a young working-girl who was sitting in front of me exclaimed with a sigh of relief : " *Akh! ya dumala chto eto pravda bili tsveti* !—Why, I thought they really were flowers !" There followed a prolonged burst of rapturous applause, accompanied by a storm of frenzied yells.

I thought of this incident yesterday, as I made my way through Lumisuo Forest towards the front line, in company with a group of Finnish officers and men. We had been walking for about an hour when suddenly the leading *sissi* halted and stood listening, whereupon all the rest of us stopped and listened intently, gazing into the undergrowth.

Around us the forest had gradually come to life. Now it was full of strange noises, of singular, mysterious sounds. It seemed as if the trees were moving, as if they were walking on tip-toe through the snow. All around one discerned a rustling, a creaking, a very faint whistling, almost a sound of breathing, as if not one branch but a hundred, not a thousand but a hundred thousand, were breaking off with a sharp, barely perceptible cracking sound here and there in the depths of the forest. It was the same mysterious sound as would be made by a crowd of people walking in silence through a wood. We stood motionless, holding our breath. And suddenly there appeared away to our right, amid the tree-trunks, a patrol of Finnish scouts, a patrol of *sissit*. They glided cautiously over the snow, their white cloaks vanishing and reappearing amid the fir trees like transparent shadows. And I, with a sigh of relief, exclaimed : " Why, I really thought the trees were walking !"—whereupon we all started to laugh. That sigh and that laughter dispelled my mental anguish. For the silence of the forest has a thousand voices, and the immobility of the forest is an illusion—it is really a fine-spun web of movement compounded of a thousand individual movements. The forest is a living thing, an enormous lurking wild beast. And the mental anguish with which it fills the uninitiated is in fact a result of this instinctive transition from imagination to reality, of this " belief ", this " feeling ", that the trees really are walking, that they have mouths, eyes, arms with which to shout at you, to watch you, to seize you.

Soon we arrived at a small encampment. Two tents stood at the edge of the path, near the graves of some Russian soldiers —the remnant of a patrol of twenty men who the day before had infiltrated through the Finnish lines and had met their death at this point. They were simple graves, freshly dug, and each was surmounted by a wooden stake stuck in the snow. From each stake hung a Tartar forage-cap made of felt. On the stakes were carved the names of the fallen, together with the names of the Finnish soldiers who had killed them.

Inside the tent a group of half-naked soldiers were huddled round one of those rudimentary stoves which are to be found in all these *teltat* and in every *korsu*. The tent was full of smoke—clear, blue smoke, laden with the pleasant scent of birch-wood—and the air was warm. As we appeared the soldiers murmured : " *Hyvää paivää*—good day," and they looked at us hard, without saying another word. (In the forest no one speaks. There is no need to speak. In the forest men are stones, plants, trees, animals, not just men.) They looked at us hard, gazing curiously at my uniform and my Alpini officer's cap. But they said nothing; they were like mute statues of granite or wood. They had only just come off sentry-duty and were standing nearly naked round the stove, drying themselves. They looked tired out. Their trousers, tunics and white cloaks hung from a wire stretched across the tent. Silently they passed from hand to hand the packet of cigarettes which I had offered to one of them. When I got up to go they said : " *Hyvää paivää*," that was all. They remained huddled round the stove, smoking. I could see their small grey eyes glittering in the semi-darkness.

I am told by the officers who are accompanying me that two Soviet patrols have infiltrated into the wood behind the front line. We set off in silence along the narrow path, walking slowly, very slowly, making no sound, keeping our eyes skinned. Bursts of rifle and machine-gun fire echo here and there in the depths of the wood, punctuated by long intervals of silence. Now and then a stray bullet whistles past our heads, from time to time a broken branch falls to the ground. During those intervals of silence we hear around us a myriad faint snapping sounds, as if some monstrous serpent were crawling through the grass. To the naked eye the forest seems deserted, the arabesque of shadows on the carpet of snow appears intact.

Suddenly a Finnish skier emerges like a flash of lightning from the white foliage of a clump of birch-trees, darting across the path ahead of us, his *konepistooli*—one of those marvellous little Finnish automatic pistols—tucked under his arm and fully cocked. Silent groups of *sissit* glide like white shadows among the trees away to our left. I can distinguish them clearly through the mist of the forest, which is growing thicker every minute. A murky light filters through the lofty branches of the fir-trees, pines and birches. A cuckoo repeats its refrain —insistent, monotonous, crystal-clear. This is the zone in which the patrol-clashes take place. It is, one might say, a virgin zone, a kind of interstice between the front line and the Finnish resistance-groups which are concealed at various points in the wood. Suddenly a guttural cry is heard : it comes from somewhere far above us. It is a hoarse sound, like the mating-call of a bird. I raise my eyes, and see protruding far above the tree-tops a trapeze-shaped wooden tower some fifty feet in height—a flimsy-looking structure of crossed beams which gradually narrows towards the top, terminating in a small aerial platform surmounted by a pointed roof like a Mongolian cap. A staggered series of ladders leads up to the platform. I am looking at one of those watch-towers which the Russians have built at various points in the woods behind the front line. Now it is in the hands of the Finns. From the top of the tower the Finnish sentry looks out over a vast expanse of forest, following with his eyes the tortuous route taken by the patrols of *sissit,* picking out the ambushes of the Soviet patrols, ready to give the alarm at a moment's notice by telephone or by firing off a red rocket. The guttural cry that we have heard is a signal to us that the way is clear. I have described it as a hoarse sound, like the mating-call of a bird. In the forest it is sometimes necessary to disguise one's voice, in the forest the cry of an animal, the creak of a branch, the sharp crack of a breaking twig, are sometimes only human voices disguised.

Presently we reach the front line. It consists of a long, zig-zag trench carved out of the hard, frozen earth—a deep trench, lined with smooth, shining twigs, some of that beautiful orange colour which characterizes the Arctic pine, the rest a whitish yellow which at once marks them out as birch-twigs. Every so often we pass an opening in the wall of the trench—the entrance to a *korsu,* a shelter, or a machine-gun, anti-tank gun, or trench-mortar post. Everything is in perfect order—clean, smooth, brightly-polished, and maintained with a scrupulous care that reflects not only the nature of Finnish discipline, which is based above all on a love of order, but the phlegmatic and punctilious character of the Finnish people—I would almost say its Lutheran character—its love of simplicity and clarity, its respect for first principles. (But having said this, I must confess that I find Finnish orderliness rather dull and unimaginative, even a little austere.)

Dotted about the wood to the rear of the trench are a number of racks approximately six feet high containing rows of skis. Beside each man's skis hang a pair of sticks, snow-boots and gauntlets, the last-named made of the hide of reindeer or dogs. The dog-skin gloves are covered with long, soft fur, and to me they are at once beautiful and repellent. (I shall never forget the shock I had when I saw, in the window of a furrier's shop in Helsinki, a dog's coat that had been dressed whole, even including the head.) In the entrance to every shelter and every *korsu,* at the top of the flight of steps leading underground, is a rack of varnished wood containing the rifles, muskets, and *konepistoolit* of the soldiers who occupy the shelter. Each rack has a little roof to protect it from the snow. The weapons have been carefully greased, they sparkle brilliantly, the wooden parts look as if they had been newly varnished, the leather belts have been thinly smeared with vaseline as a precaution against the frost. The orderliness of it all gives one a feeling of serenity, a feeling of confidence and security. Not a single rag, not a single scrap of paper, not a single piece of rubbish is visible on the shining carpet of snow, which stretches away, intact and virginal, on either side of the narrow footpaths and of the tracks worn by the skis.

We walk some way along the trench, periodically turning to study the ground immediately in front of us. Between the Russian and Finnish lines, and separated from the latter by a distance of not more than three hundred yards, stretches a chain of picket-posts or *vartiot,* each of which is linked by telephone to the front line. The distance from one *vartio* to the next is about a hundred yards, which means that they are near enough to one another to be of mutual assistance in the event of an enemy attack.

While we are studying the ground ahead of us we hear a furious burst of machine-gun fire away to our left. " There they go," says one of the officers who are accompanying me. For some days past the Russians have shown themselves nervous and aggressive. They are afraid the Finns are up to something. Their patrols try to infiltrate into the Finnish lines, in the hope of taking a few prisoners, carrying them alive to their own trenches, and making them talk. Tonight a strong Russian patrol attacked the picket-post immediately in front of us. One of the two sentries was killed, but the other, although wounded, had time to give the alarm by telephone. The Russians had tied the wounded man's hands, and were already dragging him across the snow towards their lines, when suddenly a group of *sissit* appeared and rushed to their comrade's help. After a furious struggle in which the *puukko*—the Finnish dagger—played a prominent part they succeeded in rescuing the wounded man from the enemy and carried him back to their lines. "An insignificent episode," the officer remarks to me. "The forest war abounds in these little mutual courtesies." And he adds that for some days past the Russians have done nothing but try to infiltrate and to surround the Finnish outposts.

But the Finnish soldiers around us are calm, as if nothing were toward. The machine-gunners sit beside their weapons on ammunition boxes, placidly reading. (The Finns are incredibly voracious readers. In the front line alcohol is forbidden and tobacco is scarce. The soldiers drink milk and read—mainly novels and manuals of engineering, electro-technics and radiotelegraphy.) I go up to one of the machine-gunners and look to see what book he is reading. It is a volume of natural history: *The Fauna of Equatorial Asia*. In the coloured illustrations lions and tigers alternate with elephants and snakes. And around the pages of the book, around the coloured pictures of wild animals and of plants tinged red and yellow by the tropical sun, the snow forms a hard white frame that contrasts violently with those equatorial fauna and flora.

Beside the machine-gun stands a sort of rough cupboard containing a miniature library—detective novels, volumes of history and geography, technical manuals, together with some Russian books found in the houses and schools of the villages, or in the pockets of Soviet prisoners. Ah, now we can see what the Russian soldiers read. Their books too are for the most part technical manuals. There is also a biography of Stalin, profusely illustrated. The machine-gunner hands it to me with an ironical smile. The pages of the text alternate with pages of photographs—portrait after portrait of Stalin, photographs of Stalin in every conceivable pose. One photograph, occupying a whole page, has the following caption : " Stalin and Kirov in the Park of Culture (*Fiskultura*), Leningrad ". The two men are standing side by side. Kirov is thinner than Stalin, and a little taller; his hair is ruffled by the wind. Stalin, a smile on his face, is pointing to a team of footballers. The two men have been photographed against a background of merry-go-rounds, tennis courts, football pitches, shooting-galleries—the whole vast " Luna Park " setting of the gigantic amusement-park of the Red metropolis. (Kirov, President of the Leningrad Soviet and successor designate to Stalin as dictator of the U.S.S.R., died some years ago—assassinated by Trotskyite elements.)

Last year in the Ukraine I came across many of these books, as well as innumerable wall-posters in which Stalin and Kirov appeared side by side against a background of factory-chimneys, tractors, dynamos and agricultural machines. I came across them in the Soviet Houses, in the People's Courts, in the headquarters of the Co-operatives, in the libraries of the *kolkhozi*. Kirov was the man whose loss occasioned an unprecedented outburst of grief and indignation among the Stalinist elements of the Communist Party. The reprisals provoked by his assassination were atrocious. The number of workers shot in Leningrad on the day of his funeral totalled several thousands. (It was a gigantic funeral, superbly stage-managed.) But the working masses of Leningrad have remained faithful to their own extremism, to their own Trotskyite " heresy ".

The Finnish soldier points to the figure of Stalin and smiles. Before putting the volume back in the book-case, alongside the Soviet technical manuals, he studies the last few pages with ironical thoroughness. They are full of drawings and photographs of machines. (Beneath the surface of Communism there is a surprising undercurrent of " Americanism ".) Elements of " Americanism " are very evident in Soviet life and Soviet philosophy. They recur like a refrain not only in various public assertions and well-known formulas of Lenin (his " American " definition of Bolshevism as the equivalent of " Soviet+electrification " is proverbial), but also in certain of his characteristic manias, which became more and more obtrusive during the last months of his life, when he lay dying in a villa near Moscow. In the days that preceded his death Lenin spent hours and hours stretched out in an armchair, drawing the outlines of machines and skyscrapers with a pencil on odd scraps of paper. In the Lenin Museum, Moscow, an entire wall is covered with these drawings. They include dynamos, cranes, steel bridges, and skyscrapers—scores of skyscrapers, a whole vast panorama of enormous, highly elaborate skyscrapers. Undoubtedly the man was the victim of a kind of obsession. (Incidentally, a whole literature has been written on the subject of this relationship between the American " ethic " and the Soviet " ethic ", between " Americanism " and " Sovietism " —an extremely interesting literature, comprising reports by technicians and workers from America, Britain, Czechoslovakia, France, Scandinavia, etc., who have found employment in Soviet industry. They are for the most part brief, simple documents, based on an experience—sometimes hard, but always highly interesting—of three, four or five years in the factories and shipyards, in the *kolkhozi* and mines of the Soviet Union, and published by responsible firms whose impartiality is beyond question. All are agreed on the " American " character of the Communist " ethic " and of Communist society. The reader will come to understand many things, not least about the political relations of the U.S.A. and the U.S.S.R., if he takes account of this analogy.)

We climb out of the trench and make our way through the wood in the direction of the picket-posts. To right and left of the path stretches a network of minefields. It is necessary for us to proceed cautiously, without making the slightest noise. (A few hundred yards ahead of us the Russian sentries are listening intently for the creak of our shoes.) It seems to me that the snow crunches horribly beneath the rubber soles of my *vibram*. At a certain point we are forced to spread out fanwise, so that we may avail ourselves of the cover afforded by the trees. And thus, after what seems an eternity, we reach the picket-post—a semi-circle of pine-logs, reinforced by stones and compressed snow. Leaning against the parapet, his head barely protruding above that flimsy screen, the Finnish sentry scans the wood intently. He is the " dead man ", the *vartio,* the out-sentry—what used to be called, in Italy, the " dead sentry ".

He is a man of about thirty—dark, short in stature, lean and wiry. The skin about his eyes and mouth is a network of fine concentric lines. His face is the face of an old, old man. It is the icy glint of the snow, the delicate blue light of the wood, that gives it the appearance of crinkled parchment. He stands absolutely motionless—jaw set, eyes staring. Large tears trickle from his eyes on to his wizened cheeks. He seems almost to be weeping. It is the cold, it is the nervous tension, it is the fixity of that penetrating, frozen stare that squeezes the tears from his eyes. There is something extraordinary, something mysterious and moving, about the silent, virile tears of that solitary man, standing guard in the forest with death all the while staring him in the face. He seems not to be breathing. When we come up behind him he does not even look round. He is the *vartio*—the " dead man ". All his vitality is concentrated in his eyes and ears. He is listening intently, striving to detect the minutest sounds—sounds which to my profane ear would be imperceptible.

What to me is silence is to the *vartio* a medley of still, small voices, a vast chorus of muted whispers. The *vartio* is like a human antenna that intercepts the sound-waves of the forest. The enemy is there in front of him, only two hundred yards away. Ten, twenty eyes are watching him from behind the tree-trunks. The outline of his head trembles in ten, twenty

9

rifle-sights. The *vartio* is no longer just a man, he is a wild beast. All his animal instincts are concentrated in the pupils of his eyes, in the lobes of his ears, in the ends of his nerves. He does not blink an eyelid, he does not move his head. Only the quivering of his nostrils proclaims the fact that he is alive. I have the impression that if a bullet struck him in the temple those staring eyes of his would continue to see, those blood-less nostrils would continue to quiver.

Little by little the light grows misty, it seems to rise like a thin cloud of smoke, leaving the lower part of the trees and the dark patches of the shrubs in shadow. It is a grey light, traversed by tenuous streaks of blue: a strange, delicate blue light, liquid and motionless as the surface of a lake.

Suddenly the " dead man " turns his head and fixes me with glittering eyes. That icy stare bores into me like one of those naked swords which jugglers plunge down their throats. Per-haps that is a smile which now plays about his lips, which now illuminates his tear-stained face. But it is there only for a moment, it is gone in a twinkling. The *vartio* turns his head, freezes once more into an attitude of statuesque immobility. And now little by little I too begin to discern the thousand muted sounds of the all-pervading silence.

They are like a subdued breathing, a whispering, a light rustling. A branch creaks. A leaf flutters down from a birch-tree. A large bird flaps its wings among the leafy branches. A squirrel climbs the trunk of a pine. And suddenly I " feel " the staring eyes of the Russian sentries, lurking in the undergrowth two hundred yards in front of us. I " feel " them looking at me, and I catch my breath. All of a sudden, somewhere away to our right, a long cry goes up, a mournful, strangled cry, a cry that is prolonged like a peal of laughter, like a peal of mirthless, sardonic laughter. It sounds like the cry of a squirrel. It is cut short by a burst of fire from an automatic rifle. The bullets whistle past a few inches above our heads. Someone is walking in the snow over there. I can hear the creak of branches, and the sound of heavy breathing. Then—silence.

The " dead man " has not moved, he has not blinked an

eyelid. He continues to lean against the parapet of the picket-post like a block of stone, like a tree-trunk. It is a strange war, this war in the forest. This stupendous siege has some singular aspects. Over there, beyond that screen of trees, beyond the boundless expanse of the forest of Lumisuo, one divines the presence of the mighty city, inspired by a desperate, fanatical resolve, one visualizes its suburban streets furrowed by trenches, its harbour crammed with captive ships, its railway stations cluttered up with immobilized trains and goods-waggons, its squares filled with silent crowds listening to the blare of the loudspeakers. And here in this forest—what is there, here in this forest? Only a line of " dead men ", extreme vanguard of an impassive, silent, frostbound army.

While I am pondering the singular aspects, the harsh contrasts of this siege of Leningrad, I suddenly hear away to our left a furious burst of rifle and machine-gun fire, accompanied by the muffled explosions of hand-grenades. The *vartio* detaches himself from the parapet, seizes the telephone, utters a few words in a low voice, speaking slowly and deliberately, replaces the receiver, props himself up once more against the low wall of the tree-trunks and stones. " They are attacking the picket-post to our left," whispers Lieutenant Svardström in my ear.

It is time for us to go back. Before leaving the outpost I deposit two packets of cigarettes on the parapet beside the *vartio*. The " dead man " does not even look round, it is as though he had not noticed. The delicate blue light of the forest emphasizes the deep lines of weariness that score his face, making it resemble a mask of blue parchment. And now once more the liquid silence of the forest envelops us. As we trudge in single file along the narrow path a stray bullet whistles past my ear and lodges with a ping in a tree-trunk. But I scarcely notice it. I am haunted by the memory of that wrinkled, tear-stained face, I cannot forget that weeping man, standing guard alone in the forest.

XXIX

MASKS OF ICE

Shore of Lake Ladoga, East of Leningrad, April.

WE make our way down to the lake through a dense tangle of undergrowth interspersed with enormous blocks of red granite. Everywhere the ground is pitted with the craters of Soviet shells. Suddenly there unfolds before us the vast blue expanse of Lake Ladoga—" the Caspian of Europe "—looking like a silver mirror set in the hard frame of the forest. Its still-frozen surface reflects the blue bowl of the sky with a harsh, dazzling brilliance. (This morning the ice has a glorious sheen, it is the colour of glass—the beautiful greeny-blue colour of Murano glass.) The Soviet shore, dimly visible on the horizon, is just emerging from a transparent silvery mist that sparkles like mother-of-pearl.

This is the weak point in the ring of steel that surrounds Leningrad. Here the chain wants a link. From here the vast frozen surface of Lake Ladoga stretches without interruption all the way to the German outpost of Schlüsselburg. When, last autumn, a Finnish force based on Tapperi reached this northern fringe of the shore of Lake Ladoga, and the Germans, swinging round behind Leningrad, occupied Schlüsselburg, situated at the point where the Neva flows out of the lake and heads westwards in the direction of the city, it was possible to say that the ring of steel had been closed and that the former capital of the Tsars was completely isolated. And, in fact, for some considerable time the Red Army was unable to break the blockade and to come to the assistance of the hard-pressed garrison.

But with the onset of winter the lake was soon covered with a thick crust of ice. And now there happened the thing which the German and Finnish military Commands had long foreseen : in order to reach the beleaguered city the Soviet Command tried to take advantage of the bridge of ice that Lake Ladoga had in fact become. Although daring in the extreme, the plan envisaged by the technicians of the Soviet Corps of Engineers might well have appeared at first sight to have some prospects of success. It was, simply, this : to build a double-track railway some thirty miles in length across the frozen surface of the lake. At quite an early stage British propaganda intimated that the miracle had been achieved, referring to the railway across Lake Ladoga as an established fact. But British propaganda was somewhat premature. Very soon, in fact, the obstacles to the fulfilment of this ambitious scheme proved well-nigh insuperable. True, the first section of line, some six miles in length, was laid without much trouble. But scarcely had the train scheduled to make the trial run set off on its mission than it jumped the rails.

Although it is much less uneven than, for example, the surface of the Gulf of Finland, where the sudden freezing of the waves following an abrupt drop in temperature to $-40°$ has resulted in the formation of sudden dips and steep ridges of ice often exceeding three feet in height, the frozen mirror of Lake Ladoga is by no means flat. On the contrary, it is full of undulations, full of deep furrows and high ridges that are as hard and sharp as glass. Add to this that thermic phenomenon by which the crust of ice is in a perpetual state of flux, changing its appearance nearly every day in accordance with the variations of the temperature. These variations have most marked effects on the structure of ice, the elastic properties of which are well known. So it came about that the plan for the construction of a railway had to be abandoned after only a third of the track had been completed. An alternative plan, namely to tear up the tram-lines from the streets of Leningrad and lay them on the lake, resting them on a special system of sleepers operating on the principle of a pair of scales, which would have been expected to absorb and neutralize the movements of the ice, was found to be impracticable for various technical reasons, which it would take too long to expound and clarify here. It was accordingly decided, as a last resort, to construct a dual carriage-way across the ice suitable for heavy lorries.

The problem of keeping the civilian population and the garrison of Leningrad supplied with food and munitions is formidable, and in many respects insoluble. It is not easy to supply a city of some five million inhabitants by way of a track that is exposed to constant attack by aircraft and artillery. Moreover, Leningrad lacked the transport necessary for such a gigantic enterprise. Besides mobilizing all the vehicles available in the beleaguered city it was therefore necessary to assemble on the shore of Lake Ladoga many hundreds of lorries hastily summoned from the region of Moscow, and to despatch in convoy to the head of the track a large proportion of the British and American lorries which were beginning to arrive by the Murmansk route.

It was a question not, indeed, of establishing a secure and permanent line of communication but of taking advantage of the winter months to administer a blood-transfusion to the beleaguered city. Six thousand vehicles—the number necessary for the maintenance of a shuttle-service of convoys—require at least twelve thousand mechanics, not counting those assigned to the repair-shops which the Russians have established on their side of Lake Ladoga. Notwithstanding the enormous difficulties involved, the construction of the carriage-way across the lake was successfully completed and supplies at last began to flow across the gigantic bridge of ice.

In the daytime the track appears from the air to be deserted, except for the occasional solitary vehicle and, in misty days, isolated convoys of lorries spaced out at wide intervals one from another. It is during the night that the flow of traffic across the bridge of ice begins in earnest. And night, in the depths of the Arctic winter, is a ferocious enemy. The surface of the lake is continually swept by the violent winds that blow from the north-east, that is to say from the direction of Lake Onega. These winds originate from the Arctic Ocean. They are accompanied by veritable blizzards, by snow-storms of appalling violence. Frightful blasts of air howl across the vast frozen expanse, throwing up minute particles of ice, great funnels of snowflakes hardened by the frost. The Soviet convoys venture out into the inferno of the storm along the carriage-way which, beginning in the vicinity of Kaboga and Lidnia, on the Russian side of the lake, terminates on the opposite shore at Morye, north-west of Schlüsselburg.

In the early days it frequently happened that convoys strayed from the track and lost their way, or were obliged to hang about for hours and hours in the middle of the lake waiting for help. In some cases vehicles were actually abandoned by their crews, and were bombed during the day by German and Finnish aircraft. Shortly before dawn on a morning some weeks ago a patrol of Finnish *sissit* which had ventured out into the middle of the lake on reconnaissance heard a roar of engines somewhere in the blizzard ahead of it. It was the " ice-train ", which had strayed from the track and was unwittingly approaching the Finnish lines. Gliding cautiously over the ice to the sides of the convoy the *sissit* accompanied it for several miles with the idea of allowing it to get as close as possible to the Finnish shore. But at a certain point the " train " described an ample curve and turned back. It had realized its error. It was then that the patrol attacked the vehicles at the rear of the convoy. Although they were armed only with musket and *konepistoolit* the *sissit* succeeded in isolating several lorries and setting them on fire. Altogether it was a remarkable exploit, which, having regard to the circumstances, and in view both of the fact that the *sissit* were fighting in the middle of a lake and of the tactics which they employed, is comparable in a sense to an attack by a flotilla of torpedo-boats on a convoy of ships.

Since then the convoys have been escorted by light tanks. A

line of hurricane-lamps has been installed along the edge of the thirty-mile track. Patrols of Siberian hunters, who, one might say, perform the task of traffic-police, constantly patrol the carriage-way. And, for better or for worse, the traffic across Lake Ladoga is being maintained with a certain regularity. But it would be difficult to draw up a balance-sheet of the effective aid contributed by the bridge of ice to the defence of the beleaguered city. Undoubtedly this aid is considerable; but in view of the resumption of full-scale activity which, with the advent of spring, will shortly be possible, it is not so great as to enable the Soviet military Command to count on maintaining an adequate flow of supplies of food and munitions. A clear indication of the position is provided by the fact that during the last two months the activity of the Russian artillery has been diminishing daily in a very marked degree.

From the data collected by the Finnish divisional Commands on the Karelian Front, and particularly on the Valkeasaari (Byelostrov) and Alexandrovka sectors, in other words on the two most crucial sectors of the entire siege-front, it emerges that in the month of January the Soviet artillery fired each day some fifteen hundred shells of small and medium calibre for every three miles of front: a pretty high average.

When I first arrived on the Leningrad Front, at the end of February, this average had diminished to six hundred shells a day. A fortnight ago it was down to two hundred and fifty. It is also worthy of remark that, whereas in January and February the Russian artillery repeatedly attacked the Finnish patrols, and tried to silence the loudspeakers installed in the Finnish trenches with small- and medium-calibre shells, for some two months now the enemy has been trying to disperse the patrols and to reduce the loudspeakers to silence solely by means of machine-gun fire and occasional mortar-fire. These facts suffice to make it clear that the bridge of ice has not yielded the results for which the Soviet military Command had hoped. The quantity of war material, food and ammunition introduced into Leningrad is certainly not such as to ensure a very active defence of the city.

But almost any day now the " bridge " will collapse. Already the thaw is designing strange arabesques on the crust of ice, which from the Finnish shore appears to be adorned with historical pictures like one of those Renaissance cuirasses on which geometrical motifs of a purely decorative character are interspersed with representations of human figures, with panoplies, festoons of fruit, and landscapes of fantastic design. A most beautiful " cuirass ", this, its shining surface covered with large dark spots symptomatic of the spring malady of the ice, with a kind of rash, with those fluorescent bubbles of air which at the first hint of spring form in the ice, giving warning of its impending dissolution. The movement of traffic across the lake, already reduced by the shortening of the hours of darkness (the days are drawing out quite remarkably : by now the nights are no more than brief interludes of milky twilight, of luminous dusk), is rendered perilous by the treacherous state of the " bridge ". Luminous signals appear in the sky with growing frequency at dead of night. They take the form of red, green, and white rockets, which burst unexpectedly from the frozen expanse and streak across the heavens, travelling at first with the speed of light, then gradually slowing down, and finally exploding in a shower of twinkling stars which spread through the air, merging into the mother-of-pearl translucency of the clear night.

Since my arrival on the Ladoga Front I have got into the habit of waiting for the dawn on the shore of the lake, on the little beach from which the patrols of skiers embark on their night reconnaissances. The *sissit* set out from here, from this shallow bay, which might be described as their " harbour ". For here everything is arranged as in a harbour. The rackfuls of skis and rifles and the rows of white cloaks dangling from their pegs resemble fishermen's nets hung out to dry. The piles of ammunition-boxes look like stacks of merchandise waiting to be ferried across the lake to one or other of its little harbours. The placards bearing the cabbalistic symbols of the various military Commands, the arrows indicating the minefields, the boat-shaped sledges for the transportation of wounded men,

9*

arms and ammunition (some of which take the form of inflatable dinghies of canvas or rubber mounted on skates, while others are actual wooden boats with flat keels of the type used on lakes)—everything conspires to create the atmosphere, to foster the illusion, of a harbour. Every couple of hours one witnesses the "launching" of a patrol. The *sissit* line up on the beach, enter the water, weigh anchor, so to speak, and quickly disappear into the blue shimmer of the ice. Over there on the horizon is the Soviet shore, bristling with guns installed for the defence of the "bridge" and of the Stalin Canal—the gigantic artery constructed by the Bolsheviks to link the White Sea to the Neva and thus to the Gulf of Finland and the Baltic. On these limpid nights one can distinguish with the naked eye the red flashes of the signal-lamps that guide the convoys of lorries returning across the lake to their landing-place. It is a rhythmic blinking of lights, similar to that which indicates to the navigator the position of a harbour when it is still a long way off.

It was nearly dawn this morning when a sentry announced that rockets were being fired into the sky above the "bridge". I made my way with some officers on to a promontory, from which the eye ranges far across the lake; and after a few moments I was able to distinguish clearly five, nine, twelve red and green rockets. They appeared in rapid succession, and were spaced out at intervals of about half a mile. Evidently a convoy was trying to cross the lake. But something must have gone wrong, because after about ten minutes the signals were repeated, this time at much shorter intervals.

Now the convoys are becoming less frequent; and soon they will cease entirely. Already the "bridge" is starting to creak, already the ice at the edge of the shore is splitting, becoming opaque, streaked with white scars, its surface is getting less wrinkled. As the snow melts, so the transparent crust beneath is exposed, and through it one can discern the slimy bed of the lake. (Lake Ladoga is not very deep; sixteen or twenty feet at the most.) Owing to the action of the waves the mud is all corrugated, like a starched petticoat. At some points, where the water is particularly shallow, the crust of ice touches the bottom. One sees whole families of fish imprisoned in the crystal, trapped in that gigantic refrigerator. The soldiers go fishing with picks, they break the ice with hammers and chisels, they extract the fish from it as from an ice-box.

With the beginning of the thaw the lake reveals its mysteries, its extraordinary secrets. The other day I passed near a shallow bay shaded by a dense clump of silver birches. A party of soldiers was smashing into fragments, with violent yet compassionate strokes of their picks, what looked like a large block of green crystal, within which were embedded the pitiful remains of some Finnish soldiers. (In the same way, last January, when I visited the salt-mine at Wieliczka, in Poland, I saw numbers of small fish, marine plants, and shells trapped in the crystals.) And yesterday morning, as I wandered along the shore of Lake Ladoga, near the mouth of a stream that rises in Raikkola Forest, I noticed at a certain point that I was actually walking on the roof of ice that covers the river. I heard below me the gurgling of the water, the dull murmur of the current. I looked down, and saw the stream flowing tumultuously beneath my feet. I seemed to be walking on a sheet of glass. I felt as if I were suspended in space. And suddenly I was assailed by a kind of giddiness.

Imprinted in the ice, stamped on the transparent crystal beneath the soles of my shoes, I saw a row of exquisitely beautiful human faces: a row of diaphanous masks, like Byzantine icons. They were looking at me, gazing at me. Their lips were thin and shrivelled, their hair was long, they had sharp noses and large, very brilliant eyes. (They were not human bodies, they were not corpses. If they had been I should have refrained from mentioning the incident.) That which was revealed to me in the sheet of ice was a row of marvellous images, full of a tender, moving pathos : as it were the delicate, living shadows of men who had been swallowed up in the mysterious waters of the lake.

War and death sometimes partake of these exquisite mysteries, which are imbued with a sublimely lyrical quality.

At certain times Mars is at pains to transform his most realistic images into things of beauty, as if there came a moment when even he was overwhelmed by the compassion which man owes to his like, which nature owes to man. Beyond a doubt, I was looking at the images of some Russian soldiers who had fallen in an attempt to cross the river. The pitiful corpses, after remaining trapped as in a block of crystal all the winter, had been carried away by the first spring tides that followed the river's liberation from its icy shackles. But their faces had remained imprinted on that sheet of glass, stamped on that clear, cold, greeny-blue crystal. They looked at me with serene attention, they seemed almost to be following me with their eyes.

I was bending over the ice. On a sudden impulse I knelt down and gently passed my hand across those diaphanous masks. The sun's rays were already warm, they passed through those faces and were reflected from the chuckling stream beneath, kindling as it were flames of light about those pale, transparent brows.

I returned to the glass sepulchre in the afternoon to find that the sun had almost melted those dead images. By now only the memory, only the shadow of the faces remained. Even thus does man disappear, even thus is he blotted out by the sun. Such is the transitoriness of his life. (This morning I could not bring myself to shave in front of the mirror. No, I just could not do it. I had to close my eyes, I had to shave with my eyes tight shut.)

XXX

LIKE A FACTORY YARD AFTER AN ABORTIVE STRIKE

Shore of Lake Ladoga, East of Leningrad, May.

NO one can understand the secret of Soviet social life, or the secret of the Soviet "ethic", unless he takes account of this fundamental fact: that the overwhelming majority of the Soviet people (by which I mean men and youths below the age of forty to forty-five, in other words all those who did not know the old régime, either because they were born after the Revolution or because in October, 1917, they had barely reached adolescence) have no conception of an after-world, no hope, no inkling of a life after death. They neither hope for nor believe in future glory. They do not expect it. They approach death with their eyes shut, nor do they hope that they may be able to open them once they have passed through the smooth white wall of death.

Some years ago, finding myself in Moscow, I paid a visit to the tomb of Lenin in the Red Square. I was accompanied by a worker with whom I had struck up a conversation while queueing with the crowd of workers and peasants (nearly all young, and many of them women) outside the entrance to the mausoleum. At last we found ourselves inside. In the little room, dazzlingly illuminated by the cold white glare of the powerful floodlights, Lenin appeared before me stretched out in his glass coffin. Clad in black, his beard flaming red, his massive cranium almost completely bald, his waxen face dotted with yellow freckles, his right hand resting at his side, the other

folded across his chest with the fist—a tiny, white, freckled fist
—tightly clenched, Lenin lay sleeping, wrapped in the red flag
of the Paris Commune of 1871. His round head, with its
enormous brow, rested on a cushion. ("Lenin's skull is like
Balfour's," wrote Wells.) A sentinel with bayonet fixed stood
guard at each of the four corners of the room, which is no
more than four yards square : a simple chapel, geometrically
precise of line, that might very well have been designed by
Gio Ponti : a chapel fit to enshrine the relics of a saint, the
bones of synthetic resin, of bakelite, of a modern saint. It is
forbidden to linger beside the glass coffin : the crowd streams
slowly past it in single file, never stopping for a moment. I
gazed at the embalmed corpse of Lenin : a mummy now,
impressively conspicuous in that narrow space, in that glass
coffin, beneath the white glare of the floodlights.

I said to my companion, in a reproving tone : " Why have
you embalmed him? You've made him into a mummy."

" We don't believe in the immortality of the soul," the man
replied.

His reply was terrible, but it was refreshing in its simplicity
and candour. He might, however, have been somewhat more
explicit. For it is not just a question of not believing in the
immortality of the soul. Respect for the dead, the cult of the
dead, may be a sublime and sacred thing even if it does not
imply any belief in the soul's immortality. I believe that what
is in question is the actual idea of death, in the most literal
sense of the term. Death, to the Communist, is a smooth,
compact, windowless wall. It is a cold, hermetically-sealed
sleep. It is a void—a vacuum.

I was turning these thoughts over in my mind this morning
as I entered a Russian war-cemetery. The Russian cemeteries
lie on the hills (" hills " is perhaps a misnomer : rather, they
are broad, gentle undulations, long waves of earth) which rise
at the edge of Raikkola Forest, near Lake Ladoga. They are
bare compounds, surrounded by rustic fences or by barbed
wire. *They are the concentration-camps of the dead.* At the
entrance to each cemetery stands a kind of triumphal arch, an

arch of wood painted red, with the hammer and sickle and a brief inscription superimposed in white. These cemeteries give one a far clearer idea of the Communist conception of death than do the anti-religious museums and the propaganda literature of the *byezbozhniki,* or " godless." It is an abstract conception, which in its physical, material forms has crystallized into a cold, stark dogmatism. I am tempted to say—and I hope the reader will ponder the phrase for a moment—that " to a Communist, death is like a stationary motor-car."

A stationary motor-cor—that is the right expression. A most beautiful modern motor-car of shining, almost blue steel, with its wheels, its cylinders, its valves, its tie-rods, its pistons now paralysed and lifeless. Such is death to a Communist: a Θάνατος of chromium-plated steel. Not a moral fact, but a motor-car. Not a fact of a moral order, but a purely physical, a purely mechanical fact. (And yet, even a motor-car has its metaphysical aspect, even a motor-car belongs to the world of metaphysics. But the Communists have not yet attained to this lofty conception of death as a " metaphysical motor-car ".)

Everything in the Communist ethic, in the Communist *Weltanschauung,* is related to the world of the senses, to the world of living men and of living things. I would almost go so far as to say that a Communist cemetery is, in a sense, the perfect, concrete image of the Communist abstract ethic, considered in its relationship to the world of the senses. The symbols that adorn Soviet graves, the stelae erected on the mounds in Soviet cemeteries, illustrate with remarkable immediacy and expressiveness one of the basic elements of the Communist ethic, of that " industrial ethic " which has been refined, I would almost say " stylized," by the daily contact of its exponents with machines, with " beasts of steel." One day it will be possible to assess the part played by the machine, by the Soviet man's familiarity with the machine, in the formation of the moral world of Communism. One day it will be possible to determine the extent to which the machine, and technology, have been responsible for the evolution of the Communist ethic.

The stelae have been erected on the graves in place of crosses with a strict regard for symmetry. Most of them are made of iron. A very few are of stone. (Near Mainila, on the Valkea-saari Front, I came across a Soviet war-cemetery in which the stelae were all of stone, all of that beautiful red Karelian granite of which so many of the oldest palaces and monuments of the city of Peter the Great are built. On the granite stelae were engraved the names of the dead, for the most part members of the crews of a Soviet tank-squadron; and at the top of every list of names—for each mound concealed the remains of numerous soldiers—was carved a rising sun with so many rays that it resembled a cog-wheel. The disc of the sun was adorned with the hammer and sickle. I was struck by the odd fact that the stelae were all made of stone. Then, as I walked round the cemetery, I discovered that each of them had an additional name carved on the back—a Finnish name, surmounted by an engraving of a plain Lutheran cross. Obviously the Russians had uprooted the stelae from the, so to speak, legitimate graves of some Finnish village cemetery and had converted them into tombstones for their own dead. I should add that this Soviet war-cemetery was well planned and had been laid out with a certain pious care. It was surrounded not by barbed wire but by a low railing of birch-wood; and it was approached by means of a short avenue, flanked on either side by a row of sepulchral pillars linked by a chain consisting of tracks from the gutted tanks of the men who now lay buried in the compound. But this is the only cemetery I have so far seen in which the stelae have been made of stone. In all the others they have been made of iron.)

Those iron pillars planted symmetrically in the bare earth consist entirely of strips of rough metal, trench-supports, portions of tanks, parts of the coachwork of cars and lorries, cast-iron posts picked up heaven knows where (they are of the kind that I associate with fountains in village squares), even signposts, or simple parallelepipeds of wood coated with metal. On them the names of the dead have been roughly carved, or more often painted. Those strange pillars, those rising suns resembling cog-wheels, make the cemetery look like the yard of a steelworks : one of those yards in which one sees scattered here and there, or piled up in a corner close to the boundary-wall, pieces of raw or half-worked metal, rusty machine-parts ready for assembling, and portions of old, discarded machines which have been dismantled preparatory to being sent to the foundry.

Some years ago I remember visiting Krupps' Steelworks at Essen. And now, as I look back, the immense yard of Krupps reappears before me in the likeness of an enormous Russian cemetery, littered with steel pillars, cast-iron posts, metal ingots, rusty wheels, crank-shafts, parts of boilers, sheets of tinplate, cog-wheels like rising suns, gigantic cranes. It was 1930, and Krupps' Steelworks was facing a crisis. The yard seemed deserted. The helmet of a *Schupo* protruded from the doorway of a hut situated near the entrance. From the interior of a colossal shed came a rhythmical metallic boom like the sound of an enormous gong. It might have been a sledge-hammer, it might have been a press.

And now this deep, muffled, rhythmical boom, this cadenced hammering on the grey steel plate of the horizon, reverberates amid the frozen silence not like the boom of gunfire but like the banging of an iron mallet on a strip of metal. I almost have the impression that this cemetery has just been abandoned by an army of workers. For, by a strange association of ideas, it reminds me of a factory-yard after an abortive strike : when, in the sinister light of defeat, machines, tools, everything assumes an unwonted appearance, an almost abject appearance of melancholy and desolation. At such a time the idle machines resemble strange beasts of steel standing motionless outside a closed door, before a smooth, solid white wall. They are like symbols of a vitality strained to the precise limit beyond which no machine can continue to function.

The names and obscure symbols carved or painted on the iron stelae in the Soviet war-cemeteries have the same meaning, the same significance (I say this without wishing to show any irreverence or lack of Christian piety towards those poor human remains buried beneath the rough mounds), as the red and black calibration-marks on a manometer, as the figures written in chalk on the slate that hangs beside a boiler, as the scale of a thermometer, as the numbers round the edge of the revolution-counter of a dynamo in an electric power-house, as the oscillating red arrows in the neon tubes of a radio-station. (In the same way, the cold, unwavering, pale-blue light that broods over the forest and the hills resembles in its harshness and frigidity the light of an electric power-house, of a chemical laboratory, of a rolling-mill in a smelting-works.) It is all so terribly precise, so terribly impersonal. Always this obsession with technology and specialization, always this dreary, violent atmosphere of Stakanovism.

One is almost inclined to wonder whether the symbols and names carved on these iron stelae have not the same meaning, the same significance, as the columns of figures on the wall-charts that hang inside the entrances to the various departments of a Soviet factory, indicating the levels and averages of output, the maximum and minimum coefficients of production, the degree of Stakanovism achieved by the worker and the gang. The inscriptions on the iron stelae of a Soviet cemetery should surely read, not " Here lies," etc., but " The appended figures show the maximum output achieved by the comrades buried beneath this mound," etc.

Is there, perhaps, a religious significance in these Soviet sepulchral symbols, in this passion for death, this obsession with death (a typically Russian mixture of sadism and masochism) which characterizes so many aspects of Soviet life? And this lack of faith, this nihilism, this utter hopelessness—are they not, perhaps, obscure signs of an unconscious religious feeling, inasmuch as they represent the exact converse of faith?

These Russian soldiers who die so readily, who accept death with so unconsciously eager, so avid an indifference, know no religious grammar, no metaphysical syntax. They do not even know that the Gospel exists. What they know of Christ they have gathered from anti-religious documentary films, from the puerile iconography of the anti-religious museums, from the fanatical and blasphemous propaganda of the *byezbozhniki*.

(In a Moscow church there is a crucifix with a card beneath it bearing the inscription : " Jesus Christ : a legendary character who never really existed." This fact is also recorded by André Gide in his book, *Retour de l'U.R.S.S.*) They know that they will die even as a stone dies, or a piece of wood. Or a machine.

It is not easy to determine the political and social significance of this attitude of mind, nor to assess its implications for the years ahead. So many factors in the internal situation of Russia are unknown to us that no valid judgment on questions of this kind is possible. But it is already clear that there is nothing either human or inhuman of which this people is incapable. Everything in this colossal tragedy violates the rules, and exceeds the bounds, of normal human experience. The Russians have by now become a people who hate God in themselves, and who hate themselves not only in their fellow human beings, but in the beasts.

I leave the cemetery and set off in the direction of the village. Around me, on the hills, rise the triumphal arches of the Soviet cemeteries. Raikkola Forest bars the horizon with its high blue wall. On the road I meet a group of prisoners, escorted by a Finnish soldier. Sitting rather than lying on a stretcher borne by four of the prisoners is a wounded Russian. One of his legs has been smashed to pulp by a hand-grenade. At a certain point the stretcher-bearers stop to change positions. They lay the stretcher on the snow and pause for a moment to rest. A dog comes out of a hut, runs up to the wounded man, sniffs his blood-soaked bandages. The man takes it gently by the collar and strokes it. At the same time he picks up an ice-splinter, fits it into his palm with the sharp edge protruding, and deals the animal a sickening blow between the eyes. The dog howls with pain, struggles to free itself from the wounded man's savage grip, finally succeeds and runs away with the blood streaming from its split skull.

The wounded man laughs. The prisoners laugh. " *Pois*! *Pois*!—come on! Come on!" shouts the soldier who is escorting them. The little procession continues on its way and disappears into the wood.

XXXI

GOODBYE, LENINGRAD

Byelostrov, November.

THE time has come perhaps for me to bid a cordial farewell to Leningrad. For nearly a year now, ever since I first arrived on this front, I have returned periodically to Byelostrov to look over the top of the trenches, to peer through the loop-holes of the picket-posts at the mighty city, grey and cold in its setting of forests and marshes. And always, whenever I leave this front, I am filled with an infinite sadness, I feel I am quitting a place which, paradoxically perhaps, will always be dear to my heart by reason of the memory—still, alas, only too vivid—of the hardships I endured last winter in these gloomy Karelian forests. (Leningrad is still unconquered. My forebodings of last February, when many so glibly prophesied that the beleaguered city would soon be starved into surrender, have been confirmed. In a sense, its position is far better now than it was then. The Russians have taken advantage of the summer months to evacuate a large part of the population by way of Lake Ladoga. Fresh troops have replaced the units decimated by the unprecedented rigours of that terrible winter.) Here in the sector of the " workers' fortress " the war seems to have settled into a groove. It has assumed a placid, somnolent, almost static character. It is no longer the hard siege-war of a few months ago. The heavy guns that kept up that continuous bombardment of the industrial suburbs of the south-west are silent. That ferocious alternation of attacks and counter-attacks has ceased. There is a hint of ripeness, and of weariness, in the mist that

276

now hangs above the roof-tops of Leningrad. A hint of impending doom, and at the same time a hint of blissful repose. Almost, I would say, a hint of nostalgia.

Until a few days ago the great city was languishing amid the ethereal splendour of its " white nights." But now, with the coming of the thick autumnal mists, these are slowly giving way to a livid green twilight. In this perpetual semi-darkness the shadows of the Finnish soldiers flitting among the trees have a ghostly air. And the Russian patrols that appear from time to time along the bright edge of these woods of birch-trees, a few hundred yards in front of us, move lethargically, as if weary, as if worn out by six months of continuous daylight. But very soon now winter will be upon us again—the interminable night of winter.

I should like to be able to describe at my leisure the melancholy of the cold, damp summer which followed the last savage winter. I should like to be able to describe the monotonous patter of the autumn rain on the leaves, on the tin roofs of the huts, on the oilskins of the soldiers, on the glistening cruppers of the horses. And I should like to be able to describe the great city as it appears to me today, on this singularly mild afternoon in late autumn, through the rectangular window of this *korsu,* of this front-line refuge in the forward trenches of Byelostrov. It is a small window, with a frame of birch-wood. Viewed through the slightly misty glass the city has a faded air, and it appears rather smaller, rather more remote than it really is. Set in the frame of the window, it looks like an old print hanging from the wall of the *korsu*—a dusty print, with a few patches of mould dotted about its surface.

In the top right-hand corner of the picture the sky is a little ruckled. It is a murky sky, lightened here and there by pools of bright blue—as if a river (perhaps what I can see is in fact the reflection of the Neva) had overflowed into the heavens, flooding the celestial plains, where the scattered clouds resemble islands of a transparent archipelago suspended in mid-air. I study carefully the colour of the sky, the colour of the roofs and of the woods. And I begin to ask myself : Is grey really the dominant colour in this landscape, in this old print? Or is it not, rather, pink, tempered with the vaguest suggestion of green and dark brown, discernible in the diffuse blue shimmer of the leaves? The city looks as if it had been captured by an artist's crayon in a moment of weariness and expectancy : in that precise, interminable moment in which not only human beings but, sometimes, even inanimate things seem to look back with regret, with longing, with nostalgia, to an age, at once happy and sad, that is gone for ever, or that has brought disillusionment in its train. Yes, that is the word : disillusionment. Something has withered away, something has died, in the soul of Leningrad.

A careful scrutiny of the light that pours down from the sky portrayed in this old print, a detailed study of its *chiaroscuri* and its shadows, will furnish many an indication of the reasons for this air of disillusionment—so closely allied to that kind of lethargy which at certain times of day seems to descend upon a landscape, to insinuate itself into the play of light and shade, as if the death of nature were at hand, as if some cruel fate menaced the life of the plants and animals, the enchanted prospect of trees, rocks, rivers, lakes and clouds. Is it perhaps the shadow of war that dims the lustre of this old print? Or is it not rather the presence of something more profound, the aura, the emblem of something more fundamental, more secret, more fatal?

If I look through the misty panes of the little window of this *korsu*, situated in the forward trenches of Byelostrov, I can see the city outlined against the grey horizon. For almost a year now I have been a witness of this siege, and still I find it impossible to view the colossal tragedy of Leningrad through the eyes of a mere spectator. Here the war has by now assumed a precise form, a definite character, of its own. It has become almost extraneous to us whose task is to describe it. It is a tableau now, rather than a drama : an old, faded tableau. Here, more than on any other sector of the front, it has assumed the form and the significance of an antithesis—not of the usual, too facile antithesis between East and West, between

Asia and Europe, but rather of a kind of trial of strength between the two forces that have clashed on the frontiers of Western civilization. Here the West comes face to face with itself, and that too at its most sensitive, most vulnerable point : the point where the most backward and the most modern civilizations of Europe meet, size each other up, pit themselves against each other.

It profits little to repeat the words which Gide wrote in his *Retour de l'U.R.S.S.* : " *Ce que j'aime le plus dans Léningrad, c'est Saint-Pétersbourg.*" How can one understand the drama of Leningrad, which epitomizes the whole drama of Russia, if one does not embrace with a single glance, and with a single emotion, not only the palaces, the churches, the fortresses, the parks, the monuments of the imperial city, but also the edifices of concrete, glass and steel, the factories, schools and hospitals, above all the working-class quarters, those solid blocks of rigid, precise, cold, peremptory buildings that have sprung up on the outskirts of the former capital of the Tsars, and even in the heart of the city? For it is not possible to isolate that in the destiny of Leningrad which is " imperial " from that which is " proletarian," that which is Holy Russia from that which is Communist-atheistic-technological-scientific Russia. The destiny of Leningrad offers an extraordinary example of continuity and logic. The " window " opened by Peter the Great on to Western Europe is no more than a window opened on to the sad, glittering world of machines, on to the sterile, chromium-plated world of technology. The gesture of the Tsar who opens up the " St. Petersburg window " in the wall of Russia anticipates the revolutionary purpose of Lenin, who seeks to make the city of Peter the Great not the capital of an Asiatic State, but the capital of proletarian Europe.

The huge red buildings of the Krasnii Putilovets have now shared the fate of the Winter Palace, the Taurida Palace and St. Isaac's Cathedral. The steel machines, standing idle in the deserted factories, now resemble the gilt furniture in the halls of the imperial palaces and of the princely mansions that line the Fontanka. The portraits of Lenin, Stalin, Uritski and Kirov

which hang from the walls of the factories, schools, gymna-
siums, *stolovie* and *rabochie klubi* now have the same air of
sadness and utter disillusionment as the portraits of Tsars,
princes, boyars, generals, admirals, ambassadors and courtiers
that hang from the walls of the antechambers and halls of the
Winter Palace and the Admiralty. And even the Russian
soldiers whose figures I can see from the window of this *korsu*
clearly outlined along the edge of the communication-trenches
directly in front of me, near the railway-line, are like faded
images in the margin of past history, of a discredited, already
" ancient " era : devitalized images, already " outside " time,
" outside " the time in which we are living. (The war obliterates
the milestones of the years. The siege of Leningrad seems now
to be no more than a remote episode, to belong to a remote
period of history.) They are like those human figures which an
artist portrays in the margin of a print in order to give the
measure, to indicate the proportions, of the landscape. What
I am trying to say is that in this war men do not count except
as yardsticks, as standards of comparison.

In this interminable northern twilight the cupola of St.
Isaac's Cathedral can be dimly seen, towering majestically
above the sky-line : ethereal and spectral as the cupola of a
church in a scene from a Spanish *Auto Sacramental*—for
example, in that " day " of *El Mágico Prodigioso* of Calderon
de la Barca, where the cupola of Antioch Cathedral shimmers
in a green sky behind the figures of Cipriano and the Devil, in
the " *bellissimo laberinto de arboles, flores y plantas* " : more
diaphanous, more spectral than when I saw it for the first time
in February last, standing serene and immaculate in its wintry
setting. That day the boundless expanse of white was tinged
with soft greys, split by deep chasms of blue; and when I
raised my eyes I saw the immense cupola of St. Isaac's suddenly appear above the roof-tops, looking like a bubble of air
inside a crucible of molten glass, like the larva of an insect
borne on the wind, like a jellyfish ascending from the sea-bed.
Yes : as it rose, slowly and tremulously, into the sky above the
captive city it did in fact look exactly like an enormous jellyfish.

But today the cupola of the cathedral towers ghostlike above a green and pink autumnal landscape in which everything, even the war, appears forgotten. It is in the foreground that the real tragedy of the beleaguered city acquires form and substance. That tragedy is not the war, not the siege, but the collapse of Leningrad's Western tradition. For now Leningrad's tragedy is not that of a city only : it is the tragedy of an age, of a myth. The hour, the place, the season, and this all-pervading silence, which is accentuated by an occasional solitary rifle-shot, by the occasional distant boom of a gun, suggest the motifs of a fantasy, of a detached reverie. The cupola of St. Isaac's silently dissolves in the pale sky. Inside the red factory-buildings the engines, the machines, the tools of shining steel lie dying on the concrete floors. The deserted streets, littered with dead horses and gutted vehicles, are reflected through the windows in the misty mirrors of the imperial palaces. An atmosphere of lethargy, of repose, almost of remoteness veils and softens the forms and aspects of the war. Already Leningrad has ceased to be a part of our age, already it has moved on to the margin of this time of strife.

Goodbye, Leningrad. Tomorrow I must leave for the frozen wastes of Lapland, tomorrow I must begin my journey to the far North, to the Petsamo Front. But one day I shall return to sit once more at the window of this Finnish *korsu* nestling in the front line, to contemplate anew this melancholy landscape of trees and concrete. (Every so often the sound of a rifle-shot penetrates the grey wall of the horizon, from time to time the distant thunder of the heavy guns of the Baltic Fleet rattles the armour-plating of the silence.) War knows these moments of repose and waiting, in which human consciousness, I would almost say nature itself, feels the living drama of reality less intensely; in which everything appears serene, everything is redisposed within the limits, within the framework, of a mythical, tranquil, sweet orderliness.

Or else . . .

D 764 .M323 1951
Malaparte, Curzio,
 1898-1957.
The Volga rises in Europe